S0-DSP-349

THE GLOBALIZATION OF MONEY AND SECURITIES

The New Products, Players and Markets

HG
4521
.C46x
1992
West

Dimitris N. Chorafas

AN INSTITUTIONAL INVESTOR PUBLICATION

PROBUS PUBLISHING COMPANY
Chicago, Illinois

© 1992, Dimitris N. Chorafas

ALL RIGHTS RESERVED. No part of this publication may be reproduced, stored in a retrieval system, or transmitted by any means, electronic, mechanical, photocopying, recording, or otherwise, without the prior written permission of the publisher and the copyright holder.

This publication is designed to provide accurate and authoritative information in regard to the subject matter covered. It is sold with the understanding that the publisher is not engaged in rendering legal, accounting or other professional service.

Library of Congress Cataloging in Publication Data Available

ISBN 1-55738-232-8

Printed in the United States of America

BB

1 2 3 4 5 6 7 8 9 0

Contents

Foreword
by Yoshiro Kuratani, Ph.D.

During the past ten years or so, a number of significant changes have taken place in the community of financial institutions. Among them are the globalization of 24-hour dealings in bonds, stocks and exchanges through the three major financial centers—New York, London and Tokyo, securitization of outstanding debt by banks for better liquidity positions, sophisticated portfolio management in option and futures markets by security houses, BIS agreement to ensure bank's capital adequacy, crossover of businesses between banks and brokerage houses in spite of legal restrictions in the United States and Japan, and M & A activities such as leveraged buyouts using "junk" bonds. The implications of these changes and anticipated transformations of the competitive scene in the financial world are so great that nobody can predict what impact they will have on the financial community.

Professor Chorafas, with his many years' experience and expertise, here presents a very meaningful and timely contribution to this extremely important field. His treatment of the subject matter is well thought out, arranged and presented in a logical, coherent manner. I strongly believe this book will provide a means of reliable guidance for the financial community for many years to come.

Yoshiro Kuratani, Ph.D.
Professor, Tokyo International University

Foreword
by Colin Crook

The generic requirements for general business success in the 1990s—quality, responsiveness, customer focus, short cycle times, low cost, and so on—now apply in particular to finance and banking. Unfortunately, these desirable characteristics have not always existed in the finance marketplace. Individuals and enterprises are now faced with the challenge of how to achieve these capabilities. In order to survive and prosper in the future, continuous innovation is needed together with effective management of the changes created by innovation.

Dr. Chorafas has written lucidly and compellingly on the broad issues challenging the securities industry. In addition, he has provided insight into specific issues which must be addressed.

Dr. Chorafas and I worked together over ten years ago on the innovative use of technology in foreign currency trading.

I am delighted to see that he remains at the cutting edge of innovation in finance and technology.

Colin Crook
Chairman, Corporate Technology Committee
Citibank, N.A., New York

Preface

As the securities industry grows more competitive, productivity becomes increasingly important, but not only productivity. New product development as well as ingenious marketing are just as vital. The same is true of cost control to enhance financial staying power. The drive is on for

- Innovation in financial services,
- A better market focus, and
- The curtailment of paperwork associated with trading stocks and bonds.

On the business side, debt is easier to trade on a global scale than equity, and taxation favors corporate debt. This was discovered in the 1980s; in the 1990s it is most likely that debt instruments will be the game in town. The fact is, however, that nobody can control the worldwide debt market—the key is anticipated liquidity.

The best trader is distinguished by the quick manner in which he seizes the facts and tries to reduce them to coherent patterns. Successful portfolios do not accumulate by chance. They can only develop by choice—in other words, through

- Research, development and experimentation, and
- Knowledgeable, well-informed management.

Wealth is based on knowledge and the ability to use that knowledge. Market knowledge on behalf of the trader and the investment advisor is what sophisticated clients appreciate the most. High-net-worth individuals and corporations are very demanding in their requirements and highly selective in their choice.

In 1980, AAA American companies had on average thirty-six banks to deal with. Today, this number has been reduced to nine and is still falling. Alternative means of financing further underline this reduction in the number of intermediaries. One result of high technology in banking is that the financial institution becomes its client's Assistant Treasurer. It will hold in this position only as long as it is

- Inventive in the type of products which it offers to its clients, and
- Able to keep ahead in technological know-how, so that its clients continue to need its services.

This requires innovation and management of change—two domains in which many of the larger financial institutions are weak. Such weakness is the aftermath of the "Big Company syndrome," which leads to widespread conformity.

It is illuminating to look back to the Middle Ages as well as to the 20th Century's communist regimes. One of their common characteristics is rampant conformity; another is almost total intellectual stagnation—two negative qualities which go hand-in-hand.

This book addresses itself to bankers, traders, experts of mergers and acquisitions, securities analysts and "rocket scientists" who wish to move ahead in their profession and contribute to the profitability of the financial institution for which they work. It will also be of interest to members of the exchanges, regulators and government authorities.

The theme of Chapter 1 is the infrastructure of the securities industry, with organizational issues focusing on risk management and the aftermath of growing globalization. Chapter 2 looks carefully into investment banking and merchant banking, examining both of them in light of capital markets and money markets, as well as electronic money and the specter of inflation.

Chapter 3 elaborates on financial markets, exchanges, and information providers. The subject of Chapter 4 is legislation and the role to be played by the regulatory authorities. This is further discussed in Chapter 5 which deals with the Securities and Exchanges Commmission, but also reflects the point of view of the brokers.

Chapter 6 answers the questions: Who are the Money Managers? What is their profile? Chapter 7 centers on portfolio management. The many aspects of securitization are treated in Chapter 8. This discussion is followed by a thorough example on mortgage-backed financing (MBF) presented in Chapter 9.

Chapter 10 discusses mergers and acquisitions, bringing to the attention of the reader both the good news and the bad news. Leveraged buyouts, junk bonds and their impact on liquidity is the subject of Chapter 11—including deals made to improve the product line.

Finally, Chapter 12 reviews and reconsiders the roles played by securities houses by focusing on strategies followed by financial institutions. It also elaborates on the reasons for globalization, the competitiveness embedded in high quality financial products, the wisdom of swamping costs and the dominant perspectives in risk management.

The book concludes by emphasizing strategic products. Investment bankers and brokers have to bring value differentiation to the products they are selling. High net-worth clients are sophisticated, and they have challenging questions to ask. They also appreciate the research and development spirit prevailing in the financials institution in which they place their money.

By year 2000, 70 percent of all jobs in the western world will require cerebral skills rather than manual skills. This book is an introduction to that age.

Let me close by expressing my thanks to everybody who contributed to this book. Some of the bright ideas come from Edward Dunne, UBS Seucrities in New York; Kenneth A. Hines Jr., Citibank; DuWayne J. Peterson, Merrill Lynch; Fred M. Katz, Goldman Sachs; Thomas Cranfield, Manufacturers Hanover Trust; Dr. Gabriel Jakobson, GTE Laboratories; Haruyuhi Okuda, Mitsubishi Bank; Takeshi Shinohara, Nomura Securities; Eiichi Ueda, Mitsui Bank; Mitsuru Fuji, Nikko Securities; Shojiro Ono, Sanyo Securities; Marihiro Matsumoto, Yamaichi Securities; Dr. Josef Fritz, Oesterreichische Laenderbank; Dr. Peter M. Bennett, International Stock Exchange; Mike Flinder, Lloyds Bank; John Timlin, Allied Irish Bank; Frank Shanley and Bernard Enright, Riada Securities. To Eva-Marie Binder goes the credit for the artwork, typing and index.

Dimitris N. Chorafas
Valmer and Vitznau

Chapter 1

The Securities Industry

Chapter 1

The Securities Industry

1. Introduction

During the last ten years, the securities industry has undergone radical changes. Many areas of business, in particular that of trading, show the impact of this restructuring.

Interactive computational finance is influencing the way that investment and trading decisions are made. As the market for debt and equity evolves and grows, numerous examples provide daily evidence that the most successful investment and merchant banking firms are those who have

- Flexibility,
- The ability to innovate, and
- A readiness to exploit change.

These three qualities have always characterized the leaders in the securities industry; since the late 1980s, however, another ingredient has been added to the formula for financial success—the ability to exploit science and technology. For example, option-adjusted spread (OAS) for mortgage-backed securities, uses the Monte Carlo technique that is employed in nuclear engineering calculations; twenty-four-hour banking requires the use of global networks; mapping the market into the computer, artificial intelligence (AI); and subsecond response to complex problems, the use of super-computers. In the capital-intensive economy of today, mental productivity and marketing reach, on the part of investment analysts, traders, securities salesmen, and account managers, are more critical than ever.

In the standard textbook view, the first "bankers" were goldsmiths issuing receipts, which later circulated from hand to hand, for gold. But, according to Dr. Charles Kindleberger, goldsmiths did not evolve into formal bankers until the middle of the seventeenth century in England; banking itself started much earlier in connection with foreign trade.[1]

Even in eighteenth-century England more banks developed from merchants than from goldsmiths. Moreover, many other paths led to banking; some of these included industrial firms issuing tokens to pay wages, tax collectors handling public funds, and notaries (scriveners) recommending investments and then making them for their clients. Thus investment banking originated with advisors and traders, whose descendants now manage global investor portfolios and syndicate loans.

Today, investors want advisors who have clout and experience, contacts in many industries and countries, access to a wide range of financial services, and prompt, imaginative, high-quality commercial and financial advice. They need help when things are going well and even more help when things are going badly, which they inevitably will at some stage. And they want to be in partnership with people with deep pockets.

2. Organization and Structure for the 1990s

In the months immediately following October 1987, when the worldwide boom in stock and bond markets came to a temporary but abrupt end, some ideas about the brokerage and investment banking business began to lose their appeal. One of these was the idea that doing business twenty-four-hours a day or globalization, is necessary to stay competitive.

Yet, this view of globalization is more accurate than the one that holds that the new world of competitive, high-techology financial markets would be dominated by a few worldwide, monster firms. Nevertheless, while globalization has made a comeback, most market observers no longer believe that a securities firm with a large share of any important financial market is sure to be profitable.

Profitability in the securities business, as in others, is a result of

1. emphasizing quality, not quantity,
2. having a few innovative products rather than many standard ones,
3. exercising effective cost control, not big spending,
4. focusing on economic trends rather than abstract theories.

The chart in Figure 1.1 presents a comprehensive picture of the new landscape. The "new players" in this chart are non-bank banks; the services they offer are shown in Tables 1.1 and 1.2.

To be successful, financial firms also need a comprehensive strategy for growth, a depth and range of resources, products, and qualified professional staff. A strategic plan would in-

Figure 1.1 The Expanding Horizon of Banking after Deregulation

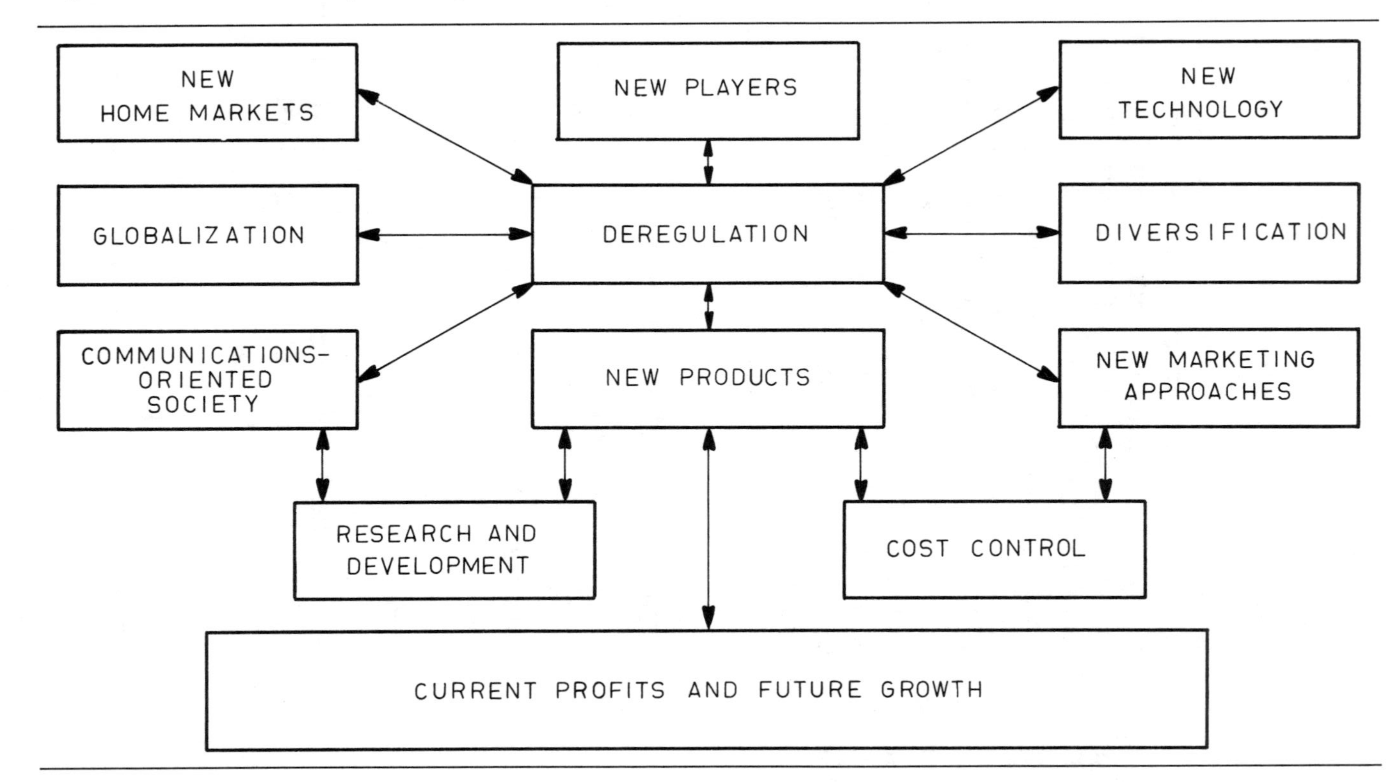

Table 1.1 Services Offered by Non-Bank Banks

Service	*Available from Financial Supermarkets*	*Available from Finance Companies*
Securities underwriting	yes	no
Demand deposits	yes	no
Interest-bearing checking	yes	no
Savings accounts		
personal	yes	no
business	yes	no
Time deposits		
personal	yes	no
business	yes	no
All Savers' Certificates	yes	no
Individual Retirement Accounts (IRAs)	yes	no
Consumer lending		
secured	yes	yes
unsecured	yes	yes
Commercial lending		
through bond purchases	yes	not exercised
through commercial paper	yes	not exercised
construction loans	yes	yes
other commercial loans	yes	yes
Leasing	yes	yes
Credit cards	yes	yes, indirectly
Trust services	yes	no
Payroll or other direct debit	yes	yes
Automated tellers/cash dispensers	yes	no

Table 1.2 Services Offered by Non-Bank Banks

Service	*Available from Brokerage Houses/ Mutual Funds*	*Available from Life Insurance Companies*
Securities underwriting	yes	no
Demand deposits	no	no
Interest-bearing checking	yes, but limited	Universal Life Policy
Savings accounts		
personal	yes	yes
business	yes	no
Time deposits		
personal	no	no
business	no	no
All Savers' Certificates	no	no
Individual Retirement Accounts (IRAs)	yes	yes
Consumer lending		
secured	yes, purchases on margin	no
unsecured	yes	yes
Commercial lending		
through bond purchases	yes	yes
through commercial paper	yes	yes
construction loans	no	yes
other commercial loans	limited	no
Leasing	no	no
Credit cards	yes	no
Trust services	yes	no
Payroll or other direct debit	yes	yes
Automated tellers/cash dispensers	no	no

clude strengthening the client base, developing specialized expertise, ensuring profit stability, and improving capital adequacy. This plan should rest on the capability of managing change. Dramatic change often comes only as a response to imminent collapse or to a corporate raider. It takes the arbitrageur and subsequent breakup to make management quickly do what it should have done long before.

Managing change means testing new ideas, developing new opportunities; it should involve people at all levels, from the top down, as well as the use of intelligent networks, steadily enriched databases, communicating workstations that present results through visualization, photonics,[2] and artificial intelligence (AI). The goal of managing change to develop systems capable of providing comprehensive support at all organizational levels.

This is necessary because even the structure of organizations is changing as the number of levels in them sharply decreases. Says Dr. Peter Drucker,[3] "The typical large business twenty years hence will have fewer than half the levels of management of its counterpart today, and no more than a third the managers."[4]

Profitable investment banks and securities houses will be knowledge-based, composed largely of specialists who direct and discipline their own performance with the help of organized feedback from customers, colleagues, and headquarters. Technology, in its many ramifications and expressions, will be instrumental in refining information.

In the last fifteen years, organizations have shifted from accumulating raw data into processing information; in the coming ten to twenty years, the focus will shift to processing knowledge. Figure 1.2 shows the technology that will be used to handle the environment. The foundation of the structure will consist of

Figure 1.2 Component Parts of a Knowledge-Based Environment

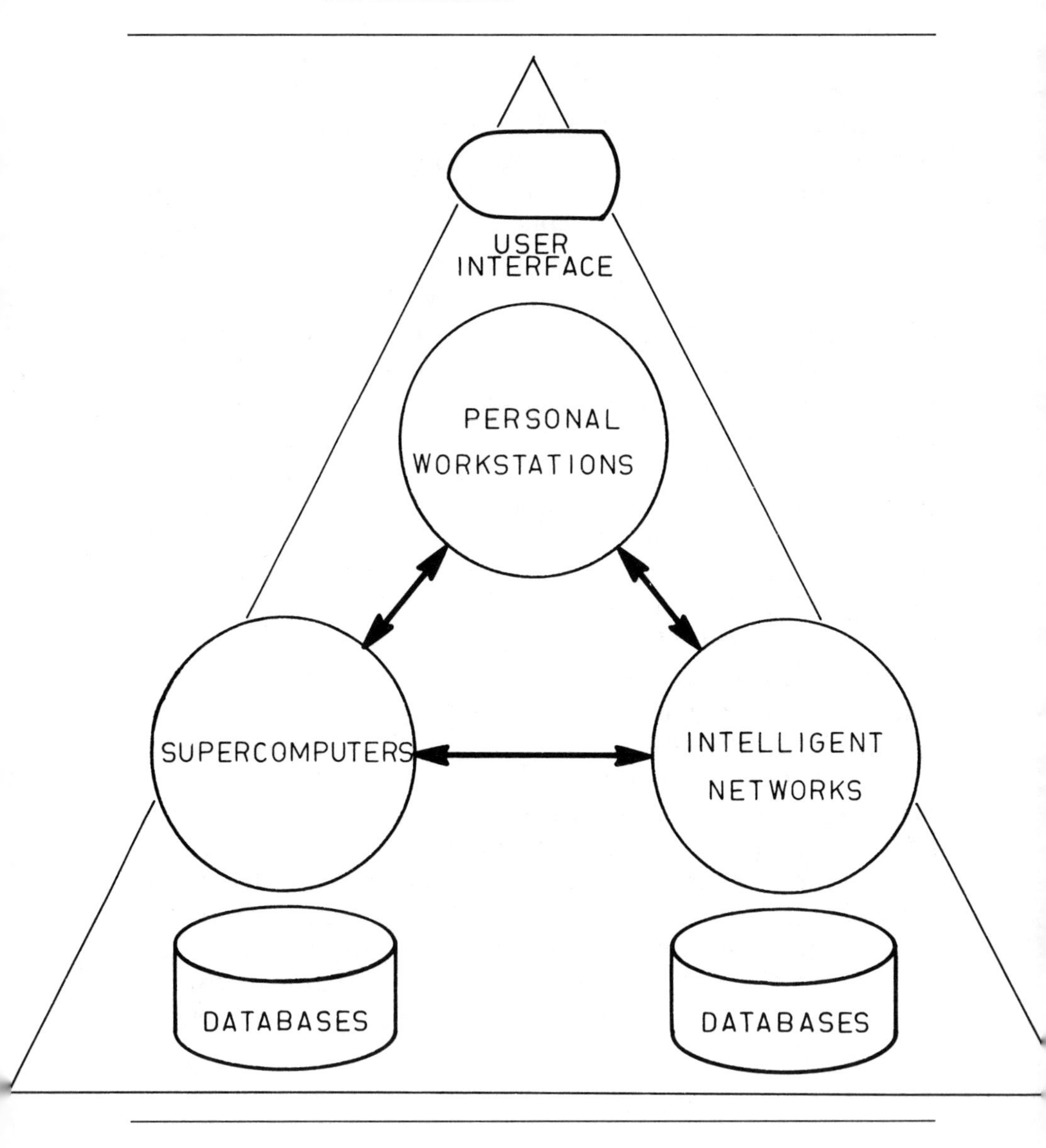

1. powerful personal workstations with agile human interfaces, internetworked among themselves and with databases;
2. supercomputers that process logical (artificial intelligence) constructs, number-crunch, and manage large databases;
3. intelligent networks linking peer-to-peer, any-to-any bank executives, market analysts, securities salesmen, dealers, back-office operators, and their computer resources.

This technological structure is fundamental to both large and small financial institutions. While smaller firms may find it costly, they benefit from it most of all—especially with the apparent trend toward brokerage and investment banking as cottage industries.

If they have saleable products, investment specialists may profit from setting up their own computer-based firms, subcontracting any bulk back-office services that they need. This is already happening in the U.S. in merger advice, with the founding of profitable firms called boutiques by specialists who have broken away from large, well-known investment houses.

In fact, large proactive organizations today are often collections of smaller firms in new structural combinations; this is called the intrapreneurial approach.

A knowledge-based financial institution will typically be peer-to-peer with very few management levels. Instead of a hierarchy of executives, this institution will use many specialists. Dr. Drucker compares this structure to that of a large symphony orchestra, with a large number musicians on stage playing under one conductor.

The organizational structure will be flat, and the high-grade specialists will need to work in synergy. As the activities in which they will engage will require a growing amount of know-how and intelligence, the CEO/conductor and his or her domain experts will have to be networked in real space.[5]

Earnings will be higher because the costs will be lower, management layers being one of the main contributors to costs. The higher the level of motivation of the specialists, the greater will be the firm's ability to capitalize on business opportunities.

There are many reasons why traditional firms miss opportunities for new solutions. In a typical situation, no top-management decisions are made on satient issues, no clear ideas about how to reach goals and no grand design exist—only the order to "do something." Incorrect messages are given about risks and benefits. There is often conformity rather than constructive competition, inadequate preparation, and an unspoken rule against trespassing on the "fiefs" of colleagues.

All this ends in mismanagement of corporate expectations—which no financial companies can afford, particularly in the turbulent markets of this decade. Nor can an investment bank survive by falling behind competition in its usage of high technology.

Vincent T. Pica II, managing director of Prudential Bache's financial strategies group, says, "The securities industry has seen a tremendous revolution in its analytic capability to respond to the regulatory and investing needs of our clients. We have responded with new structures for financing and investment. This is where interactive supercomputing will make a difference. This is where the industry is going."

3. The Financial Markets of the Starting Decade

The world economic system of the 1990s will inevitably make international economic and political relations more complex. Changes brought by rapid market evolution, as well as international economic relations, will increase the level of absolute wealth but also increase the gap between rich and poor countries. This will be even more true when technology is used less for producing weapons systems and more for producing and exporting goods and services.

With intensified competition for jobs, skilled workers will find markets willing to pay ever larger sums for their skills. Unskilled workers may find themselves competing with people, often from other countries, who are willing to work for a fraction of what the former earn. While many skills will be portable, at least among countries of the First World, others, such as client handholding and trading conventions, will be specific to certain markets.

There will as well be a vital issue in customers' perception of a financial institution's dependability. In their home market, customers tend to migrate toward investment companies they trust the most and with which they are most comfortable; thus, some observers feel that at least part of the financial services business is not particularly conducive to competing successful in foreign markets.

Tokyo-based Nomura Securities, the world's largest stockbroker, closed its equities unit in New York after failing to persuade American institutions to trade domestic stocks through its brokerage house. Daiwa Securities, also of Tokyo, has been forced to cut back operations at its U.S. subsidiary in an attempt to keep it afloat.

In Tokyo, of the foreign financial institutions that rushed to open shop after a mild deregulation, a large number have registered heavy losses, and some have even withdrawn from that market. They failed because they could not convince prospective clients that they were both dependable and permanent fixtures in the Japanese market. For the same reason, they could not attract top Japanese bankers, traders, and computer specialists to their organizations.

In spite of this problem, the internationalization of all domains of financial activity is taking place. Because all firms are each others' subcontractors, the concept of trade imbalances must be redefined. This is not to understate the impact of mismatched trade flows, but the way markets are forming; they tend to promote globality, including

1. expanding business opportunity,
2. greater potential for profitability,
3. possible gains through securities trading and foreign exchange,
4. diversification and spread of risk,
5. increasingly international control of settlements,
6. possibilities for market growth, and
7. account control.

These reasons extend beyond the concept of a bank as a financial intermediary. They help explain why knowledge and information are vital commodities. Knowledge advantages apply throughout financial markets, and in particular to three product lines, securities, forex, and options, all of which, to a large measure, interact and share common ground (see Figure 1.3).

Knowledge and information are the foundation for the trend toward mergers in the United States, Europe, and Japan. As mergers create big conglomerates, however, smaller firms are gaining a place in the market.

Ironically, spin-offs and concentration happen at the same time. Already one-quarter of the gross national product of the First World (other than agricultural) is produced by multinational firms. But, globalization is also inseparable from the development of the worldwide information networks and computer systems made possible by technological progress.

Figure 1.3 The Three Most Profitable and Risky Trading Decisions: Forex, Securities, Options

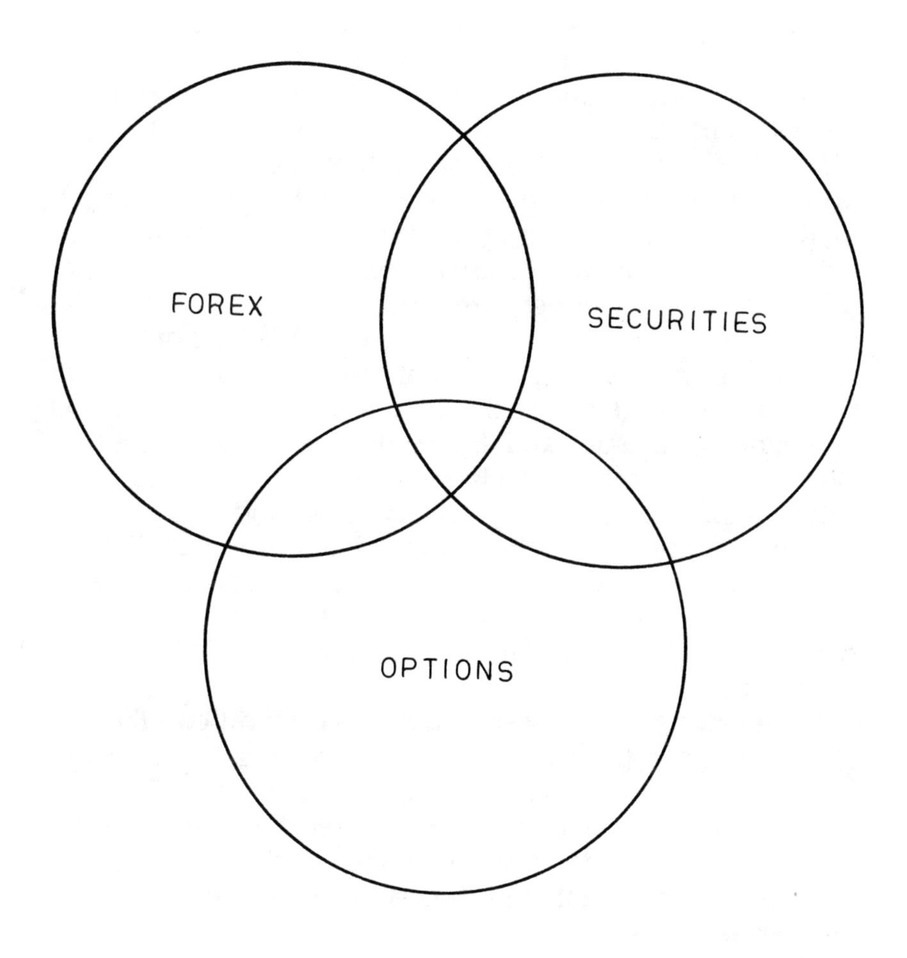

Because what happens in one part of the world now spreads around the globe instantaneously, financial markets greatly influence one another worldwide. Transactions are managed internationally, and there is an increase in the number of dealings that are unrelated to real economic fundamentals. The force of international financial movements has now become stronger than the power of national governments, even those working in concert.

Large currency trades are made every day in foreign exchange markets around the world. A year after the October 1987 market crash, $4.2 trillion worth of stock was switched on the world's major stock exchanges. The growth in such markets has been geometric, as global trading, new technologies, and new instruments share new buyers.

A small number of very large transactions dominates the market. Of the orders going through CHAPS (in London), a small fraction (less than 1 percent) represents 95 percent of the value. Every night CHIPS in New York handles 750,000 orders on the average and 1,200,000 orders as a maximum. With the mean value of each transaction being $3.2 million, this translates to $2.4 trillion as an average and $3.84 trillion as a maximum. Today, the gross national product (GNP) of the U.S. is $5.3 trillion; therefore, on the average, nearly half of the American GNP is switched in the financial market, which talks volumes about both the importance of this market and the risks being taken.

The greatest of these risks is what has been called a Follow-the-Sun overdraft, which relates to the financial responsibility of the correspondent, resulting in default risk being imported. An educated guess is that somewhere this risk will hit the system. Among the issues to be addressed is the question of who is liable in the event that something really big goes wrong.

Technology is partly responsible for this risk. Systems interconnected on-line are so complex that it is difficult to determine when a settlement has taken place. Due to a lack of universal time stamps, which are at least at therblig (1/1,000 of a second) level, it is virtually impossible to untangle completed settlements and to roll back transactions. Aside from this technical challenge, there is a need to redefine the concept of financial integrity in a global sense.

4. Risk and the World Economy

What makes financial markets powerful is not as much their size as their immediacy. Markets react instantly to news, and because that news is widely available, the markets have become the world economy's transmitter.

Through the financial markets, every policy initiative receives a judgment and every action, a reaction. Thus, the financial markets in the 1990s will function as a pressure valve, allowing the economy to let off steam, transposing volatility and swings in activity from the real economy to the financial economy.

For the dollar, the pound, gold, the bond market, and the stock market, the fluctuations of the 1990s will likely be dramatically larger than those of the 1960s, 1970s (when fixed exchange rates were abandoned), or even the 1980s (when financial deregulation gained momentum). By contrast, the fluctuations in the real economy are expected to be relatively few and rather smooth.

In business life, risk exists in any a situation and regards decisions, positions, or choices that involve potential financial loss. In the financial markets, this potential loss is apt to be substantial. Hence, risk management should start with resource management (see Figure 1.4).

In the next step, commitment tracking as well as advice on investments can be strengthened with expert systems support; although, the final decision is with the executive, the trader, or the investment banker. By contrast, transaction

Figure 1.4 Risk Management Is a Critical Part in the Able Handlings of Financial Resources

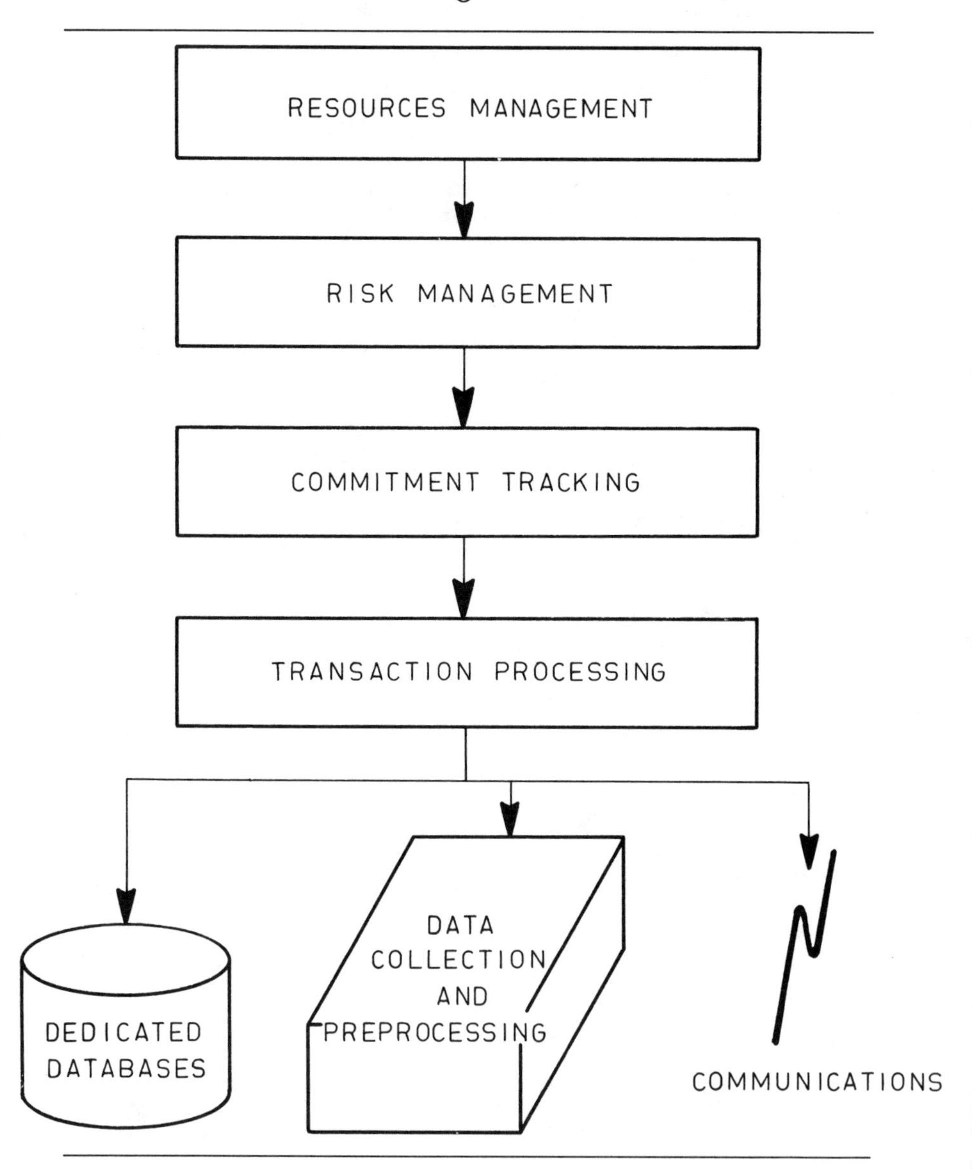

processing should be fully automated; for example, the administration of payment documents can be effectively handled through imaging—that is, photonics.

Today imaging is an innovation, as were expert systems until recently. Innovations must offer real added benefits to potential users if they are to succeed. People will not rearrange their life-styles just to use a product; nevertheless, at times they may need to restructure their way of thinking to incorporate an indispensable concept, and this is the case with the new approaches necessary to manage risk.

Leading bankers and securities experts agree that in order to face the challenges of the 1990s, the financial industry requires

1. a global and polyvalent control of risk,
2. major improvements in the quality of financial services,
3. intelligent networks that provide worldwide trading, monitoring, and compliance,
4. photonics solutions, from imaging to communications,
5. the automation of payments documents—a job which is still largely manual,
6. human windows to make man-machine interfaces user-friendly and agile,
7. expert systems implementation at better than state-of-the-art level, with risk control being one of the focal points.

Risk is not a new notion in the financial industry, particularly in the securities market. "But," says Kenneth A. Hines, senior vice-president of Citibank, "while the management of risk is our business, it is an impossible management task without the technological infrastructure....It is most difficult to quantitatively measure and forecast risk without tools."

This is true at both macroeconomic and microeconomic levels. The world economy today is based on gigantic debts which support each other in a fragile equilibrium. These include not only Third World sovereign loans, but also the debts of the agricultural and real estate industries. The savings and loan associations have long been in trouble in the U.S., and leveraged buyout has created a pyramid of corporate debt.

The world has been replacing equity with debt. There are also millions of players speculating in currencies and stocks. With one financial market or another always open for business around the globe (as an effect of globalization), there is no visible end to the game of speculation which is made easier by a credit mechanism that permits one to buy without paying and to sell without holding.

It is best to be wary of the amount of leverage used in some deals. "I look at the numbers, and I have a very difficult time understanding some of them," says Ira Harris of Lazard Brothers. "We are going to wake up one day and find ourselves with a lot of problems on the financial side of deals that come at the end of the business cycle."

"Many of our growing difficulties," says French economist and Nobel Prize winner Maurice Allais, "result from ignoring a fundamental fact—that no decentralized market economy system can function properly if the uncontrolled creation of new means of payment postpones necessary adjustments. That happens every time that people cover their spending, or their debts, with simple promises to pay, without any effective direct or indirect counterpart."

From this point of view, the current credit mechanism considerably amplifies market disorders. And it should not be forgotten that all the great crises of the nineteenth and twentieth centuries resulted from excessive expansion of credit, that is, from promises to pay and their monetization, as well as accompanying speculation.

Investors have little confidence in any level of stock prices because they worry about the intentions of other investors and of traders. Even small changes in prices can become highly leveraged when these intentions (signaled prices) may have to fall considerably before bargain hunters begin to buy stock, or they may have to rise considerably before investors become willing to sell their shares.

To the uncertainties inherent in national exchanges has been added speculation on foreign stock markets and options markets, a result of globalization. This is speculation amplified by a fundamental contradiction between short-term capital movements and the independence of national monetary policies. Such policies can magnify the potential instability of the entire world economy with a significant effect on the financial system.

This situation was not created overnight. It arose as a result of practices that flourished in the 1970s and 1980s. During the 1970s, for example, the money center banks significantly increased their deposits without having corresponding increases in capital. The ratio of loans to capital in some American banks had risen to as high as 25 to 1. Because many money center banks were lending other people's money transnationally, the security of the financial system was increasingly linked to the interdependence of nations; at the same time, the banks themselves became overexposed.

During the boom years of the 1980s, it became increasingly apparent that in order to prevent a market crisis from hitting the entire financial system, global securities markets need supervision of the kind developed in the banking industry.

The 1989 Financial Market Trends, a quarterly survey published by the Organization for Economic Cooperation and Development (OECD), stated that the existing regulatory environment is a patchwork that was put together when securities markets were less sophisticated, interlinked, and exposed than they are today. OECD noted the growing concentration of the securities industry, the predominance of twenty-four-hour banking, the level of the risk now being borne by intermediaries in the securities market, and the strong links between the securities market and the banking and payments system. As a result, it suggested that serious problems in securities markets would have the potential to destabilize the entire financial system.

5. The Aftermaths of a Growing Globalization

Most First World countries now have integrated their economies into the global economy, thus reaping the benefits of access to fast-moving international markets (although some national economies are not able to adjust to large new capital flows in purely monetary terms because their fiscal policies are out of synchronism.) Global convergence, and the subsequent integration of the worlds' major product and financial markets, will result in spreads among national interest rates and much narrower inflation rates.

This started in early 1990, with U.S. interest rates influenced not as much by domestic fundamentals as by developments in Japan and Germany. A 50 basis point hike in Japan's discount rate caused an equivalent rise in U.S.-government-bond yields, as the interest rates in America moved in concert with those overseas. The global interest-rate level is increasingly driven by global inflation and global economic growth. The rules of the game are changing.

In the trading and brokerage of shares and bonds, a large market share may not yield similar profits to all dealers. This is because affordable computer power and efficient telecommunications give the advantage to those traders who are able to invest in technology and back their trading positions with huge amounts of capital.

The microchip has made information available to everybody at a low cost. Corporate treasurers and institutional investors can now pick and choose between brokerage firms rather than using one supplier. Also, they look for added value from specialized intermediaries.

This value can be expressed on an innovation grid, which divides product and market perspectives into the phases of (see Figure 1.5) evolution, expansion, consolidation, and breakthrough moving counterclockwise.

Each of these phases has challenges with which brokers and investment bankers must come to terms as globalization forces itself upon them. The focus is on the fundamentals, that is, the quality and skills of the people who work in securities firms rather than the size of the trading floor. With information available to all, what counts is the understanding that knowledge and information produce new ideas about business, enrich trading and account management, and make it necessary to cultivate personal relationships with clients much more deeply.

The most successful investment banks are leading corporate finance advisors, as well as specialists in fund raising, mergers, and acquisitions. Some also develop a range of services, such as personal banking and leasing, beyond stock brokerage.

These products of vertical integration will not necessarily be made available in a global sense, as globality is demanding in terms of its prerequisites. To a great degree, these prerequisites are a result of the dramatic growth in the interdependence of markets.

To justify the new prerequisites, investment banks are exporting financial research and development (R and D) to their subsidiaries overseas. One example of this is the simulation of interest rates and exchange rates for forecasting purposes; another is the use of mathematical repayment models in mortgage-backed financing. Approaches such as the Monte Carlo method, binomial lattices, and multiple

Figure 1.5 An Innovation Grid in the Financial Industry

STRENGTH	EXPANSION - EXISTING RESOURCES - NEW MARKETS	EVOLUTION - NEW RESOURCES - NEW MARKETS	CHANGE
	CONSOLIDATION EXISTING RESOURCES TO EXISTING MARKETS	BREAKTHROUGH NEW RESOURCES EXISTING MARKETS	

regression analysis are being used in much the same way that they are used in nuclear engineering and aerospace research. The reason for this emphasis in analytics is that

1. bonds, warrants, and index futures markets respond to movement in underlying equities, which, in turn, must be thoroughly investigated;
2. equities respond to movements in the bond market; hence, there is a feedback between financial sectors;
3. both bonds and equities are affected by changes in the currency market, which has been in steady flux since the institution of flexible exchange rates.

Being able to follow the flow of news and its impact on different diverse markets, some of which may respond to cultures other than the firm's, has become a major consideration for all top-tier securities houses. Another important concern is creating a trading center with all trading functions under one roof and in one open, interactive area. At the same time, given the market environment that is currently unfolding, advanced technology is necessary to augment the trader's capabilities. This means having intelligent networks, distributed databases, and expert systems.

The value of high technology comes into play in meeting the increasing needs of customers. When the markets began to deregulate, clients began to expect comprehensive services from securities houses; also, growing diversity of client needs is a product of the institutionalization of the market, a trend that, at least for the time being, seems to be irreversible. Customers now demand from their brokers and investment advisors, not only expert knowledge but also steady and actual information and execution flows.

Institutions are now responsible for most of the trading activity of the market; it is projected that by 1994/95 pension funds alone may represent more than 50 percent of the business of a brokerage house in the First World. This development will have far-reaching implications for the future course of the securities industry.

Investment houses should as well realize that it is equally important to maintain enough breadth in outlook to weather any dramatic shifts in market sentiment. The trading center should provide a strong foundation for investment diversification, particularly in keeping the firm active in retail, institutional, and foreign business.

In the retail sector, the securities firm should enhance its ability to handle both large-volume, small-lot trading and a small number of big trades. In dealing with institutional and international clients, it is necessary to handle complex intermarket information and execution flows and provide a twenty-four hour trading capability, most often in large lots. For every client and every market, the office automation effort should be focused so as to swamp costs.

6. The Big New Player in the World Economy

With the information it imparts through price swings and a growing transaction volume, the global financial market is the newest and most powerful player in the world economy. As such, it is putting new pressures on national economies, including that of the U.S. which up until now has been relatively sheltered from such intrusions.

As well as altering the rules of the game, this new player has introduced constraint factors and business opportunities to the market. For example, investors are reassessing the risk of holding paper that could become junk bonds virtually overnight. As a result, if investors deem a company to be at risk of downgrading through takeovers or management buyouts, its bonds drop in value.

Some of the few companies not susceptible to these downturns are industrial giants such as IBM, General Motors, and General Electric, which are considered by many too big to be taken over—although, in the present economic climate, even this is not certain. Thus, investment banks often avoid making new investments in corporate issues and are rethinking positions still held in portfolios.

American bankers say that to overcome the current hostility of domestic and international investors, U.S. industrial firms will be obliged to provide bond holders greater protection against so-called event risk, that is, the danger of credit downgrading because of a takeover that is not reflected in the balance sheet or profit-and-loss statement. They can do so through more tightly worded bond contracts.

What may yet emerge is a new standard of language that triggers a put when an outside party acquires 20 to 50 percent of a company's outstanding common stock. But, although the inclusion of strong put language may save most industrial issuers some 30 basis points on a long-term financing, it may also precipitate a greater financial crisis in case of an LBO.

Of the new bond covenants devised to offer some protection to debt holders, many are one-sided. They offer the holder compensation if management deems a deal to be hostile, but not if either management or a friendly buyer puts the company in hock to take it private. Nevertheless, there is pressure on companies to tighten up the protective language in bond indentures. For example, if a company is taken over or taken private, the bond will often pay a new, higher interest rate.

These are sugar-coatings offered to the purchaser by bond issuers; in fact, most securities markets have none of the procedures developed by bank supervisors to monitor risk.

With new types of risk, such as LBOs, steadily appearing, this could be detrimental to the health of the market.

A safety net for some types of risk may be particularly important for the small shareholder or bondholder who does not have the capacity to absorb failures in the market. (Were stocks time deposits, in the event of an accident, central banks would step in to protect depositors from loss. No such lender of last resort stands behind the securities markets.)

As evidenced by their behavior in the New York stock market, small to medium individual investors deal with uncertainty badly.

Since 1985, small investors have been liquidating stock holdings at an unprecedented rate. Supervisors can work to change this trend and bring confidence to the market by establishing common standards on measuring risk and by clarifying responsibilities.

With small investors marginal players at best, the behavior of institutional investors plays a growing role in the global financial market. These investors have an international perspective, as well as the know-how necessary to deal in diverse markets, different currencies, and a variety of financial instruments.

Private investors usually transfer funds from low-yielding, fixed-rate savings accounts into higher-yielding financial instruments by making many moves of small value. Institutional investors do so with fewer moves, each with a large value.

The regulatory climate is favorable to such moves. Every financial institution and exchange in the First World encourages nonresident corporations and public entities to raise funds in the market. Institutional investors become more powerful by developing specialized financial instruments to absorb the large pool of funds seeking higher rates of return.

This system works well as long as there is fair play. A healthy global market should provide growth opportunities for its participants; when lust and greed overtake prudent logic, however, financial markets can become dangerous.

This does not mean that full-fledged risk coverage is necessary but rather that there is a need to redefine exceptional risk and financial responsibility.

As things now stand, it is doubtful whether the banking, securities, and payments system could be shielded from the consequences of widespread insolvency in the financial markets. This phenomenon would in fact inflict fatal losses on a large number of intermediaries simultaneously. Even widespread illiquidity poses severe problems, as became evident at the end of January 1990, when the bond market crashed.

New, global financial regulation should be implemented, not to eliminate risk, but to clearly define, on an integrative basis, the rules of the game regarding

1. the banking system as it is known today,
2. the securities markets and exchanges,
3. forex transactions,
4. options and futures,
5. off-balance sheet items,
6. some chapters in the treasury side,
7. reserves required from whomever engages in financial transactions above a certain level and at a frequency greater than an established benchmark.

Regulations should ensure that some of the reserve money is globally administered so as to establish a lender of last resort to securities firms but without the unwanted effect of encouraging intermediaries to take even greater risks.

Beyond that, international coordination is vital. The securities business is evolving in such a way that exercising national control has become progressively less feasible. Investment banks are therefore increasingly active in several national markets, including the international secondary market in equities, the Eurobond market, and different securities and commodities exchanges.

Each of these has already outgrown national boundaries. As a result, the nature of the risks currently assumed by securities market intermediaries could, in a crisis, impose unacceptable external costs on the entire financial and payments system and, ultimately, on the whole First-World economy.

To recapitulate, in order to capitalize on business opportunity and growth, financial market exchanges will likely continue to deregulate. Their challenge is to synchronize, in a short period of time, global activities in such a way that no major loopholes or unsettling, destabilizing factors will be left uncorrected.

Big changes may not happen daily, but news and transactions travel fast; therefore, an intelligent communication network built for the global market should provide instantaneous regulatory linkages. Also important is that expert systems be used to assist in all transactions, check on compliance (particularly in the case of big-ticket operations), and fully automate low-value deals.

These guidelines are relevant not only for exchanges, but also for individual firms. To become and remain a low cost/high quality producer and distributor of securities services, a financial firm must develop a strong in-house capability relative to high technology.

Endnotes

1. Charles P. Kindleberger, *A Financial History of Western Europe.* (London: George Allen and Unwin, 1984.)

2. Optical disks, optical fibers, optical anything.

3. A native of Austria and journalist by profession, during and after World War II Dr. Drucker became one of the fathers of modern American management theory.

4. "The Coming of the New Organization." (Paper delivered at Corporate Leaders Forum, Harvard University, Cambridge, Ma., 1989).

5. This defines a whole topology in which the financial institution operates in real time on a twenty-four-hour-per-day basis with the market mapped into a super computer through mathematical models.

6. See also Dimitris N. Chorafas, *Risk Managment in Financial Institutions* (London: Butterworth, 1990).

Chapter 2

Investment Banking

Chapter 2
Investment Banking

1. Introduction

Banking has existed for at least thirty-seven hundred years. Historical evidence indicates the presence of banking organizations for nearly two millenia before Christ. One of the earliest evidences of banking regulations is contained in the Code of Hammurabi (1728–686 BC), the founder of the Babylonian Empire; it consists of a set of legally binding standards for banking procedures.

Banking in antiquity was done without the aid of a currency; the standard unit of value was variously defined as an established weight or measure of agricultural produce or of some precious metal.

During the Renaissance, the Italians, the first modern bankers, transferred money in international trade and handled the substantial payments received and dispensed by the Catholic Church in Rome. Italian bankers spread throughout Europe, establishing correspondents in Avignon, Barcelona, Bruges, and the Champagne fairs.[1] Financial outposts were instituted in Amsterdam, Antwerp, Besancon, Hamburg, London,

Lyons, and elsewhere. In fact, Lombard Street in London is named after the Lombards of northern Italy.

During the industrial revolution in England, the bank and its financial services were restructured along the lines of capital formation and usage. This enhanced the bank's role as an intermediary between society and industry, as well as lenders and borrowers.

Today, industry uses accumulated capital to invest in producing goods and services. From the largest commercial banks and brokerage houses to the smallest credit union or savings and loan association, the essential function is to collect money from people and institutions who have accumulated a surplus, (i.e., creditors) and deliver it to those who need to use it (i.e., debtors).

Financial institutions also invest their own assets to make a profitable return, but the core of their business is managing the net wealth of others by giving investment advice, arranging terms, and collecting a percentage for their services.

This fee may be either a fixed commission or interest-rate spread (i.e., the difference between what the financial institution pays to borrow the funds and what it charges to lend them out again).

The bank accumulates capital from depositors or borrows funds from other financial institutions. The role of an intermediary is to correct a mismatch between where the capital is available and where it is needed.

Today this intermediary role has been taken on by department stores, acceptance corporations, telephone companies, brokers, and other money market players. Nevertheless, banks have expertise that non-bank organizations lack; during their years of experience in the financial markets, bankers have accumulated a large store of knowledge regarding where and how to invest wealth.

Managing money is not for everyone. Thus, it is inevitable that members of the high-net-worth population—people and companies—will get to know each other. They are trained in each others' behavior patterns and understand each others' operating habits, market perspectives, and financial networks. The composition of this population, while dynamic, is shrinking.

The Wall Street Journal asked a former securities regulator where financial control was concentrated today, and was told that there is no longer a following of "thousands of anonymous stockholders" owning publicly traded companies. "There are a limited number of shareholders, and they know each other," the former regulator said. They also need each other in order to stay in business.

2. Money and the Essence of Finance

In essence, finance is an exchange across time, involving transactions between the past and the future. The surplus accumulated from past enterprise, and stored in the form of money, is made available to new ventures with the promise of future rewards. Investment banking is that simple; the past and future determine the basis of an agreement and define its terms. Then money changes hands, or more precisely, is invested.

Money facilitates arrangement among several parties; hence, it is a sort of communications medium. The inventor of money has not been determined—likely candidates, however, include the Chinese, Sumerians, Babylonians, Hittites, Assyrians, and especially the Lydians.

The first widely used currency in antiquity was the unit of coinage established by Gyges, King of Lydia, in 687 B.C. It was an alloy of gold and silver cast in a uniform shape and weight. This marked a milestone in financial history; money had now begun to assume the function of an instrument of transfer (i.e., one used for transacting business). Money made it possible to make remittances from one place to another without transporting bulky commodities over long distances.

Once an accepted unit of value had been established, business could be transacted by an exchange of liabilities. Thus, money evolved from a concrete, or tangible, entity to an abstract, intangible one.

Nevertheless, one might still ask, "What is money?" Is it an entity whose value is determined by a government or reserve bank, or is it a representation of choices made in, and the shifting values of, the market?

Money can be defined in more than one way, and these definitions are complementary rather than contradictory. Money is, as discussed, a means for transacting business and, because it is limited in supply, a store of value. It is also the raw material of the banking industry; without it, banks cannot act, as financial intermediaries, to promote capital investment.

Money is, as well, a unit of measurement; it makes it possible to apply metrics, to have reference points, and to apply debits and credits. As such, money is an instrument used by a government to regulate its economy.

In the U.S., this power is exercised through the Federal Reserve System, and in other countries, through central banks. Fifty or more years ago Marinner Eccles said, There is no limit to the amount of money that can be created by the banking system, but there are limits to our productive facilities and our labor supply, which can be only slowly increased and which at present are being used to near capacity.[2]

Government monetary policy is to be distinguished from fiscal policy, which relates to taxation and the budget. Furthermore, monetary and fiscal policy often come in conflict, usually for political reasons.

For example, monetary policy contracts the money supply while fiscal policy is expansionist, as attested to by budgetary deficits. An analogy might be that of a street car going down a steep hill with its conductor applying the brakes only to the left wheels.

William Greider illuminates the nature of this conflict with an example from post-World War II U.S. economic policy: Yet Treasury wanted to keep interest rates low, both to hold down the cost of government borrowing and to encourage private economic activity. It was, Eccles acknowledged, a conflict of responsibilities. The Treasury's primary job is to finance the government at the lowest cost at which it can....The Federal Reserve has the job of regulating money and credit in such a manner as to help maintain economic stability.[3]

Monetary policy must ensure that the currency of the country, in this example the dollar, functions as both a store of value and a unit of account. If it does not, the production and consumption sectors of the economy start to spend dollars as fast as they are received, on occasion daily; prices are then fixed on the basis of the value the monetary unit is expected to have tomorrow, since its intrinsic value has been eroded through inflation. This process leads to hyperinflation.

Monetary authorities can regulate the available money supply not only by stopping the printing press, but also by reducing the velocity of circulation of money. Thus,

Money Supply = Monetary Base x Velocity of Circulation of Money

In the U.S., the monetary base has been classically followed through M1, which represents the spending of money in the form of currency and most checking account deposits. There are, however, nine different measures of M from M0 (currency only) and M1, to M2 and M2′ all the way to M7—and all of them can be distorted as the financial system changes.

The French use M2, which includes all small savings accounts and time deposits at banks, to calculate the monetary base; the Germans use M3, which is a broader aggregate; the

Spanish use M4. There is no agreement among economists on which is the best measure.

Most economists agree, however, that excesses in the monetary base always find their way into the financial markets. During the 1980s, in the U.S., this excess drove up paper prices and allowed Wall Street's great rally; but ten years earlier, in the 1970s, the excess accelerated the velocity of circulation of money and led to two-digit inflation.

Both in the sense of metrics and in terms of transacting business, money is now often regarded as financial information. Walter Wriston, the former chairman of Citibank, says, "Information about money is becoming almost as important as money itself."

Actually, this idea is not new. In the early 19th century, the Rothschilds made their fortune by being better informed than other bankers about the outcome of the battle of Waterloo. In this case, the messengers were pigeons; this trend in being better informed than competitors accelerated with the telegraph.

According to Dr. Charles P. Kindleberger, the telegraph made possible for the first time efficient, direct manufacturing operations based in one country and controlled from another. Success in money and banking operating in a number of countries, before the telegraph, required having a large number of brothers or cousins, with a single combined interest and thinking more or less alike, to solve the agency problem.[4]

Today, this role is played by intelligent networks. Technology not only helps to inform bankers and investors, but also interconnects markets, sometimes magnifying interim tactical market corrections, achieving resounding new bottoming effects, or amplifying worldwide a notion of euphoria regarding investments.[5]

Increasingly, money is handled electronically, by being stored in databases, manipulated by computers, and transferred through networks. Money in the form of information can be embodied in a cheque, a banknote, a bill of exchange, a debt instrument, an electronic funds transfer, or in any of a variety of specialized text and data exchanges. It can be presented as a written instruction relating to an account, or transmitted over lines and visualized on a workstation.

3. Investment Banks and Merchant Banks

The business of both investment and merchant banking is financial engineering. As do their merchant banking counterparts abroad, investment bankers in the United States go beyond the traditional risk-taking of market-making and underwriting. They invest their capital in restructuring established companies and funnel seed money into venture-capital fledglings.

Pure underwriters do not usually invest on a long-term basis, monitoring the progress of the company. Investment banks, however, hold on to shares, underwrite more shares or bonds, and arrange mergers.

To do this job, investment bankers require a considerable amount of real-time information from around the world. Thus, investment banks must have rich databases with listed companies and corporate loans, as well as on-line access to public databases.

Figure 2.1 shows, in the form of a block diagram, component parts of an information system that can help an investment bank to prepare new offerings. This real-life application is networked through the main money markets in which the bank operates and is supported through artificial intelligence (AI).

Financial markets today are significantly influenced by networks, databases, and AI because institutions program their computers to take advantage of opportunities or trigger automatic Buy and Sell commands. Knowledge-engineering

Figure 2.1 An Information System for Underwriting Enriched with Knowledge Engineering Modules

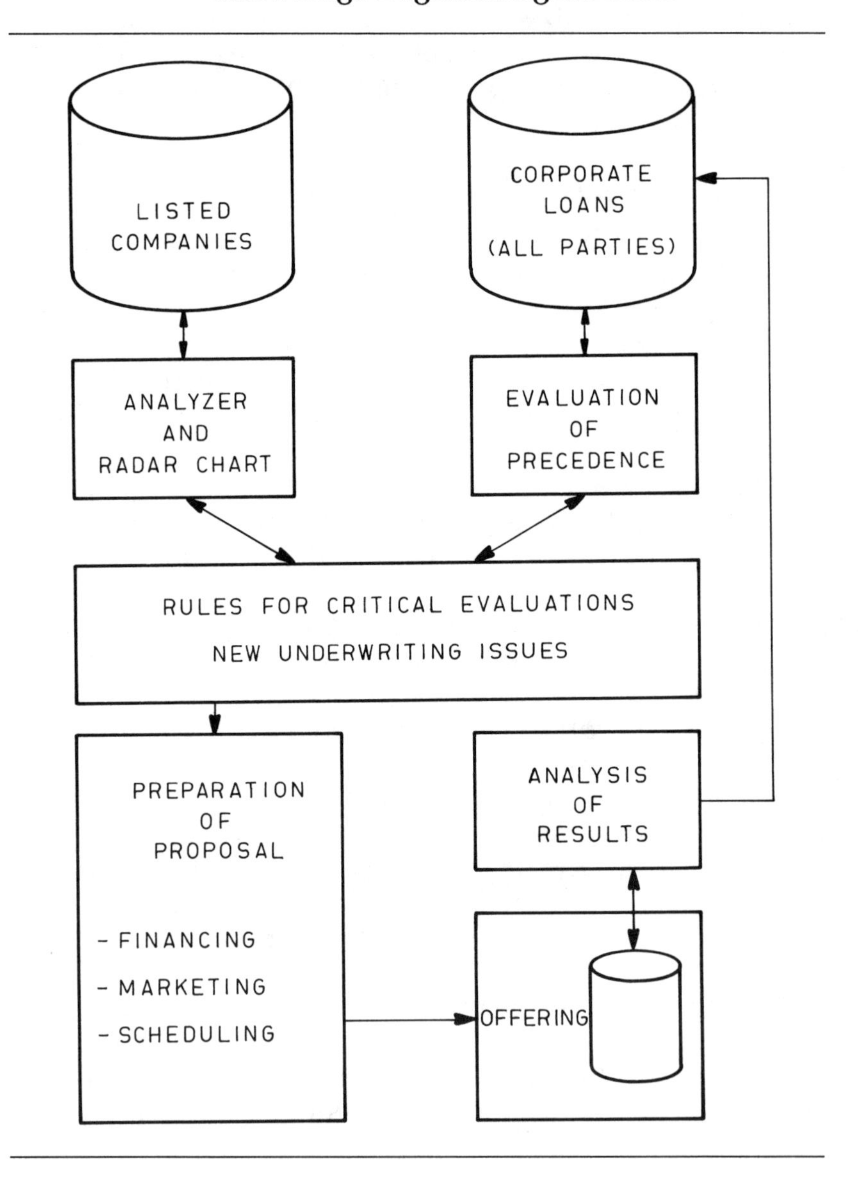

support is indispensable because handling markets efficiently involves not only reading information on a screen, but also performing AI-enriched pattern recognition and processing logical inferences.

For example, when the lows within a pattern begin to form, the operator knows that a business opportunity is developing and must be exploited immediately. Technology also aids in creating accurate client profiles of high-net-worth individuals and customer companies. Aggressive investment banks focus on a system that includes the business environment and the individual customer.

The environment acts on the foremost financial institutions as an agent of change, impacting both on their own executive style (therefore, culture) and on their organizational structure. They know that if they don't keep both of them dynamic, they will not survive.

But, the investment bank's individual customer also has a major impact on the financial institution requiring individual attention which must be flexibly adjusted to stay in tune with his or her values.

Because they have developed expertise in working with environmental conditions, finding sources of money, and developing business opportunities, investment banks are the financiers of capitalism. Besides trading securities, they raise funds for corporations with stock and bond issues. The late J.P. Morgan, the best known of the 20th Century's investment bankers, once wrote, "My job is more fun than being king, pope, or prime minister, for no one can turn me out of it, and I do not have to make any compromises with principles."

In the seventeenth and eighteenth century, the nearest equivalent to a merchant bank was a merchant who undertook lending. A merchant bank in the twentieth century is like a private bank with partners. American-style merchant banking covers the spectrum from giving investment advice to engineering mergers and acquisitions.

This approach began to take on its present dimension in 1985, when Merrill Lynch offered to put up a $1.2 billion loan to help in a takeover of Miami-based Storer Communications. In a number of buy-outs since then, Wall Street investment banks have assisted managements with very large loans, in return for owning a part of the company being acquired.

The lines dividing merchant banking from investment banking—particularly in the U.S.—are hazy. Dr. Carmine Vona, of Bankers Trust, considers the merchant bank more transaction-oriented. He believes that a successful merchant bank will have

1. the ability to spot financial opportunities;
2. a fast reaction time, because the mismatched conditions that create opportunities tend to reach equilibrium quickly, then disappear;
3. the ability both to test new products on a trial basis and to transform them into a volume operation to keep up with expanding market demand if they succeed;
4. the know-how to withdraw and absorb the losses if the product does not find market acceptance.

Because of the rapid pace and global nature of merchant banking, Vona suggests that its practitioners must constantly monitor positions, as well as credit, rate, and liquidity risks, all of which have a major and lasting impact on bank profitability.

Both merchant and investment banks must be able to design, sell, and deliver, any product, any time, anywhere in the world. Thus their aim is to develop an environment that makes fast-paced product creation and delivery possible; otherwise, they may wind up with a portfolio of non-liquid, low-quality, long-term assets with insufficient yields.

Also, corporate clients may become competitors of both commercial and investment banking institutions if they have (along with investment expertise) cultural background, a client investor base, financial staying power, and the ability to sustain a stream of new financial products.

No financial institution or non-bank bank can survive without new financial products, and these demand research and development. An R and D organization should be similar in scope to a lab such as Bell Telephone's, even if smaller. New product planning also requires specific policies, structures, and procedures.

Figure 2.2 shows the matrix organization that must be involved in product planning (PP). Since software should be used to fine-tune the financial products, the personnel of merchant banks and investment banks need a greater degree of technological literacy than that generally exists in the commercial banking business. Managers and professionals at all levels must be able to use technological tools effectively.

Those who go into investment banking should also have a creativity, ability to work under pressure, and a sense of personal responsibility. They should also think and act as entrepreneurs; their job will require negotiation skills and emphasize factual and documented decision making.

Investment banks need highly qualified investment advisors and risk management tacticians with a feel for customers' needs. Also necessary are personnel qualified in administration and capable of setting up control systems, as well as executives who can follow up with any necessary corrective action in order to make the bank a low-cost producer and distributor of financial services.

4. Capital Markets and Money Markets

Capital formation is the reason for the existence of the banking system, particularly merchant banks and investment

Figure 2.2 A Matrix Organization for Product Planning in the Financial Industry

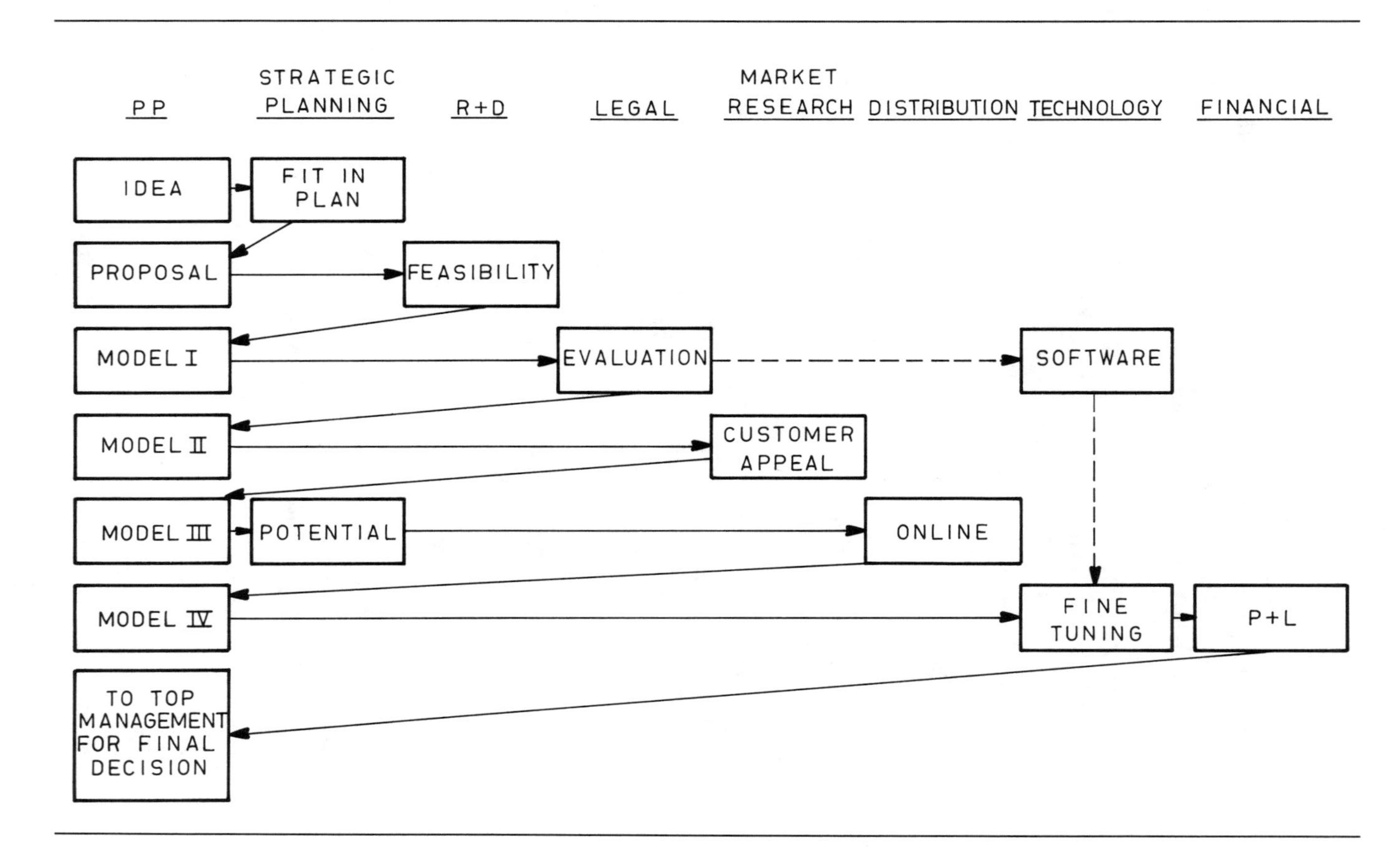

banks. Capital formation goes beyond accumulating savings into creating new productive facilities to allow wealth to be generated through investments. As such, it determines the pace of expansion that creates new services, which, in turn, generates jobs. A good example of the process is Sweden, where a proliferation of banking institutions in the 1850s was succeeded by rapid economic growth that transformed the country from one of the poorest in Europe to one of the richest in the period from 1870 to 1914.

Sweden transformed itself through hard work and financial engineering, an activity that addresses itself to all facets of the banking business, including the institution's internal operations as well as its external interaction with the client base, the development of capital and the know-how necessary to manage it, wholesale and retail trade, and capital markets and money markets.

Today, all the largest banks and securities houses operate as multinational financiers; wealth flows across national frontiers without losing its value, seeking opportunities wherever it finds the highest return, the least risk or both. Global banking takes place in both money markets and capital markets. Capital market transactions are typically medium-to-long term, and a major activity is that of issuing bonds and promissory notes.

Securities transactions are part of this market. In the widest sense, securities are documents giving title to property or claims on income that may be used, for example, as security for a bank loan; but, securities are also income-yielding financial paper, or debt and shares, traded on the stock exchange or in secondary markets.

On Wall Street, the bond market is where judgments are made about the long-term future of the economy. The bond market is also the place where a skeptical audience of trading experts continuously assesses the government's and the Federal Reserve's performance. When bond traders bid up interest rates, it means that they do not trust the regulatory authorities to protect the future value of money; when asset managers foresee a liquidity crunch, they quickly convert to cash rather than having the market downgrade their investments. In the interests of capital formation, bond traders, through the sale of their financial products, offer their services to both private and institutional investors.

The Federal Reserve Board, after examining all financial assets held by Americans, calculated the average net worth of American families (their assets minus their debts) and the following portfolio can be profile developed:

- Of the total net financial assets, 54 percent were held by 2 percent of the families.
- The greatest amount of such assets (86 percent) was held by the top 10 percent of families.
- Another 35 percent of the families shared among them the remaining 14 percent of financial assets.
- This leaves 55 percent of the families in the sample with zero or negative net worth.

Thus, capital formation typically occurs at the top of the financial pyramid, and the few lend to the many.

Directly or indirectly, high-net-worth individuals own most of capital, including bank-holding companies, insurance firms, and other financial entities. Pensions and life insurance, however, are also indirect forms of personal savings and are distributed much more widely among American families than stocks and bonds.

A mutual fund is a financial organization that makes investments on behalf of individuals and other institutions. The investor buys shares of the fund, and each share represents ownership in all of the fund's underlying securities. Any dividends and capital gains produced by these securities are paid out in proportion to the number of fund shares owned, after managerial bonuses and general expenses have been deducted.

During the mid- to late-1980s, mutual fund assets experienced significant growth. Various factors have led to this surge in funds sales, including deregulation, which enabled mutual fund companies to advertise, thus enhancing their competitive edge. (Nevertheless, mutual funds still represent only 6 percent of total financial assets in America; bank savings accounts and other low-return investments account for a greater percentage.)

Besides dissolving barriers between banks, brokers, insurers, funds, and so on, deregulation has led to growth in the number of outlets for financial products and promoted the creation of a large array of services that can respond to the needs of a broader base of investors.

Deregulation helped the educated consumer and led to disintermediation. When the high interest rates of the early eighties made money market funds more attractive, many investors switched their money into these accounts; then, as interest rates declined, investors, accustomed to high returns, began looking for solutions with higher returns than savings and time accounts.

Short-term debit instruments are issued and traded in the money market, in which transactions are usually for terms considerably less than a year. This market became important with the deregulation of the banking industry. It flourishes unless legislation (e.g., Switzerland's stamp duty) penalizes the short-term transaction, and, as with capital market operations, it can be divided into domestic and foreign segments.

A certain intensity of capital- and money-market transactions characterizes a financial center. Today, legal and tax conditions rather than location, increasingly determine the development of these centers. This shift is largely owing to the worldwide use of electronic money, an that issue will be discussed in the last section of this chapter.

5. Investing under the Spectre of Inflation

All investors, large and small, institutional or personal, have one thing in common: a fear of inflation. Millionaires and low-net-worth savers, young or elderly couples accumulating a modest nest egg, giant insurance companies, mutual and pension funds are all subject to the effects of the shrinking dollar.

When inflation fever reigns, precious metals and real investments, such as estates, are the options of last resort. Those who know better appreciate that there is really no safe place in the financial markets, and no way to protect financial assets against the excesses of government.

Nothing panics financial markets more than subversion of the currency, uncertainty, and inflation. The domestic and international repercussions of a collapse in financial markets, including the inflationary psychology that settles in, can be serious indeed.

There is a long history of proposals to stabilize currencies with commodity reserves; except for the use of gold, however, this method does not appeal to the market. Bondholders depend on a government and a reserve bank to protect their wealth, because inflation cheapens the value of money and erodes their long-term financial assets.

Inflation happens when a government succumbs to pressures put on it by various sectors of the economy, each of which tries to resist major portions of the burden falling on it or to gain a competitive advantage. This typically includes resistance to taxation, which swamps the government's revenues. In order to maintain its share of real output, the government runs deficits and covers them by printing money.

Inflation can be stopped by making the weakest sector (typically, consumers) pay for it. "We must tax the poor," said Andre Tardieux, a former French Socialist Prime Minister. "They are the most numerous."

Deflation, or the measures taken to stop inflation, may succeed if unemployment and wage reductions can be imposed upon labor. This solution can be avoided if foreigners fail to recognize what is going on and contribute resources in the form of capital inflow. But when that contribution to government deficits stops, the monetary system has to be fixed, which could prove quite painful.

The German hyperinflation of 1921–23 was much more than a financial phenomenon; it was rooted in the sociopolitical condition of post-World War I Germany and its people, who were unwilling to bear the burdens of a lost war and its reparations. The short-term approach was that of printing money and letting fate decide the outcome. This started a recession that led to World War II.

Generally speaking, violent changes of major economic magnitude occur during wartime periods and in a relatively short time. Thus, they can be thought of as a means of testing the structure of a monetary system and its resilience.

For this reason, wartime periods provide fertile ground for economic studies. Dr. Milton Friedman analyzed the data from three wartime periods of the United States—Civil War (CW), World War I (WWI), and World War II (WWII)—in respect to prices, income, and monetary changes. The price peak came approximately at the end of the CW, with a ratio of 2.32 to the price at the start. About a year and a half after the end of WWI, the price peak also reached a ratio of 2.32. Three years or so after the end of WWII, the price ratio was 2.13.

Thus prices at the peak were almost identical in these wars—2.13 to 2.32 times their level at the outbreak. Given differences in the duration of each of the three wars, the rate of rise was successively lower though the immediate reason for the increase in prices and money income was the same: the diversion of resources for wartime use. Slightly over half of one year's national income was diverted to the war budget during the CW and WWI; this figure went as high as 166 percent of the national income during WWII. On a per-year base it was 14 percent in the CW, 9 percent in WWI, and 18 percent in WWII.

Three facts are generally cited as explaining part of the better performance in terms of inflation in WWII.

1. A larger portion of government expenditures was financed through taxes.
2. There was a significant increase in output.
3. Greater direct controls were exercised over prices, wages, and the distribution of goods.

Direct controls were completely absent in the CW, they were present to some extent in WWI, and they were excessive in WWII. The major way in which direct controls can reduce inflationary pressure is by stimulating increased purchases of government securities. But direct controls, Dr. Friedman suggests, did not ultimately affect the magnitude of the price rise.

In these three war periods, total Federal tax receipts averaged 1/5 of total expenditures in the CW, 2/5 of total expenditures in WWI, and 3/5 of total expenditures in WWII. Despite this increase in taxation, the deficit in WWII was greater, reaching 13 percent of the yearly national income. The cumulative total deficit was three times as large in WWII as in WWI. The cumulative excess deficit was twice as large.

During WWII, the substantial rise in real output eased the physical and psychological problems created in attaining such an impressively large war output. The increase in real output added to the factors of production an increase in income paid but, since this was absorbed by the government for war purposes, there was really no increase in goods available for purchase in the market.

From the point of view of the quantity theory of money, increasing output helps to curb inflation related to the gross national product. The government can then finance part of its expenditures by creating money without great inflationary pressure on prices.

Although wars destabilize currency and, therefore, the economy, they have other after-effects, some of which may help the country on its way to recovery. During most of the post WWII period, a cheap currency gave the Japanese a tremendous advantage in world trade. When the yen turned strong in the mid-1980s, cheap credit fueled the Japanese miracle machine.

At the same time, world economic history shows that cheap and easy credit inevitably leads to inflation as well as excessive speculation in financial assets and real estate. Eventually, credit becomes expensive and harder to obtain.

The idea that inflation and interest rates are inexorably linked dates back to the theoretical work done at the turn of the century by one of America's great monetary economists, Irving Fisher (1867–1947). Fisher argued that the interest rate consists of two components—a real rate and a premium for expected inflation.

The real rate reflects long-term factors such as the productivity of capital and the saving habits of the public. The more productive the nation's capital stock, the more companies will demand funds to invest and thus bid up the price of money. On the other hand, if people save more of their income, more money will be available for lending, and rates will decline.

These fundamental factors, Fisher argued, only change slowly, so real rates hardly move at all; what really makes rates bounce is inflationary expectations. As inflation speeds up, lenders refuse to accept current rates because they expect to be paid back in cheaper dollars; thus, they automatically add in an inflation premium.

As Fisher saw it, a 1 percent increase in expected inflation would push up rates by an equal 1 percent, and vice versa. According to his analysis, the Federal Reserve could not affect the real rate of interest at all and could have only a miniscule, short-term influence on market rates. If the Fed pumped in money in an attempt to lower rates, investors would quickly raise their inflation projections and demand higher rates for their money, thus offsetting the Fed's actions. Like it or not, said Fisher, the monetary authorities could affect only inflation, which would then be translated back into interest rates via the inflation premium imposed by the market mechanism. Unfortunately, as logical as Fisher's ideas sound in theory, they do not always work in the real world. One critical notion is that the public will refrain from lending at current rates if it believes inflation is accelerating; this assumes that people have attractive alternatives, which in general is not the case. In fact, the lending public may gain from inflation, at the lenders' expense—though it will lose from high interest rates. William Greider presents the following example:

- A middle-income family that purchased a $35,000 house in 1969 would have been at that time making monthly payments of around $400. A decade later (because of inflation), the house may be worth as much as $90,000 and the family's wages may have doubled; the monthly mortgage payment, however, is still $400. The mortgage payment is actually shrinking as a share of the family's income.

- On the other hand, if the interest rate is not fixed but variable, then a $40,000 home purchased with a mortgage interest rate of 9 percent will commit the family to a monthly payment of $322. When the mortgage rate goes to 15 percent, the monthly payment rises to $506—an effective

> price increase of nearly 60 percent. At the level of 15 percent mortgages, about three-quarters of American families could no longer afford a $40,000 home.

Inflation is also cheating depositors. For example, before the U.S. rate ceiling was liberalized on some savings accounts in 1978, small investors were in effect forced through most of the previous decade to accept interest rates of 5 percent—even though inflation was running at twice that figure.

Still it is the bond market, whose long-term interest rates the Fed cannot directly control, that may suffer the most under inflation. When bond traders bid on investments of ten, twenty, or thirty years' duration, whether it be government bonds to cover the federal debt or corporate bonds to raise capital for new factories, they are implicitly making a forecast on future inflation. These forecasts are also a judgment on how well the Federal Reserve is doing its job.

A similar scenario exists in the stock market. Inflation can clobber stock prices, as investors have learned to their dismay, over the years. The Dow Jones average of thirty industrial stocks, was trading around 900 in mid-1979, no higher than the level it had reached ten years earlier. But a $100,000 of investments in stocks was worth a lot less in 1979; an investor who bought a portfolio based on the Dow Jones average in 1969 and held on to it for ten years would have lost about half of the value of his or her money.

Corporate balance sheets are also undermined by inflation. These glossy annual reports may show ever-rising profits in current dollars, but this is mostly an illusion, concealing the damage to the companies' real assets. Because of inflation, the replacement cost of productive equipment becomes much greater than the depreciation that firms deduct each year on their existing plants and machines.

It is no small irony that as investors wait for a market rise, the market seems to require, as a precondition, decline in the rate of inflation, the cost of money, the incidence of business failures, and the projected federal deficit. From time to time, prospects may look good with respect to the first three trends; the fourth refuses to fall in line, mainly because of a factor that Fisher overlooked—that of fiscal policy.

6. Capitalizing on Electronic Money

Though its form has changed from gold and silver coins to paper, and from paper to electronics, money remains an instrument for storing and exchanging value. What is important to remember is that money is information and information is money.

Unfortunately, many banks are not equipped to take action based on this concept. The majority still program their computers to function on a sequential rather than inferential basis. The programs they use screen numerical data, such as Dow-Jones points and earnings, but don't make qualitative comparisons on even relatively straightforward processing techniques, such as monitoring the patterns that develop in the market.

Few investment banks have understood that they can value-differentiate their business, and gain an edge over their competition, by capitalizing on the concept of electronic money.

This means combining new product planning with the appropriate technological infrastructure in an integrative way (see Figure 2.3). An approach using mortgage-backed financing (MBF), a relatively new product in securities, will involve

1. conceiving and simulating the product, then experimenting in order to determine its marketability;

Figure 2.3 Merger Product Planning and Technology: A Product Goal and Supporting Services

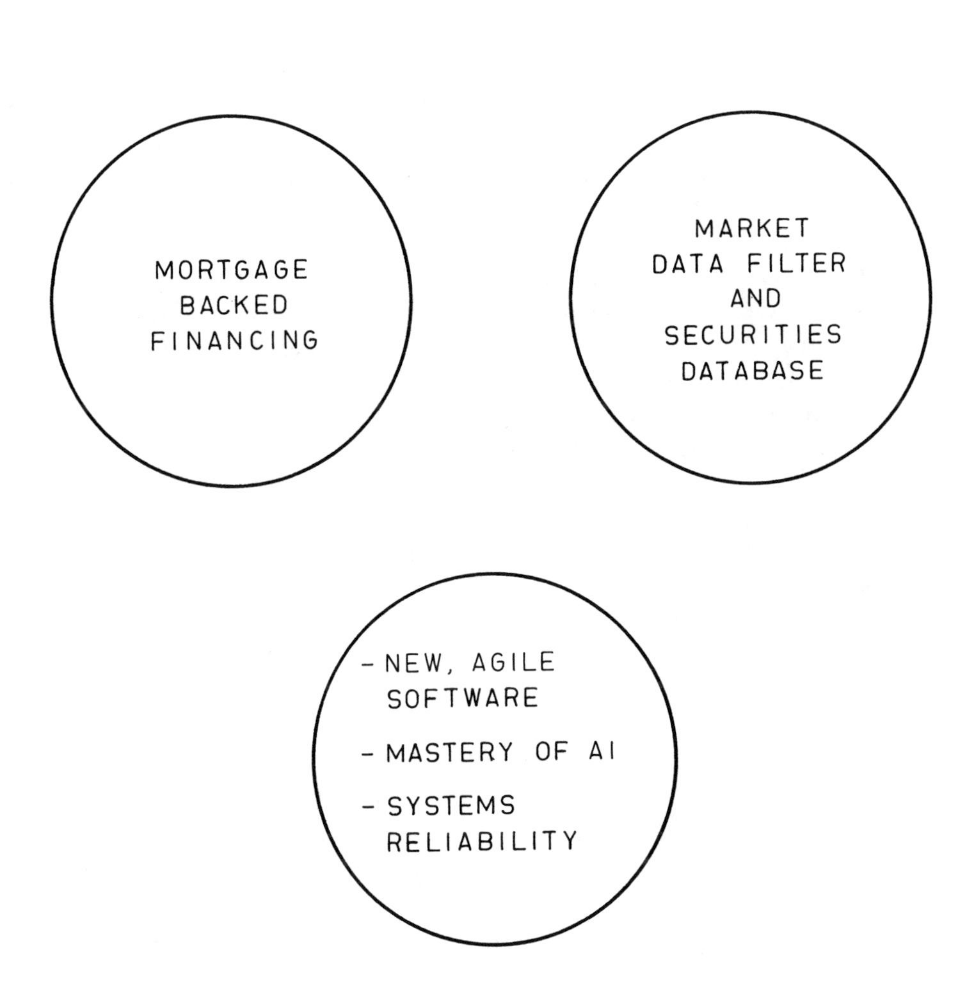

2. the use of supercomputers and AI to construct a market data filter, as well as to help in managing a securities database;
3. the development of new types of software by using knowledge engineering to map the best expertise in the organization into the computer;
4. the use of reliability engineering to assure uninterrupted operations—a "must" in twenty-four-hour global banking.

In other words, capitalizing on the new money management perspectives requires more than electronic funds transfers (EFT). It is necessary to exploit the intelligence that exists in information about money, and this requires a great amount of know-how and high technology.[6]

It is important to understand the significance of electronic money; its invention laid the foundation for a new generation of banking products.

In the late 1960s and 1970s, the growth in the international banking business began to exceed the capabilities of paper-based systems and the manual handling procedures to cope with it.

The need for a fast, safe, and universal means of transferring funds from one place to another grew to paramount importance. This need seemed to be filled when EFT was developed.

Many firms established proprietary computers and communications-based systems to speed operations among their worldwide locations. (Today, nearly half the financial transactions and messages of money center banks—as well as about 85 percent of the money value that these represent—travel over their proprietary international networks.[7]

During the 1970s and early 1980s, financial institutions discovered that while EFT is necessary, it is not enough. The emphasis should be not only on data transfer, but also on the handling of compound electronic documents.

This changed the picture, as payment documents include signatures as well as alphanumeric characters. Automatic signature recognition calls for mastering neural networks, which are second-generation expert systems.

Also, the on-line storage and retrieval of compound electronic documents necessitated the use of imaging, or optical disk technology. In turn, because of time constraints, documents needed to be transmitted over short and long distances required in megastreams (millions of bits per second) and eventually gigastreams (billions of bits per second). This emphasized the primary role of networks.

Megastreams can be supported by coaxial cables and satellites, and gigastreams, by optical fibers and a new generation of satellites. In the second half of the 1980s, however, it became evident that systems developed to handle electronic money need to be personalized to clients, whether they be the corporate treasurers, high-net-worth individuals, or others.

This problem was solved with the development of the customer profile analyzer, which makes it possible to identify the personality traits of a client by using a process of successive evaluation steps as Figure 2.4 shows. This process is fully automated.

Artificial intelligence has made it possible to create a quality database in conjunction with the current portfolio profile. Thus, the bank can build an investment planning and control process which is automated yet personalized by client.

In general, solutions based on AI, simulation, quality databases, supercomputers, and intelligent networks help bankers to make investment decisions based on real-time market reality, not hunches about how things are going. Furthermore, the use of these tools is critical for an expanding financial organization that operates in different tax jurisdictions throughout the country or across countries, uses a variety of funding sources, and has to take into account the

Figure 2.4 Working Online with AI Assistance, from Profile Analysis to Investment Committments

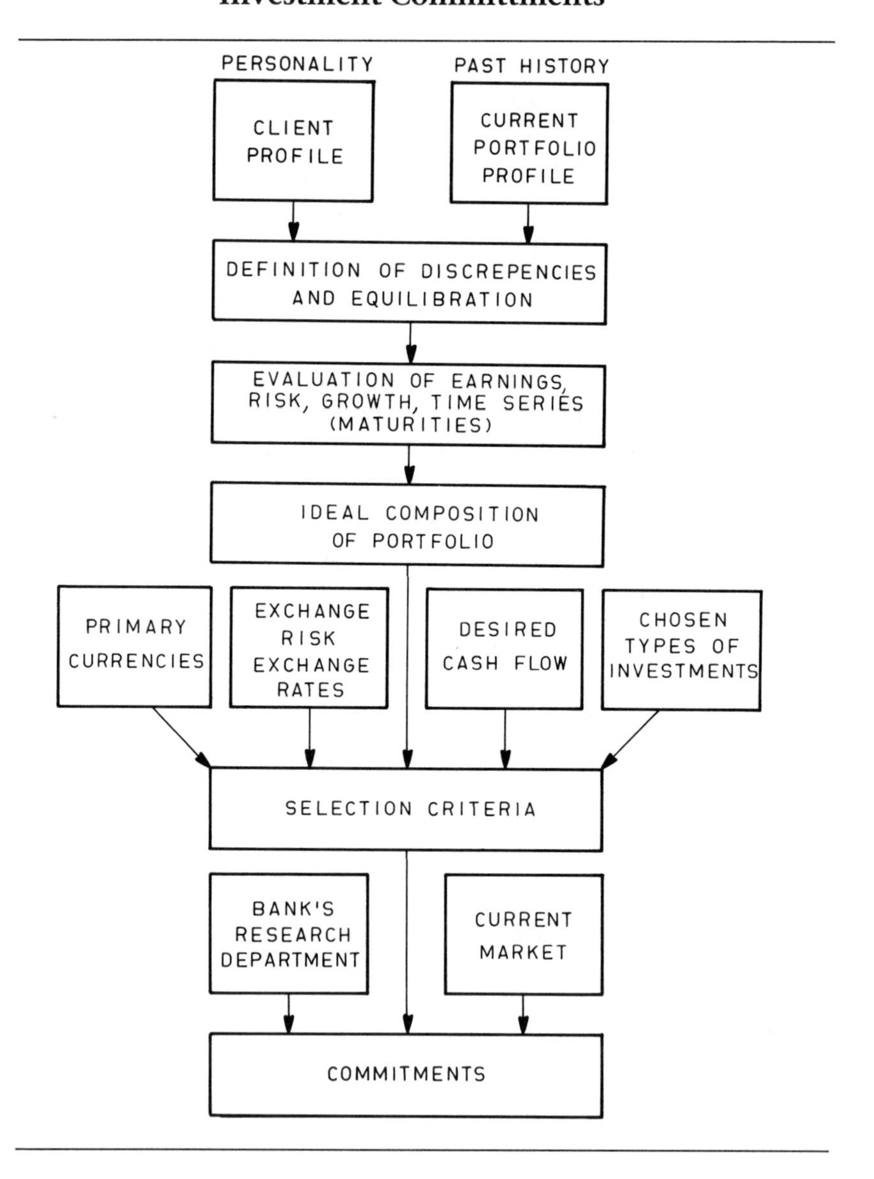

impact of product deregulation and new competition in the financial services industry.

New technology has opened many doors; for example, with information about money digitized, it is possible to exploit this information in many ways that might never have occurred to professionals and managers using paper-based processes and serial thinking. Supercomputers, another major component of the new technology, make it possible to think in parallel, or combine into one set different financial markets, thereby exploiting their opportunities. Patterns can be examined, and business and resource-allocation decisions made, on an integrative and consistent basis.

Yet another new tool is a client mirror, which provides an investment bank or securities house with a pattern of profit and loss (P and L) by individual customer, type of account, and origin of transactions and investments. The customer mirror can reflect all transactions and investments by type, size, cost, risk (to the bank and to the client), income to the bank, profit margin, and realized profits to the bank and to the client.

These evaluations can be extended to comparisons with results obtained by competing investment banks in areas including securities trading, investment analysis, Forex, cost control, P and L, and market share and account management. The goal of these optimization models is to help users make the right choices.

Endnotes

1. Medival and Renaissance fairs held in Champagne, France.

2. Marinner Eccles was Chairman of the Federal Reserve Board from 1933 to 1948.

3. William Greider, *Secrets of the Temple: How the Federal Reserve Runs the Country* (New York: Touchstone/Simon and Schuster, 1987).

4. *A Financial History of Western Europe* (London and Boston: George Allen and Unwin 1984).

5. See also D.N. Chorafas and H. Steinmann, *Intelligent Networks*. (Los Angeles: CRC/Times Mirror, 1990).

6. These subjects are elaborated in two books by D.N. Chorafas and H. Steinmann: *Expert Systems in Banking* (London: Macmillan, 1990); and *Intelligent Networks* (Los Angeles: CRC/Times Mirror, 1990).

7. The other half goes over the network of the Society for Worldwide Interbank Financial Telecommunications (SWIFT), which also handles the money (transactions and messages) traffic of lesser banks that are connected to interbank operations.

Chapter 3

Markets, Exchanges, and Information Providers

Chapter 3

Markets, Exchanges, and Information Providers

1. Introduction

A portfolio is a list of the stocks, bonds, and commercial paper owned by a private investor, an institutional investor, or a bank. Typically, a portfolio contains equities, debt, and cash; but, it may also have other assets, such as precious metals.

The portfolio is structured around a set of securities (bonds, stocks, etc.) that have been bought in various quantities and at different prices. Each security is called a position. For reasons of both analysis and management, a securities database needs to record when each position was bought and for how much. In the case of bond positions it must also recall not only the maturity of each, but also whether it is callable.

Public and company debt is issued to the market through bonds. Bonds are corporate, sovereign, or other debt obligations with a legal claim on the issuer's assets in a default; thus, they are presumed to be safer than stocks, which represent equity in a company.

As a loan from the holder of the bond to the issuer, the bond specifies a sequence of payments of principal and interest according to a schedule. Factors determining this schedule may include the issuer and type of bond, its face value, the conditions of payment (if any), whether it is callable or a bullet, whether equity-linked or not, and the maturity date.

Whether they know or not, most Americans today depend on the bond market to finance their retirement, their hospitals, their schools, their jobs, their productivity, even their defense. The same is true for citizens in all other First World markets.

There are market leaders and followers, whether they be investment houses or markets, in different types of securities. For example, bonds denominated in Swiss francs and issued in Switzerland by non-Swiss borrowers represent the world's second largest international bond segment after the Euromarket.

Some exchanges, like the Chicago Board of Trade and the Chicago Mercantile Exchange, specialize in trading commodities. With commodities, moneys, options and futures, equities and debt, there is no high-return, low-risk investment, except in wishful thinking.

Trading advisors cannot eliminate the risks inherent in trading commodities, equities or debt; they can, however, apply their skills and experience to the task of reducing risk and improving an investor's chances of enjoying the benefits of the futures market. Successful trading employs the results of thorough research into economic and financial conditions. Highly structured research, or financial engineering, now offers expertise and insurance against the danger of emotional decision making that is the downfall of many amateur investors.

2. Why the Market Matters

Theoretically, a prerequisite to a healthy market is to have a reasonably stable medium of exchange, traded at a rate that more or less reflects the true value of the currency. Nevertheless, the money markets of the First World, which are presumably healthy, have wide swings in exchange rates.

These swings take place for a number of reasons, the most important of which are psychological (though traders prefer to analyze swings in terms of fundamental and technical factors). While real interest rates, (the difference between interest rates and inflation) among other factors, play a key role in promoting or dropping a currency, market sentiment and echo effects play a decisive role in the pricing of currencies by the market.

In order to follow and analyze market behavior, it is necessary to use metrics. One of these, the dividend indicator, is employed to determine whether stocks are cheap or dear. (Its use is now being challenged by non-traditionalists.)

The market's dividend yield is a percentage figure, which is computed by dividing the amount paid in a market index by the number of companies in that index. Other factors being equal, the market's yield sinks as stock prices climb.

It is considered to be a bad sign if the dividend yield on stocks is low, especially when compared with yields on alternative investments, such as bonds and Treasury bills. Figure 3.1 shows yields on the S&P 500, based on cash dividends, over a twelve-month period. As is evident, there has been a steady degradation of dividends; stock buy-backs practiced throughout the eighties did little to alter this trend.

Prior to a leveraged buy-out, RJR Nabisco announced it would purchase up to 20 million of its shares at prices between $52 and $58 a share. A month later it bought even more—21 million shares—at $53.50 each. RJR Nabisco, which had

Figure 3.1 Yields on the S & P 500, Based on Cash Dividends

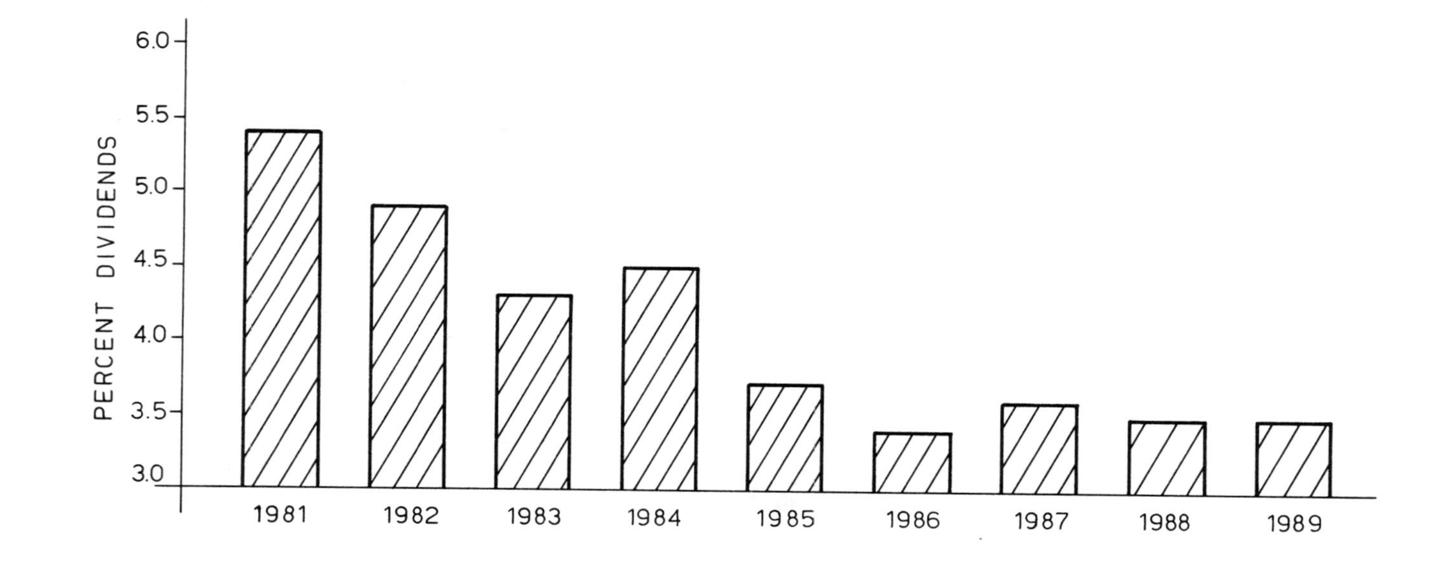

traded around $52 a share in anticipation of the buy-back, immediately fell back into the mid-forties. Johnson (RJR Nabisco's CEO) had spent more than $1.1 billion buying stock, and its price was lower than ever.[1]

Stock prices, according to theory, represent the present value of future corporate earnings and are indicators of the state of supply and demand in the economy. This is not always true.

In the U.S., and to a lesser degree in Europe, it is the current year's (and to some extent, the next year's) earnings that count. In Japan, the frame of reference in evaluating earnings is the long term—ten, fifteen, even twenty years.

In the Western world, earnings have great impact on stock price which, in turn, influences another indicator—the cumulative value of listed companies in a stock exchange, or market capitalization.

Market capitalization is used as a metric of financial strength. It is also a volatile issue; an example of this is given in Figure 3.2 which shows dividends, net profits, and market capitalization in the first half of the 1980s, on the Zurich stock exchange.

When each year's rate of growth or decline is compared with that of the preceding one, it becomes evident that there is an erratic variation in all three factors, and in particular in market capitalization. Furthermore, while many securities analysts believe stock market prices move in sympathy to one another, the graph shows that in at least two out of five years (1981, 1984) they have been uncoupled.

There has been a gradual but steady change in the U.S.'s level of market capitalization. In the mid-1960s the capitalization of IBM on the New York Stock Exchange was equal to the market capitalization (in the Frankfurt Exchange) of the whole German industry. But such times are past; both the value of the American stocks and the strength of the U.S. dollar have greatly declined.

Figure 3.2 **Dividends, Net Profits and Market Capitalization on the Zurich Stock Exchange**

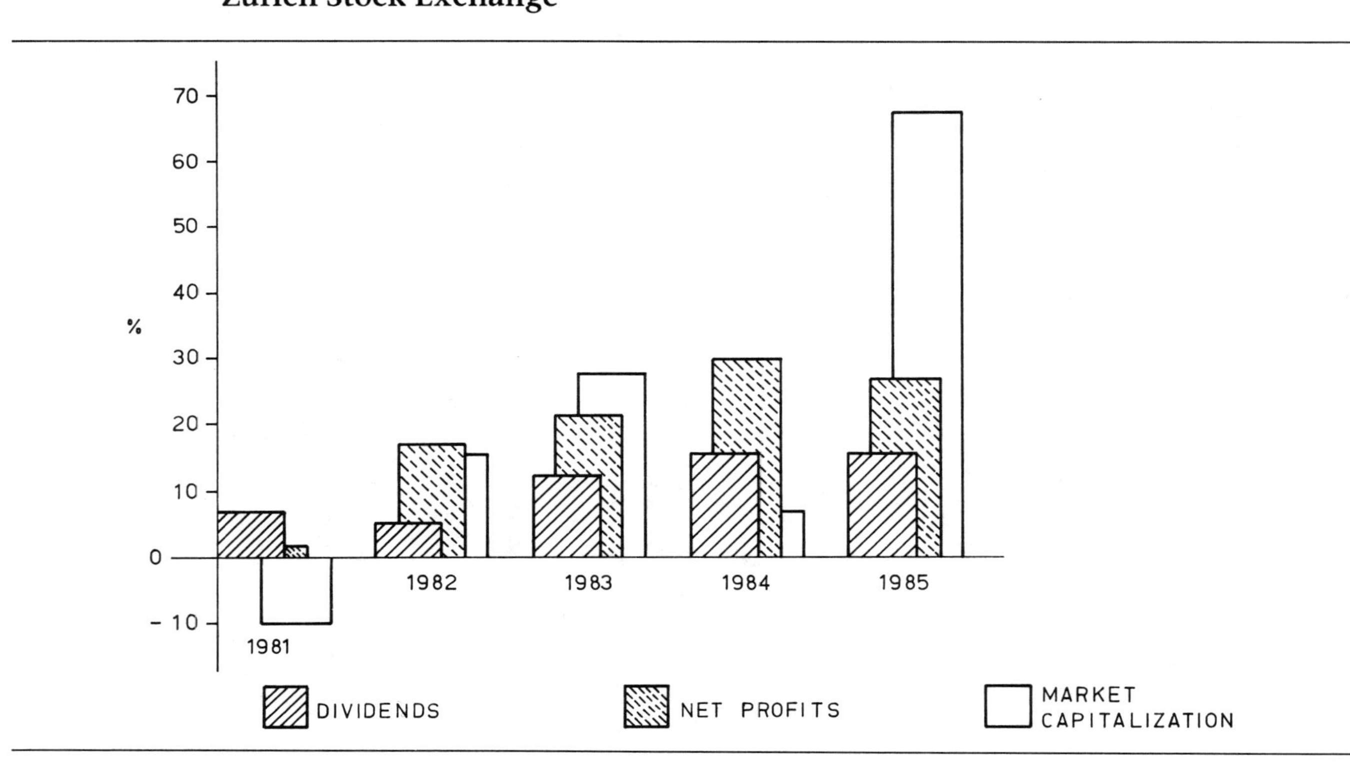

By the end of 1989, the total market capitalization of U.S. companies stood at $3 trillion, while Japanese companies were valued at $3.9 trillion. The U.S.'s share of worldwide market capitalization shrank to 29.4 percent in 1988 from 53.6 percent in 1978, while the corresponding metric in Western Europe shrank only slightly, from 20.9 percent in 1978 to 19.9 percent in 1988. Over the same timeframe the capitalization of the Japanese industry grew from 17.8 percent to 44.2 percent.

The appreciation of the yen against the U.S. dollar has inflated some comparative statistics, but clearly the Japanese have targeted financial services as a strategic international market. Already number one in terms of market capitalization as well as volume of equities and bond trading, Tokyo has surpassed New York as the world's premier financial center.

This dramatic change is shown in statistics released by Morgan Stanley Capital International (see Figure 3.3). Though these are percentages, in absolute terms every market grew. The market value of equities was $1.4 trillion in 1978; it became $8 trillion in 1988. Even adjusted for inflation, $8 trillion is an impressive multiple of the 1978 market value.

Another significant change to be noted is the shift from equity toward debt. In the New York stock market alone, corporations have since 1984 retired more than $600 billion in equity while raising more than $1 trillion in debt from banks, institutional investors, corporations, and the public.

The growth of currency debt markets around the world has accelerated as technology hastens the flow of capital across borders.

Computers and communications have made trading both speedier and cheaper, enabling investors to use new financial instruments. Also, as markets grow more sophisticated, they are increasingly being dominated by the institutional investors, whose behavior tends towards wide swings rather than stabilization.

Figure 3.3 Market Capitalization in Equities in the U.S., Japan and Europe: A 10-Year Change

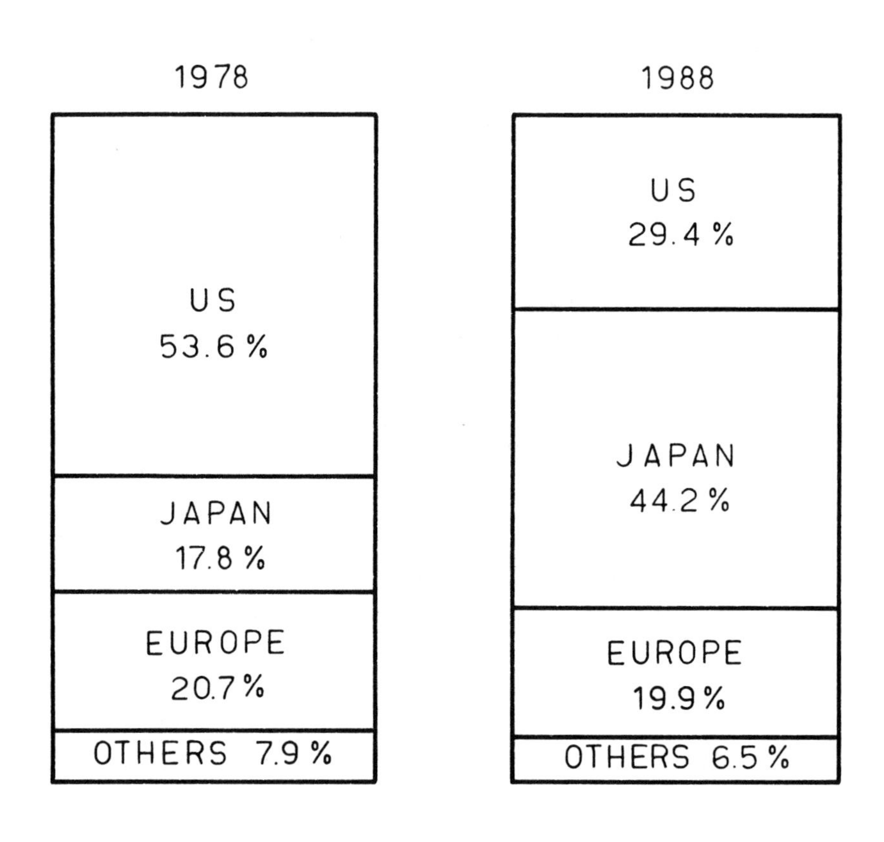

Wide swings bring hardship not only to investors and brokers but also to the market mechanism as a whole. Brokers hold their clients' positions on margins, and when the market turns sour, some of their clients are not able to face the effects of leveraging.

Charles Schwab and Company, America's largest discount broker, suffered heavy losses in late 1987 because one of its customers failed to meet a margin call of $80 million. The firm's potential loss was believed to be at least $40 million. According to Wall Street sources, Schwab asked Security Pacific and other banks for help.[2] That same week, faced with a $44 million loss, L. F. Rothschild and Company, a middle-sized investment and brokerage firm, announced 150 layoffs.

Direct financial losses were not the only immediate aftereffect of 1987's Black Monday. Just as significant was a 35-percent drop in retail trading activity. Investors who called their brokers afterwards encountered a substantially leaner securities service industry geared to wringing more profit out of a narrower retail customer base. At some brokerages, particularly the discounters, that translated into higher trading commissions and also meant less personal service for all but the biggest customers.

In England, big securities houses took a critical look at their operations, and a few dropped out of the private client business altogether to focus on more profitable financial services. Others decided to serve only wealthy private customers, preferring a niche market to the risks of a wider one.

Many securities dealers are currently avoiding executing trades for individuals; instead, they are focusing on the economies of discretionary money management. There are, however, brokerage services who cater to the less affluent. For individuals who feel confident about making their own investment decisions, some investment banks offer execution-only services, while some of the more profitable securities houses insist on targeting a carefully defined slice of the market.

3. A Global Structure for Stock Exchanges

When we speak of twenty-four-hour banking our axis of reference is London–New York–Tokyo. Originally, the London Stock Exchange, the International Stock Exchange (ISE), has always been a hub of world trading, with its position becoming stronger in recent years. Figure 3.4 shows its emblem.

The deregulation of the British securities market known as Big Bang brought new international business to ISE. Today the stock exchange in London is the third largest in the world and, as such, is Europe's door to Japan and the United States. It is also the largest exchange in terms of trading shares in companies that are not headquartered in its home market.

Being a major outpost in global twenty-four-hour trading, ISE hopes to cash in on the European Commission's determination to break down the barriers between Europe's stock exchanges. To maintain its position, it is tooling up its computers, communications, and expert systems services as part of a long-term project to automate the entire trading process, including activities such as the entering of share price information, order placing, purchase authorization, and back-office operations regarding stock transaction.

At ISE, this process of gradually eliminating paper-based business is being called dematerialization. The Big Bang created an electronic marketplace. This eliminated the need for market makers and their customers to meet face-to-face on the trading floor.

According to the board of ISE, high-technology solutions are necessary to handle both domestic and foreign securities efficiently. This is particularly true in London, where 25

Figure 3.4 Logo of London's International Stock Exchange (ISE)

percent of ISE activity is now in foreign securities, compared with 5 percent in New York, and 20 percent in Tokyo.

Thus, it is not surprising that London is at the forefront of deregulation and technology. As Dr. Peter Bennett, ISE director of Strategic Research, aptly remarks, three forces—internationalization of the securities business, deregulation, and innovation due to technology—are combining to challenge and destabilize the traditional framework for the operation and development of the securities markets. Exchanges have to be not only reactive but also proactive within this framework.

Financial institutions as well as exchanges need to function in a proactive and synergistic manner. Cooperation among banks can be effectively based on what J. Michael Williamson calls the devolution principle. In British EFT/POS, for instance, each member bank will operate its logical network with the national EFT/POS structure acting as a big switch.

A similar approach can be taken with investment banking and brokerage networks. As another example of the devolution principle, in mid-1989 five major competitors on Wall Street—Morgan Stanley, Goldman Sachs, Salomon Brothers, First Boston, and Drexel Burnham Lambert—joined forces (and budgets) to develop a sophisticated communications network that will enable them to compete with domestic and foreign giants.

In London, Tokyo, and New York, real-time networking and computer-assisted trading is fast replacing the telephones and telexes that were the main links between dealers in the 1970s and early 1980s. This has changed the dealing landscape. In Forex, for example, because there was time enough in the past to shop around for the best offer and keep the books in order as well, traders would wait days after a purchase for the currency value to rise before reselling at a profit.

Now, however, the Forex market does some $500 billion in daily trading; these large volumes make hourly currency fluctuations of even a 1/1,000 of a dollar profitable. Millions can be made or lost within seconds; hence, both banks and financial centers are upgrading their technology in the battle for profitability and market share.

Furthermore, nobody in the First World has the luxury anymore of saying, "Markets are closing at 3 o'clock. We can settle the books later on." All major brokers and Forex operators are trading around the clock and the books have to be kept up in real time.

The Pacific Basin stock markets provide a good example of both the rapid growth of the stock market and some of the problems this growth has engendered. In 1982, stock markets in Japan, Hong Kong, Singapore, Australia, New Zealand, and Malaysia accounted for about 21 percent of total world market capitalization. By the end of 1989, because of the growth of regional economies and appreciating national currencies, these countries accounted for some 48 percent of world market capitalization (44.2 percent of which is in Japan).

While it may seem monolithic to some, the Pacific Basin is not one entity; thus, it must contend with cross-border settlement of trades. Banks can exchange currency quickly, but it takes days to settle securities trades, since there are transfer agents involved, multiple brokers speaking different languages, and so on. Transborder settlements are also hampered by the lack of a recognized international numbering system and significant variations in the type and amount of information available to investors.

Investors attach great importance to timely and accurate information, as their judgment on buy or sell depends on it. A valid judgment can rarely be formed based on one type of security. As discussed in Chapter 1, international portfolios are just as sensitive to the price of equities and debt as they are to exchange rates.

Figures 3.5 and 3.6 provide some interesting statistics. They concern total return for investors as a function of changes in the price of securities, the income they provide (in dividends for stocks and interest for bonds), and the effect of variations in the exchange rate of moneys relative to a reference currency.

Notice the difference in the histograms. The upper part in each figure shows results in local currencies ($, L, Yen, DM, and SF). In the lower part income is reported in terms of dollars, or as it would be seen by investors who are U.S. dollar-based and would like to know how they fare in terms of investment in their base currency. (The graphs do not take into account taxes or inflation.)

Doing comparative analyses across stock exchanges can be difficult, because reporting requirements vary widely by country.

- In the United States, quarterly and semiannual corporate financial results must be filed within forty-five days of the close of the quarter.
- In Japan, quarterly reports are not required, and semiannual reports must be filed within ninety days of the half year's close.
- In many other places requirements are simply ignored; for example, in Malaysia in 1988, nearly half of the 350 companies listed failed to file final 1987 results within the required six-month period.

There are also variations in how financial instruments are traded and the way dealing is done. Japan's over-the-counter (OTC) stock market, once a wasteland for little-known stocks, is now booming.

OTC has enjoyed a seven-fold expansion over the past five years, fueled both by companies eager to sell shares and investors ready to buy. "It took a hundred years to see sixteen

Figure 3.5 Equitites—Total Return in Local Currency and in U.S. Dollar Terms

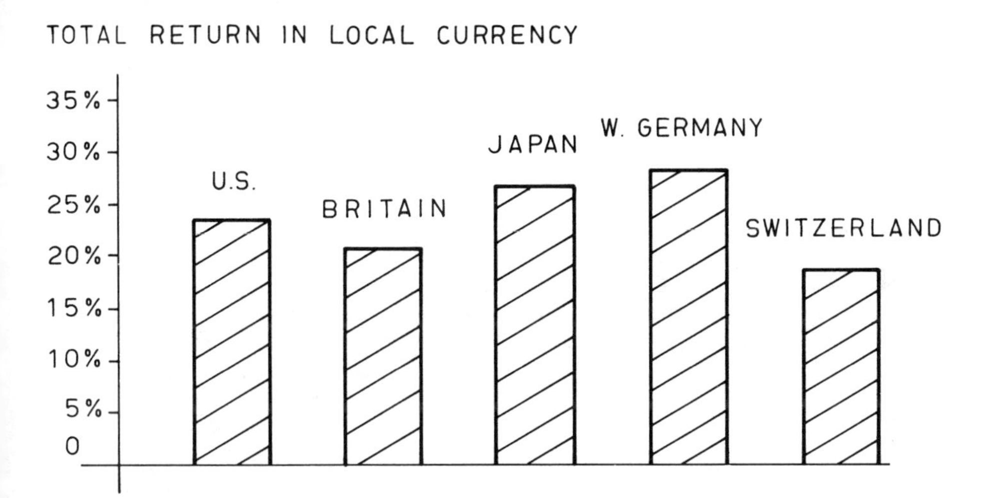

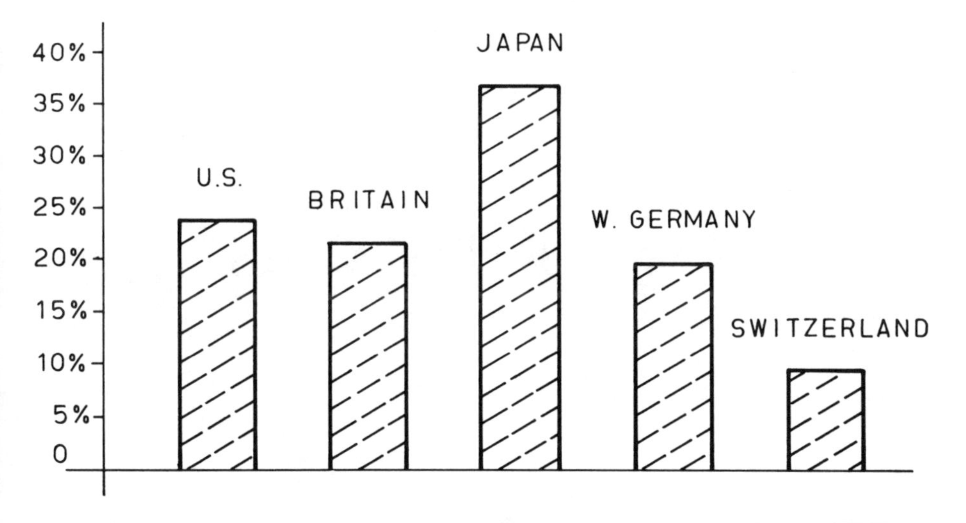

Figure 3.6 Bonds—Total Return in Local Currency and in U.S. Dollar Terms

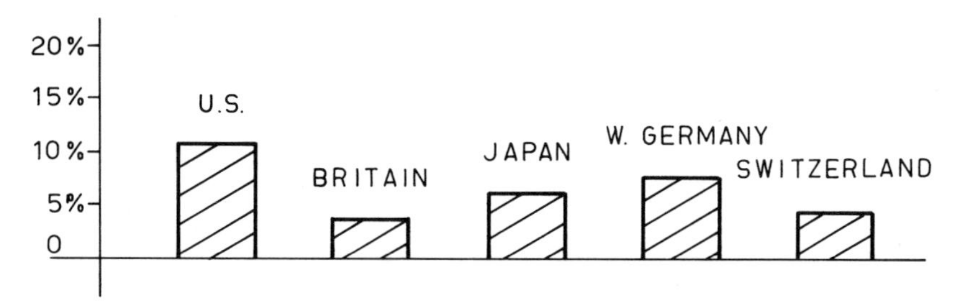

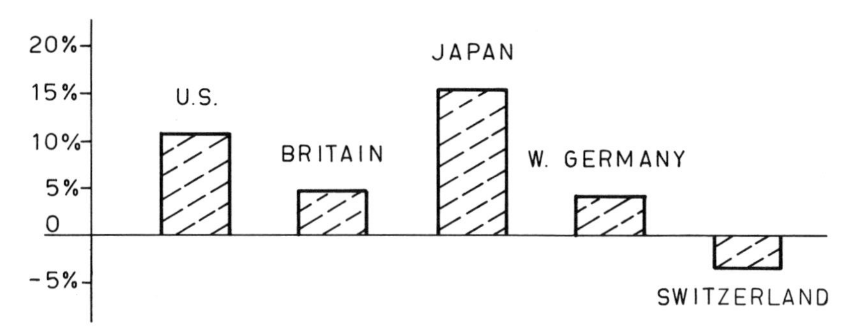

hundred companies list on the TSE [Tokyo Stock Exchange]," says Kojiro Watanabe, president of the Tokyo Investment Information Center. "But it will take fifteen years for the OTC market. This is a revolution. The OTC index will outperform the TSE index over the next two to three years."

Capitalization has ballooned to about 7 trillion yen (about $51 billion) from one trillion in 1984, making OTC bigger than the New Zealand stock market and four times the size of London's second section. In fact, Tokyo's OTC enjoyed a boom in the early sixties, but faded just as fast. Until a few years ago, brokerages were not allowed to recommend OTC stocks or to distribute their reports. But, things have changed.

4. Automating the Exchanges

On-line trading, involving computers, communications, and software technology, has altered the methodology of the exchanges and in a number of cases the practice. Today, many of the New York Stock Exchange's small orders are routed through a network of computers that handles tens of thousands of transactions each day.

Figure 3.7 shows two paths that can be used. In the top path, which reflects current practice, the investor calls the broker to give an order. The broker has market data instantaneously updated by information providers (IP), such as Reuters, Telerate, Quotron, and Telekurs. The problem with IP services is that investors also have real-time access to such data, simply by subscribing to the IP services—and many do.

In the bottom path, the broker's manual interface is replaced with a knowledge-based system, providing the basis for value-differentiation.

According to analysts in New York, within the next 3 years, brokers will be using expert systems to select at least 80 percent of equities, even if overall supervision is under the fund manager's control.

Figure 3.7 A Three-Way Interaction: Investor, Broker and Exchange Floor

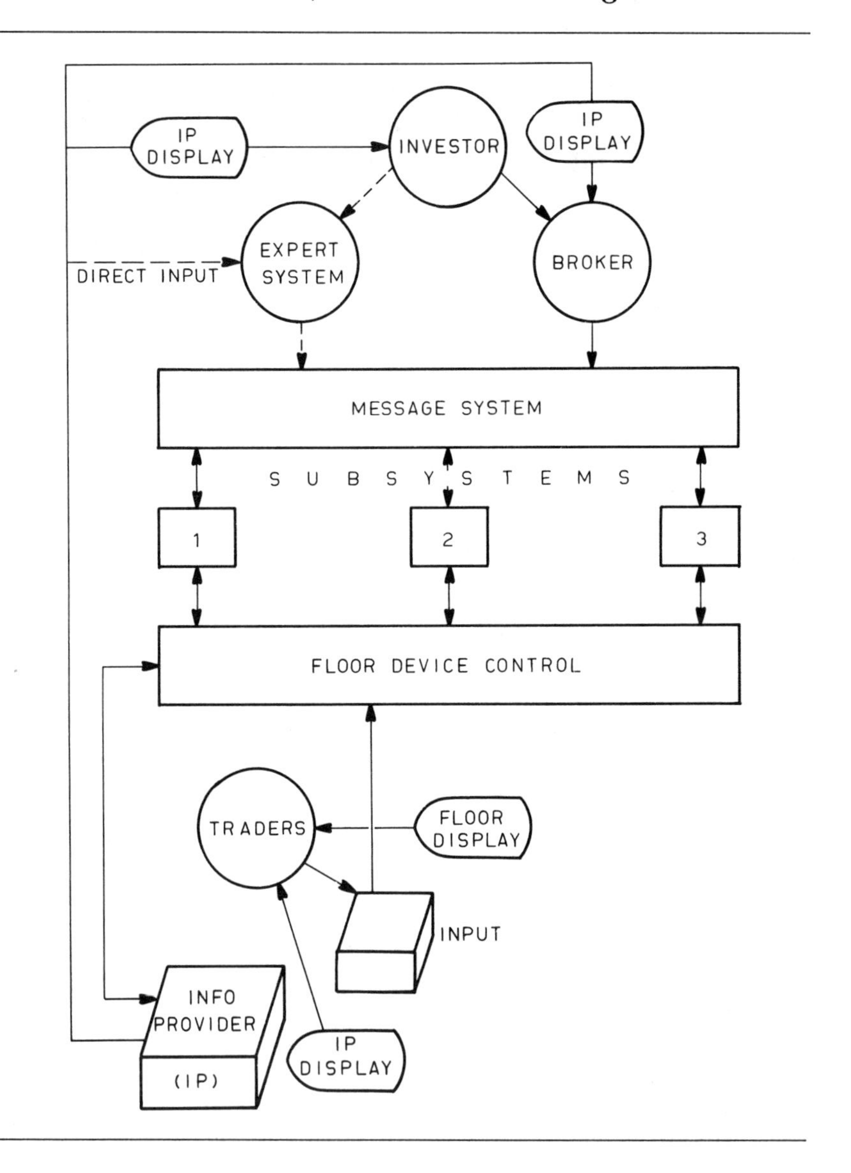

Whether through the broker or by means of an expert system, the input has to be channeled through a message-switching link. Today, this is a traditional technology communications network. Tomorrow it will be an intelligent network.

Brokerage houses that think ahead of the market trends are eager to capitalize on the business opportunities such a network can offer. Capital Link Securities, a company owned 20 percent by J. P. Morgan, is gearing up to let institutional investors bid competitively via computers for public bonds of blue chips. By cutting costs through automation, CapitaLink will charge less than half the Street's typical fee. Furthermore, this is a commodity-type business that corporations can run as efficiently as Wall Street can.

Under plans currently being developed by some stock exchanges of the First World, expert systems at an electronic switchboard will take messages from brokers and translate them into trading language. They will also return information from the exchange's computers to the brokers. Depending on the type of orders placed by brokers, knowledge engineering constructs will be able to

1. automatically handle most orders placed during trading day and all those placed outside trading hours;
2. address itself to Buy and/or Sell (limit) orders from brokers, with action engineered through program trading.
3. specialize to odd-lot transactions, (purchases or sales of less than 100 shares) to minimize handling costs.

Floor control routines at the electronic switchboard will convert orders into metaphors, that is, language understood by equipment on the trading floor. This will be an emulated trading floor enriched with AI contracts.

Today, when a trade is completed, a card is dropped into a reader that scans it and enters data into the reporting system. Video displays show prices, outstanding orders, and other information affecting the market. Data travels back to brokers through the computer system of the exchange, and updated stock quotes are released to wire services and other information outlets. (This function was originally performed by the serial ticker.)

In addition to NYSE and American Stock Exchange (AMEX), New York has a large over-the-counter market where transactions occur under the National Association of Securities Dealers' Automated Quotations (NASDAQ) system. The majority of foreign companies whose shares are traded in the U.S. are quoted on NASDAQ rather than on one of the two major exchanges. This is primarily due to NASDAQ's rather limited financial reporting requirements, as well as the on-line handling capability that this trading network has built over the years.

The minimum criteria for listing a foreign company's common stock on the various exchanges are given in Table 3.1. Both the NYSE and AMEX listing criteria for foreign companies are designed to encourage non-U.S. firms to list their shares by focusing on worldwide rather than strictly U.S. distribution of a foreign company's equity. Non-U.S. companies may also elect to qualify for listing under each exchange's U.S. domestic listing criteria, but few do so.

Technologically more advanced than its competitors, NASDAQ has implemented one of the best networks for on-line trading purposes. Real-time, computer screen quotations can be obtained on the National Market System (NMS), an electronic service that has evolved into a sophisticated and organized market. A company's common stock may qualify

Table 3.1 Minimum Requirements for Listing at the Stock Exchanges in New York City

Criteria	*New York Stoock Exchange*	*American Stock Exchange*	*NASDAQ*
1. Number of shareholders	5,000 worldwide, each holding 100 or more shares	2,000 worldwide each holding 100 or more shares	300
2. Number of shares publicly held	2.5 million worldwide	1 million worldwide	100,000
3. Total market value of publicly held shares	$100 million worldwide	$20 million worldwide	No specified minimum
4. Balance sheet criteria	$100 million net tangible assets worldwide	$24 million stockholders' equity	$2 million total assets and $1 million stockholders' equity
5. Pretax income	$100 million cumulative for the last three years*	$30 million cumulative for the last three years**	No specified minimum

*With none of those three years less than $25 million
**With none of those three years less than $7.5 million

for inclusion on the NMS by meeting relatively simple listing criteria.

In other exchanges, too, a gradual introduction of electronics-based trading is in process. In Zurich, for instance, this is expected to dispense with regional rivalries among trading floors from bank and brokerage offices throughout the country. Switzerland also has a fully electronic Swiss Options and Financial Futures Exchange (SOFFEX)—a fully computer-based futures market from trading through to settling. Introduced in mid-1988, SOFFEX operates under the control of leading exchanges and banks, with traders and market makers connecting on-line with computer partners.

The NASDAQ and SOFFEX example are not the only ones in the First World. The trend on all major and some of the minor exchanges is to gradually automate both operations and surveillance activities.

Work done along this line at the New York Stock Exchange is leading to speculation that the Big Board is becoming Big Brother. For example, as part of its market surveillance operation, NYSE has compiled a massive database as well as developed sophisticated software that allows it to spot trading by a corporate officer's relatives, neighbors, college classmates, and fellow club members.

To do that, NYSE had to gather a large amount of private information about half a million individuals, the majority of whom have never been accused or even suspected of committing a minor crime. That information goes into the Automated Search and Match (ASAM)—a quality database (see Chapter 4).

Officers in corporations, every accountant associated with one of the Big Eight accounting firm, every lawyer who is registered by the state, every investment banker who is a member of the exchange, employees of companies that are members of the exchange, and many others are included. The database has information such as home address, wife's maiden name, relatives, civic organizations, college graduating classes, employment history, and so on.

According to New York law, such monitoring of individuals is apparently legal, though some people say that it violates the spirit of the U.S. Privacy Act of 1974, which was passed in the wake of the investigatory abuses of the Nixon administration. At the time, Congress did not envision what would be possible with computers; thus, there are database-related loopholes in the act.

For greater cost effectiveness, ASAM works in tandem with another NYSE computer that creates continuously updated profiles of trading in all listed stocks. This system, known as Stockwatch, analyzes trading patterns and sends up red flags whenever price changes, or volume or other factors violate certain parameters.

There is an algorithm that alerts NYSE executives that they should be looking at a particular stock. It reads prices every day and looks at how they have moved. Altogether, the algorithm watches eighteen parameters and sends out an alert whenever any of these are violated.

With or without sophisticated watchdog activities, the stock exchange is one area in which investment banking and brokerage merge. With automation, the field of market transactions has become extremely impersonal; thus, first-class technological solutions can provide a competitive edge, particularly when operating in a global market.

5. The Changing Role of Information Providers

A financial services intermediary, whether it be a broker, bank, or any other party, needs not only to market and administer an increasing spread of products (in an ever more crowded marketplace) but also to be informed in real space about prices. Reuters and Telerate, followed by Quotron in the U.S. and Telekurs in Europe, were the first to establish a network that could ensure real-time service for prices.

Today Reuters and Telerate dominate the world's electronic markets in foreign exchange as well as U.S. Treasury bonds and bills. These firms hope to lead the markets in stocks, futures, and commodities as well. Realizing that the financial information business is booming, thanks to deregulation of markets and the ability of computers and networks to process information quickly and affordably.

In the two most dynamic trading sectors, foreign exchange and money markets, a virtual duopoly has been created by Reuters, a British firm, and Telerate, a U.S. firm.[3]

Reuters, the most powerful firm in the business, rose to prominence with the dismantling, in 1971, of the Bretton Woods system of fixed exchange rates. A couple of years later, Reuters launched a terminal-based service for exchange rates based in London. This service quickly spread around the world. Today about a third of the international foreign-exchange trade is done on Reuters' estimated ten thousand dealing screens, and another third is said to be done over telephones after consulting a Reuters screen.

Clients, who include most of the world's banks, pay rent for the screen and a fee for each service. Profit margins are hefty because once the telecommunications network is in place, profits from the sale of Information Provider terminals increase drastically.

Reuters and Telerate have been able to maintain their duopoly in the markets because it is costly for would-be rivals to develop new price quotation systems. However, competition is mounting; both Telekurs[4] and Quotron[5] have entered this business, the latter with value-added services.

Building up a new name, a new network, original IP resources, and a following is altogether an expensive proposition; thus, whichever information provider gets to the markets first has a good chance of building up an impressive client list quickly, provided this firm can convince traders that its product is indispensable.

A couple of years ago Reuters and Telerate secured a base for terminals and new business opportunity in Japan. At first, because of protectionist barriers on overseas telecommunications carriers, this process was slow; but, now that these problems are more or less over, Japan is the fastest-growing securities exchange in the world.

There are also other functional markets for financial information, such as equities and commodities. But, at least in the American equity market, information supply is dominated by Quotron. Reuters is also working on automated trading, through which foreign exchange, commodities, futures, and shares can be dealt with simply by posting bid and offer prices, which are then matched automatically.

In 1988, Reuters finalized a deal with the Chicago Mercantile Exchange (Merc) to develop an electronic trading network for futures contracts, through which deals can be transacted automatically outside of the Merc's regular trading hours. The concept behind automated trading is to network with the exchanges on a global basis and provide a whole spectrum of services, such as quoting prices, providing pump and quotas, filtering important news through expert systems, and providing access to historical and other public databases, through an integrated workstation.

One promising automated after-hours futures and options trading system is Globe. Projected to start operations in 1990, it still has problems. "Globex is the best technological and commercial answer to the challenges of internationalization and automation," said Gerard Pfauwadel, chairman of MATIF, the French financial-futures and options exchange.

MATIF, which has had Europe's highest trading volume in futures and options in the last three years, is the first exchange to join Chicago's Mercantile Exchange on Globex. The French exchange will initially list at least two contracts, National

Treasury bond contract and Paris interbank offered rate (Pibor) contract, on Globex, in both futures and options form; links for Globex in Japan have yet to be secured.

Because a global trading network operates twenty-four hours a day, it offers major advantages to traders. Its implementation, however, requires significant skill. To acquire such know-how, Reuters put Instinet, one of its subsidiaries, to the test as a small electronic noticeboard. The product was buying and selling shares in America and in England.

Because they key into a vital part of the securities business, twenty-four-hour trading networks set up in the dealing room substantially enlarge the IP's role. The next stage may be to try to tie these systems more closely to the back office, thus providing matching and clearing and truly automating paperwork. To be successful, this approach must integrate functions that are now supported through separate networks. In any financial market, there are essentially two communications systems: one for dealing, and one, the back office, for settling trades.

So far, efficient, automated handling of financial payments documents has not yet been attempted. The problem is beyond the scope of classical data processing; a solution will likely require a massive use of imaging (optical disks) and expert systems, as well as considerable know-how.

Monitoring, supervision, and settlements must be attended to. Coopers & Lybrand worked with Bear Stearns to develop an expert system able to expedite the monitoring of brokers' discretionary accounts by managers. (These accounts allow brokers to invest clients' funds without prior investor approval.)

In the securities industry, all firms expect their branch managers to be responsible for monitoring broker activity; but, a typical branch may register 20,000 discretionary transactions per month. The expert system maintains a profile of each broker's activity throughout the year; thus, it can quickly identify items that a compliance manager would otherwise have to search for.

In recognition of the need for automating supervisory functions, researchers are developing expert systems that can act as "assistants" in areas such as investment management, unit trust administration, personal equity plans, and cash management. Each of these modules, all of which can stand alone or be networked, has a full range of features for its domain specific task.

Today, expert systems are developed by investment banks, securities firms, and other financial institutions. Tomorrow, IPs could provide them through downloading, with customization included.

Typically, expert systems are modular constructions and can be fully integrated with other applications; thus, they can provide a single, AI-enriched solution to the problems of managing in a financial services environment. For example, one application for unit trust management includes functions for unit pricing, dealing, and debtor and box administration.

Commodity software, though not traditionally offered by IPs, could prove to be a significant source of business for them. Customers may not be appealing to larger financial institutions, which have their own knowledge engineering teams, but to smaller brokers and local banks. Solutions offered could provide the capability for switch dealing (with full incorporation of management fees into bid and offer prices), the ad hoc derivation of bid and offer prices at any time during the day with real-time pricing capability, and obtaining dividend information by using a specialized investment management knowledge-based module. Information providers could also offer advanced software that supports their clients' decision-making ability by incorporating knowledge-enriched information. Income modeling, for example, would allow subscribers to see the effect upon yield of proposed changes to a particular portfolio. Without commitment, users can investigate how selling stock A and buying stock B might affect income. Modeling results can be kept in computer memory and retrieved for later comparison. Other modules would help optimize brokers' commissions in purchase and sale.

6. Forecasting the Stock Market

One of the most essential of knowledge-enriched services is forecasting. Investment banks and securities houses provide such information through weekly and monthly reports, which they distribute to their clients, usually free of cost, as an investment service.

Compiled by economists and market analysts working for the investment house, these reports can be instrumental in determining where the financial market is heading. Needless to say, they do not agree among themselves; this divergence of opinion is exactly what makes a market.

For example, in late 1989 Prudential-Bache stated: "Consensus has shifted 180 degrees since last year (1988) and so have we. Last Thanksgiving, we were the cheerful ones, in part because the consensus was preoccupied with a three-pronged scenario of doom." According to this economic analysis document, in late 1988

1. the majority of market analysts believed that the economy was beginning to heat up and inflation was going to increase at an uncomfortable rate;
2. interest rates, which had been rising for several months, were forecast to further rise sharply;
3. the stock market was expected to do little on the upside, and competitor economists were projecting that it would weaken further.

In late 1988, Prudential-Bache, on the other hand, had expected rates to come down and the market to be strong. But in late 1989, this view shifted 180 degrees when the economy seemed headed for a soft landing and possibly for a recession.

But this again was a contrarian view; the majority of other economists and financial analysts were not worried about the threat of inflation in the context of the weakening economy, and with interest rates already sharply down, it was difficult to find anyone who was forecasting a long bond of 9 percent. The Bache specialists were diametrically opposed; they expected reinflation and rising interest rates, neither of which bode well for the stock market. In fact, the liquidity crash at the end of January 1990 justified this view, though it was the bond market that suffered the most.

Prevailing stock-market theories, as well as quantitative and qualitative models written to forecast market movements, will be discussed in other chapters. The aim here is to show how expert opinions can vary, and how some events may precipitate a change in sentiment.

In October 1989, NYSE had a mini-crash. It came almost on the anniversary of the major October 1987 market downfall and prompted many on Wall Street to search for comparisons between 1987 and 1989. Yet, less than two weeks earlier, in an investor newsletter dated October 1, Shearson Lehman Hutton had cited twelve ways in which the bull in 1989 seemed more likely to last. Among other things, the firm noted that

1. the ratio of stock prices to corporate profits was at an inflated 22 to 1 in 1987, almost twice the 1989 level;
2. interest rates were rising in 1987 and falling in late 1989;

3. investor sentiment was wildly bullish in 1987 and far more cautious in 1989.

Yet, the 1989 rally seems to have rested on some shaky foundations. Major among them has been the relentless pace of corporate takeovers, which enriched everyone on Wall Street from stockholders to investment bankers, but also raised the question, Who will pay the bill?

This wave of buyouts was fueled by financing from a junk-bond market that was severely weakened when Canadian developer Robert Campeau nearly defaulted on $1.27 billion of debt payments. He had used these loans to acquire Allied Stores and Federated Department Stores, and there were liquidity aftermaths similar to those in the case of the Australian "tycoons."

"A scarcely perceptible development in Australian life of the 1980s has been the way we have become anaesthetized to the real meaning of big money," suggested Australian Business. "Expressions such as A$18 billion [about $14 billion U.S.] trade deficit and the A$108 billion foreign debt roll all too smoothly from newsreaders' tongues. And nice round numbers make great newspaper headlines."[6] But they don't make a great economy, nor do they provide for continuing business health.

Australian Business went on to suggest that billion dollar figures may be economically important, but they seem to be a part of a dream world which is "distant and meaningless." What is near and meaningful is the collapse of business empires built on sand, which creates an earthquake in the financial system.

In Australia, for example, Hooker's collapse dealt a huge blow to the local banking industry. Domestic banks such as Australia and New Zealand (ANZ) and Westpac were exposed to the downfall of the Hooker group for A$113.5 million and

A$100 million respectively, with the company's shares their only security on those exposures.

In the case of the National Safety Council, the State Bank of Victoria is unlikely to retrieve a cent of its $100 million exposure, secured against nonexistent assets. But foreign banks have been hit too, with the Industrial Bank of Japan at A$15 million, Credit Commercial de France at A$10 million, Barclays at A$10 million, and Boston at A$20 million.

Born out of greed for greater but elusive profits, the practice of debt financing has caused hardship for many financial institutions. When the wave begins, the news spreads fast and many firms try for a piece of the action. Unfortunately, as soon as repayment problems surface, financial backing, both for supporting new takeovers and for salvaging the falling empires, begins to dry up.

What happens in Australia is quite relevant to the U.S., because international financial events influence Wall Street in real time. Also, events can compound; for example, in October 1989, United Airlines said in a three-paragraph statement that a labor-management group headed by chairman Stephen Wolf had failed to get enough financing to acquire the air carrier. (Several banks had apparently balked at the deal, which was to be partly financed through junk bonds.)

Stock-market response was immediate. For some time at NYSE, airline stocks had looked like attractive takeover targets. With the United deal in trouble, investors started to speculate on whether other deals might not go through, and the market went through the floor.

Economist Milton Friedman took an optimistic view of this event: This is a particularly big fluctuation, a very substantial decline in percentage terms, but the market will recover from it, just as it recovered from the one-day, 508-point decline in 1987. There is nothing about the decline in the market, in and of itself, that need give any concern about the economy.

Ravi Batra, in his book, *The Great Depression of 1990* gave a contrarian view: "Whenever wealth is concentrated in countries among very small minorities," he said, "a stockmarket crash can occur and this could lead to an economic depression. Over the next few years, I think the market will decline by more than 50 percent."

Financial analysts' opinions vary; sometimes they are exactly the opposite of one another. In certain cases, some will advise buying, others selling; and the information they give to justify their opinions may be the same—or very similar. But, it is their interpretation of the information that differs. This is what makes a market.

Endnotes

1. Bryan Burrough and John Helyar, *Barbarians at the Gate: The Fall of RJR Nabisco* (New York: Harper and Row, 1990.)

2. *Business Week,* 9 November 1987.

3. Owned at 56 percent by Dow Jones.

4. This firm is sponsored by the major Swiss banks.

5. Formerly an independent company, Quotron is now owned by Citibank.

6. 20 September 1989.

Chapter 4

Legislation and the Role of a Capital Base

Chapter 4

Legislation and the Role of a Capital Base

1. Introduction

Regulation need not be oppressive. On the contrary, it should be dynamic and adaptable to the changing market landscape. Nevertheless, there must be a clear and precise regulatory framework for the proper functioning of the financial market.

One issue addressed by regulatory measures is the type of activity in which a financial institution can engage; another is the capital requirements that it should observe. On the other hand, there are no regulations regarding the type of technology that a bank or a securities house should use.

Hence, the technological infrastructure presents a significant opportunity for gaining leadership,[1] since no bank or securities firm is obliged to maintain a minimum standard—with the exception of some reporting requirements.

Many regulations in the financial markets were originally put in place to protect the markets against catastrophies, like the crash of 1929. But while already-established regulations may work well in a stable environment, they may not be suited to one that is dynamic and fast-changing. Successful regulatory measures need to be adaptable to economic and technological developments, yet impose controls to prevent behavior that is contrary to the good of the market.

For example, regulation Q, which was effectively applied in the United States for two generations, prohibited banks from paying more than a set amount of interest on demand deposits. This rule was effectively neutralized by the rise of the Money Market.

After years of waiving interest-rate ceilings (which created economic distortions in the seventies), the Bank for International Settlements (BIS) introduced new requirements centered on bank capital.[2] Some reserve banks, such as the Bank of Italy, have for two decades raised the loan reserve requirement of the regulated banks any time they saw the danger of inflationary escalation.

Nevertheless, antiquated regulations eventually become counterproductive. One result of Regulation Q was that bankers stopped putting in effort as the spread between cheap deposits and loans became by itself enough to cover costs and still leave a good profit. As a result, many financial institutions that ignored innovations suddenly discovered that electronic banking had left them far behind.

2. Banking, Securities, and the Glass-Steagall Act

One of the most famous legal barriers to competition was America's Glass-Steagall Act of 1933. It erected a wall between commercial and investment banking by prohibiting banks that take deposits from underwriting or dealing in corporate bonds, corporate equities, and some types of municipal securities. The act had three objectives—to discourage speculation, prevent conflicts of interest, and promote the soundness and stability of the banking system.

Supporters of the act believed that the activities of the securities affiliates of commercial banks had contributed to the stock market crash in 1929 and caused the bank failures of 1932 and 1933. They argued that a commercial bank's soundness could be threatened both by direct losses on any securities it held and by damage to public confidence should its securities affiliate falter.

It will soon be sixty years since the Glass-Steagall and McFadden acts, among others, broke up America's banking conglomerates. These acts also restricted commercial banks to branches in their home states and set up the Federal Deposit Insurance Corporation. This eliminated banks' monopoly status, and the accompanying profits, and led banks to greater risk-taking.

In 1991, the Bush administration sent to Congress proposals for changing the old legislative structures. These seek to restore bank profitability by letting financial institutions spread their risks. Proposals include dropping the barriers to interstate banking and allowing commercial banks to pursue other businesses, such as securities. (Some feel that in the time it will take Congress to act on such legislation, technological advances will have rendered the issues covered in these proposals obsolete.)

If legislation is to successfully divide banking activities over time, it is necessary to define what is and what is not included in dealing in equities and debt. As Figure 4.1 demonstrates, this is not easy, as many concepts are interlinked. Thus, it is important to distinguish between financial products and their packaging, the markets for which these products are targeted, and the distribution channels that are used to sell and deliver them.

Every year the distinctions between financial product lines get fuzzier. Securitization, as well as the ways in which banks arrange loans, are making it more and more difficult to distinguish the loans department of a bank from a securities

Figure 4.1 A Financial Product Has to Be Packaged, and This Can Be Done in Many Ways

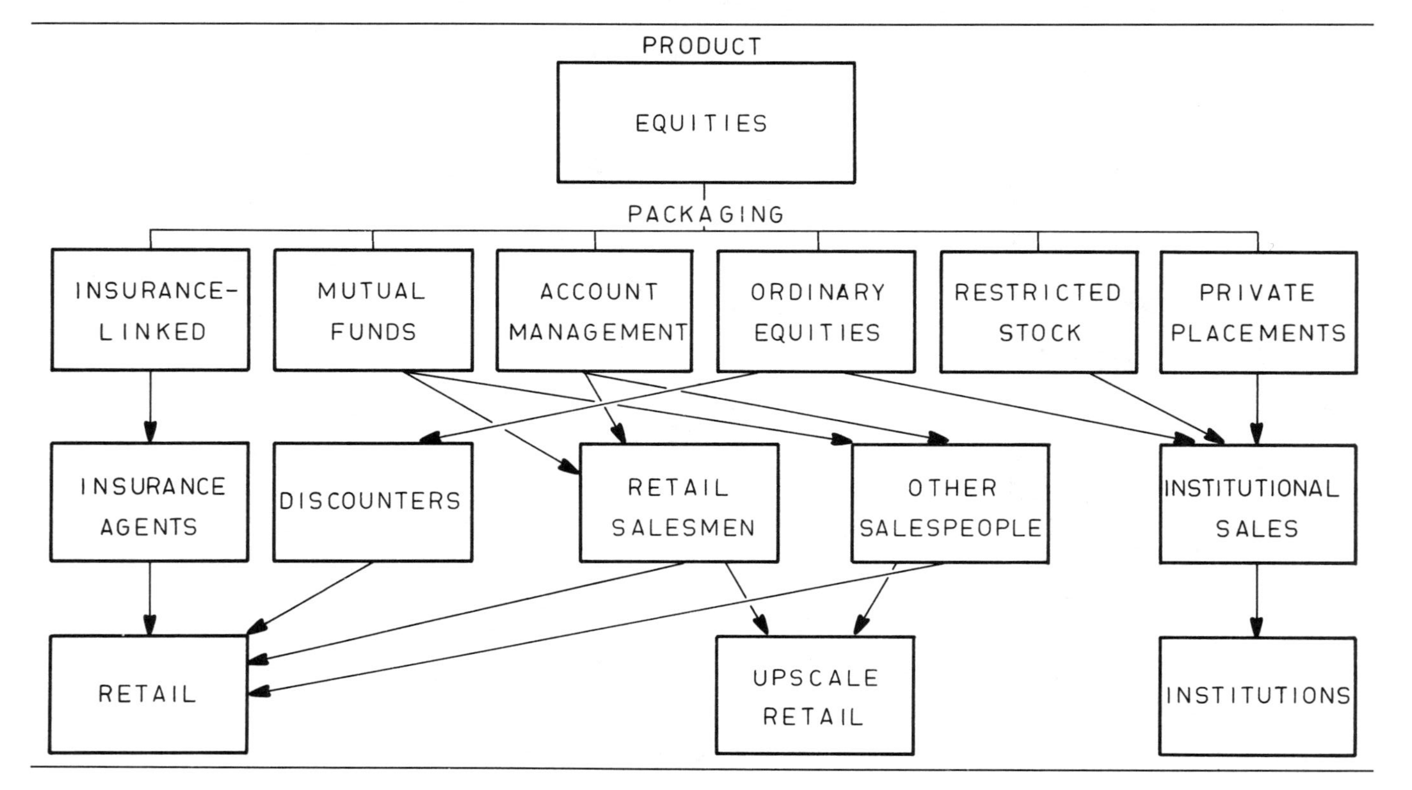

house. Also, global markets are rapidly reducing the importance of whatever restrictions may exist in individual national markets.

Though the Glass-Steagall Act in America and Article 65 in Japan formally provide for legal aggregation in the two biggest financial markets of the world, there is de facto noncompliance with the strictures of the acts.

Until quite recently, when a bank made a loan it usually expected to keep it on its books until repayment. Now many commercial banks are under pressure from regulators to increase their ratio of equity capital to total loans; and since it is hard to persuade investors to buy bank shares in the current economy, many banks consider it more expedient to reduce loans than to increase equity.

Thus, loan liquification is becoming increasingly popular. Although there are legal problems barriers to making bank loans fully tradeable, an active market has developed in packaging and transferring them from one bank to another. This is also true of mortgage-backed financing (and asset-backed financing [ABF]).

Banks with capital constraints, if they want to make room for new business, will sell loans or swap them to other banks that still have room for fresh lending. They also sell packaged loans to institutional investors and insurance companies, thus tapping major financial resources through securitization.

Securitization is a new product, and one that can be developed through value differentiation (see Chapter 13). Investment banks realize that there is no copyright in the banking business.

Financial activities will pay dividends only if a bank can come up with new (or apparently new) ideas, for which it can then charge a premium or earn specific fees. As a result, in the big investment banks, corporate finance departments are now feverishly working on developing products that are both tailored to individual customers and not available from most other banks. These products could be anything from exotic new types of securities to proposals for mergers and acquisitions.

Thus, the line dividing banks from the securities trade has, to all intents and purposes, disappeared. And it may soon be abolished legally; in April 1987, the Federal Reserve decided that the Glass-Steagall Act allowed bank subsidiaries to underwrite commercial paper, municipal revenue bonds, and mortgage pass-through securities, as long as this business generated no more than 5 percent of their revenue. (In June 1988 the U.S. Supreme Court quashed a legal challenge to this interpretation.)

Bank lawyers believe that this limit of 5 percent will eventually be raised to 10 or even 20 percent. They also predict that corporate debt, a big-ticket item in underwriting, will eventually be added to the list of securities. A new asset-backed securities market is now developing in emulation of the fiercely competitive and lucrative mortgage-backed securities market.

Exceptions made to existing legislation are accelerating deregulation. In October 1987, the U.S. Supreme Court ruled that the Glass-Steagall Act's barriers between commercial and investment banking do not apply to state-chartered, non-Federal-Reserve-member banks (SCNMs). This affected thousands of banks in America.

Specifically, the Court refused to hear a challenge to lower court rulings that the act does not apply to SNMB securities affiliates and subsidiaries that operate within the laws of their home states. An estimated nine thousand SCNMs in America are now able to take advantage of this ruling. These, however, are relatively small banks, and even if a number of them take advantage of the decision, the impact on the securities industry will be minor.

More intriguing is the possibility that large state-chartered banks will now enter the securities business. To do so, these banks may have to drop Fed membership as well as circumvent possible bank-holding-company bans on securities. (Table 4.1 shows the strategic considerations involved in this proposition.) Nevertheless, the Court does not create law; it interprets it. True deregulation would mean repealing the Glass-Steagall Act, establishing interstate banking, and observing tougher capital requirements.

Ironically, the October 1987 crash, the liquidity crash of January and February 1990, and the debt of the Third World appear to have accelerated congressional moves to ease the Glass-Steagall Act. Because banks need greater room to diversify and strengthen their earnings, regulatory reforms may be a good solution to the problem of losses on loans.

New forms of security-based lending have grown to the extent that Congress now has no alternative but to allow commercial banks to move into the securities business. Nev-

Table 4.1 Strategic Considerations in Capitalizing on a 1987 Supreme Court Ruling

Reasons to move	*Practical Issues*	*Risks*
Overcome Glass-Steagall restrictions	Drop Federal Reserve membership	1. Wholesale funders feel less secure.
Escape from bank holding	Dissolve holding company	2. Payments systems access becomes more difficult.
		3. Loss of flexibility, and of tax shelter in Delaware.

ertheless, the Glass-Steagall Act may yet remain on the statute books, albeit with major alterations to account for the merging of financial industries and the subsequent redefinition of financial responsibility that will be necessary.

3. The Merging Financial Industries in Europe, the U.S., and Japan

For some time, banks' and insurers' businesses have overlapped. In fact, in Europe both operate on a system that promotes the merging of activities (see Figure 4.2). Thus, the polyvalent aspects of competition have become increasingly relevant.

The struggle for market share in the growing common zone of financial activity is becoming keener and tougher, particularly with recent changes in legislation. In Switzerland, for example, the legislators gave official recognition to the so-called second and third pillars of the Swiss social-welfare system.

- The first is the State pension for the aged and their dependents.
- The second is the pension paid by the now legally compulsory pension funds to which employer and employee contribute.
- The third is the income from the retired person's own savings.

According to Dr. Alfred Wenger, General Manager of Vita Life Assurance Company, life assurance in Switzerland, besides providing risk coverage, has always done business in the area of savings.[3] Competition between banks and insurance firms is, therefore, nothing new. Nevertheless, since the 1970s, marketing considerations have increased in impor-

Figure 4.2 Banking and Insurance Have Many Common Grounds, both Being Financial Industries

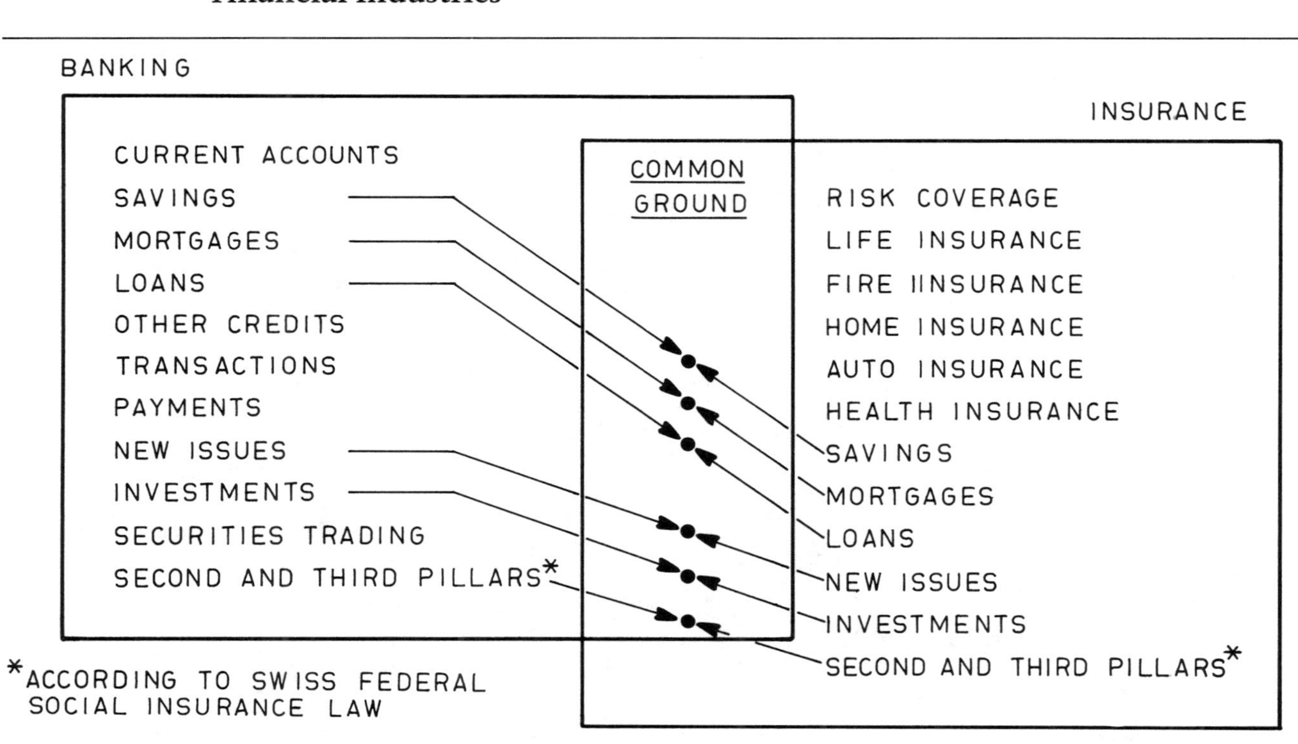

tance in the sector of financial services, with major overlaps being the result.

Mixing different lines of business is not necessarily a competitive strategy; rather, it is a result of companies perceiving a need to offer their customers complementary and ancillary services.

In the U.S. and Germany, a number of banks sell insurance as an ancillary service. For example, in 1989, the Deutsche Bank (Germany's largest) began selling insurance through its branch offices.

Insurance companies in the meantime are doing banking mainly because it is a part of their business. In America, Prudential Insurance handles between two and three hundred thousand checks a day, more than the amount processed by most American banks.

Since insurance companies have no legal constraints on operating in the interstate market, interstate banking is being introduced by non-bank banks. Meanwhile, a Federal Reserve Board ruling now allows the leading bank holding companies—Bankers Trust, Bank of New York, Chase Manhattan, Citicorp, J.P. Morgan, and Security Pacific—to buy and sell corporate bonds. This decision has caused consternation in some quarters. "The Fed is on its way to giving banks an invitation to shoot craps with the taxpayer's money," says John Dingell, chairman of the House Energy and Commerce Committee.[4]

Nor is the Securities Industry Association (SIA), which represents most investment firms, very happy. The increased competition may reduce profits in a business that already operates on thin margins. Wall Street is also concerned that the Fed will deregulate banks even more. Edward O'Brien, SIA president, says, "It represents piecemeal dismantling of the separation that exists in the financial-services industry, a system that has worked exceedingly well for more than fifty years."

Similar comments are being heard in Japan. "The securities are very strong and much more progressive in their implementation of high technology because they make very good profits," says an executive of Kyowa Bank. "Nomura has more profits than all other securities firms taken together."

At the end of World War II, the U.S. government designed and ratified a new Japanese constitution, which including two important provisions—the Japanese could not build an offensive military capability; and the securities industry and commercial banking industry would be separated by law. These were reflections of the state of affairs at the time in the United States under the Glass-Steagall Act. Nevertheless, despite the restrictions of Article 65, and thanks to the crossbreeding of Japanese firms, Japanese banks and others have for some time been making inroads into the securities business.

As one of many examples, Yamaichi Securities, the No. 4 securities house, belongs to the Fuyo Group. There are also seven banks—Fuji, Yasuda Trust, Chiba Kogyo, Ogahi Kyoritsu, Shikoku, Higo Bank and Higo Family Bank—in this group. (Fuji is the No. 3 city bank.) There are also three insurance firms, two leasing companies, and Tokyo Tatemone, Japan's leading property developer.

Furthermore, a loophole in the law allows associates of the banks to have an interest in brokerage firms. Banks exploit this by dispatching staff to the securities houses under their control.

4. Adequacy Defined by BIS and the Quality of Capital

Three times a year, the supervisors of the major eleven national central banks meet at the Basel headquarters of the Bank of International Settlements. The object of these meetings is to compare notes on international lending and to exchange views on the world's financial situation.

The BIS Committee on Banking Regulations and Supervisory Practices has been instrumental in having minimum capital adequacy requirements set for international banks. This is a standard set up to assess capital in relation to credit risk (though it does not necessarily address issues such as interest-rate risk or investment risk on securities).

Capital adequacy is now measured on the basis of consolidated accounts, with capital being defined as issued ordinary share capital, noncumulative perpetual preferred stock and disclosed reserves. This is core capital, or Tier 1, and at least 50 percent of a bank's capital base should consist of this basic element; supplementary capital will be admitted into Tier 2 up to an amount equal to that of the core capital.

By the end of 1992, under the new supervisory rules, international banks must have equity capital equal to a minimum of 8 percent of their risk-weighted assets. This is the fundamental notion behind the Tier 1 and Tier 2 definitions.

Tier 1 (core capital) is a type of equity that determines how fast the bank can expand, since core capital has to account for at least 4 percent of the total 8 percent. As discussed, it must consist of either share capital or disclosed reserves—and no gimmicks such as perpetuals (see Section 5).

Because supplementary capital is a somewhat fuzzy notion, it has been restricted to counting for no more than half of a bank's equity capital. Such supplementary capital may consist of undisclosed reserves, revaluation reserves, general provisions such as loan loss reserves, perpetual debt instruments, and subordinated term debt with maturity over five years. Debt capital cannot account for more than 50 percent of core capital.

According to the agreement worked out by the Cooke Committee, deductions from capital should be made with respect to goodwill and investments in subsidiaries engaged in banking and financial activities, which are not consolidated.

Weights (0, 10, 20, 50, and 100 percent) are assigned to different types of risk assets, including off-balance sheet items. The weighting scale ranges from advances to cash and Central Bank balances; but, BIS has adopted a somewhat ambiguous approach with regard to holdings of government stocks (gilts). It allows national governments to apply weightings of 10 or 20 percent, depending on the life of the stock, in order to reflect interest-rate risk.

While a minimum ratio of capital to weighted risk assets of 8 percent is to be achieved by 1992, national authorities are free to adopt higher standards. It is also likely that these minimum criteria may be increased over time. For instance, the requirement that capital must be allocated to off-balance sheet activities is likely to result in substantial cutbacks in low-margin treasury operations and international lending.[5]

The risk/asset ratio (RAR) has been adopted as the key for determining required capital, with the needed amount of capital set in relation to the sum of risk-weighted assets. Off-balance sheet and contingent liabilities are included in the RAR.

The BIS agreement is the culmination of several efforts directed toward creating a greater degree of regulatory convergence between countries. Emphasis is on the capital regulation of banks rather than on the banking business as such. This immediately raises the issue of whether competitive distortions (whether desired or unintended) are created between banks and alternative suppliers of banking services.

A welcome policy resulting from the BIS effort is that the quality of capital is as important an issue as its quantity. Emphasis is placed on core equity (Tier 1) capital, which must be held at specified levels in relation to assets. This quality of capital is quite important because banks the world over have been diversifying their range of business, and, as discussed in the previous section, classical lines of financial activity based upon specialist institutions have been steadily eroded.

Reregulation at an international level is strongly advised, because banking has become increasingly complex, and there is no precise parallel between type of financial activities and type of institution. As emphasized throughout this book, with the creation of new instruments, global financial markets, and extensive finance facilities, the eighties have been a decade of unprecedented financial innovation.

All this has relevance for bank capital in many respects. Most important, with the incorporation of a wider range of contingent liabilities, the risk characteristics of a bank's balance sheet have become more complex. Also, many of the new instruments (and markets) enable risk to be imported and exported.

Furthermore, because some innovations have enabled banks to raise capital in new ways, supervisors have to determine the amount of risk associated with each one of them (see Section 5); plus, the trend to inflating off-balance sheet accounts has introduced new types of risk for both financial institutions and manufacturing and distribution companies.

Why does a bank need capital? Capital is necessary for at least eight reasons:

1. A bank's capital creates a public confidence factor. Capital attracts capital; that is the essence of banking. A strong capital base is an indication that shareholders are prepared to make funds permanently available to support the business of their bank.

2. Having adequate capital makes it possible for a bank to explore business opportunities without having to add up every small expense.

3. In terms of day-to-day activities, from loans to investments, capital is necessary to absorb operating losses. As with any other industry, finan-

cial staying power enables a bank to remain active in the environment in which it operates.

4. Adequate capital enables a bank to take long-term risks, sustaining possible (and hopefully temporary) shocks while continuing to operate successfully.

5. Capital is necessary to support the bank's basic infrastructure and make its continuous improvement possible. (The technological infrastructure should not be financed by deposits, as the required financial investment is quite significant.)

6. Adequate capital enables assets to be written off as the need arises; thus, tough management decisions become possible.

7. Capital provides long-term funds to alleviate the hazards of maturity transformation.

8. A sound capital base permits the bank to buy time, enabling management to adjust to changing market conditions and patterns of business.

To perform these functions efficiently, bank capital should be permanently available and based on equity rather than debt; there should also be a reasonable balance between the level of capital and the degree of risk being taken.

Of course, having too much capital may be as much of a problem as having too little; it becomes easy to look at own capital as an internal insurance fund for covering risks not included in the bank's pricing scheme. As a professor of banking once said: "A lending officer who has no bad loans may be as poor a decision maker as one who has too many bad loans—because he is losing lots of business."

Losses in banking can come from a number of sources. With all loans there is an expected average loss on a portfolio, but there are also unexpected losses. If capital adequacy is substandard, losses may become disastrous if there is a high covariance between different risks. This is a common factor in most bank failures.[6]

5. Perpetuals and Basic Capital Requirements

The global financial landscape is more precarious than it has been for fifty years. Thus, as discussed in the previous section, bank regulators from eleven countries have been working out common standards for the amount of capital required to be in the reserves of international banks. For example, banks will have to start putting aside capital when they engage in currency swaps, interest-rate swaps, and back-up swaps.

Such off-balance-sheet instruments help grease the wheels of international finance, providing hedging for clients who borrow in one currency and pay back in another. But for the bank they involve exposure, hence risk. To counteract such risk, regulatory rules make these services more expensive.

Bank regulators are, however, at a loss as to how to approach the growing trend of turning loans into securities. Preston Martin, vice-chairperson of the Federal Reserve Board, Robin Leigh-Pemberton, governor of the Bank of England, and Gerald Corrigan, president of the Federal Reserve Bank of New York, have all raised questions about the way this trend is blurring the boundaries between commercial banks and securities houses.

New technology increases a bank's reach, but at the same time undercuts its traditional role as intermediary. The banker's skill in matching borrowers and lenders is fundamentally based on having superior information. But information on who is willing to borrow and lend, as well as what terms are being offered by whom in which market, can now be obtained more quickly, and at less cost, from an electronic screen than from holding banking meetings. That is why the technologically advanced Japanese banks have taken over their European competitors and, to a lesser degree, their American counterparts in a leverage worldwide.

The economy of the First World today operates quite differently than it did only a decade ago. Financial deregulation has changed the manner in which markets behave. Legislation has not matched the pace of major technological advances, nor has it addressed itself to the new wave of financial fraud. Recently, there have been $10 million frauds at Security Pacific in Los Angeles and at a major London bank. An American survey shows there are tens of cases involving the loss of $3.5 million or more. In Britain a study demonstrated that a third of all cases of computer crime now center on financial institutions; altogther they are the biggest single group of victims.

In practically all countries, current law regarding fraud relates adequate only to property that is visible and tangible, not to the invisible and intangible property represented by databases, workstations, and networks. Thus, insurance underwriters often have to determine the ground rules by themselves.

There are also questions regarding financial responsibility and capital adequacy. Banking supervisors recently had to decide whether commercial banks should count as core capital the money raised through the sale of subordinated perpetual floating-rate capital notes.

Perpetuals look like bonds but are considered to be equity, with the additional aspect that the borrower can decide to repay; but, in most cases, the investor cannot ask for repayment.

Obviously, these terms are unfavorable to the investor; this is reflected in the pricing. Perpetuals pay considerably better than a regular bond issue.

Subordinated perpetual notes are a relatively new instrument and are "perpetual" in name only. Essentially, banks are selling fifteen-year floating-rate notes at a 1 to 1.1 percentage point over the London interbank offered rate. This is more than the return on traditional floating-rate instruments.

In exchange for the higher return, investors run the risk that the interest may not be paid. Although the specific wording of the loan agreements is not always the same, the general thrust is that interest payments may be skipped if the issuer runs a loss and omits paying a dividend on its common stock. Also, there is no obligation to make up any missed interest payments once the issuer is operating profitably again. A missing coupon deadline can also make perpetuals look risky and losses in market value can be considerable.

Interest payments officially cease after fifteen years, at which point holders can exchange their notes for cash. Redemption is made possible because the issuer never receives the full amount of the money raised.

The perpetuals are initially sold at a discount of about 20 percent to the underwriter; the notes are then sold to investors at face value and the underwriter uses the 20-percent difference to set up a special trust, which then invests the money in zero-coupon U.S.-government bonds. After fifteen years, the maturity value of the zeroes is equal to the amount needed to redeem perpetuals. Thereafter, the special trust owns the perpetuals, which are essentially worthless.

The issuer can afford to pay a high rate of return on the perpetuals because interest payments are a tax-deductible expense, whereas dividend payments on common stock or preferred shares are not. This is similar to the inverted logic of switching equity for debt in leveraged buyouts (LBO). It is a tax loophole, which explains why some banks are willing to use the perpetuals formula.

To better understand the perpetuals business, one should examine its origins. In 1984, three British banks came up in the Eurobond market with what was called perpetual floating rate notes. The first financial institution on record to offer perpetuals was National Westminster, followed by Barclays and Standard Chartered.

The practice of perpetuals grew in 1985 and 1986, as some companies began underwriting perpetual debt. Within a few years, there were several loans of that type of instrument, with three classes of perpetuals being distinguished, featuring—

1. revised interest rate on a ten-year period, but without accounting for debtor quality (Examples are 5 3/4 SAS and 5 3/4 New Zealand Railway, both of 1986.);
2. traditional fixed interest (such as the 6 1/4% Air Canada, 5 1/2% World Bank, 5 3/4% KLM issued in 1986);
3. Foreign Interest Payment Security (FIPS), which has the peculiarity that the principal is in one currency (such as Swiss Francs) while interests consist of a fixed sum in another currency (such as dollars).

With FIPS, the issuer reserves the right to pay back the capital, hence lendors also face the risk that repayment will not permit them to profit from a change in exchange rates—or in interest rates. Many perpetuals include such call options.

However, where there is risk one can also find opportunity. Japanese investors, for example, are buying low-cost subordinated perpetual floating-rate notes on the assumption that subsequent hikes in the coupon will drive the issuers to redeem the paper. Other bankers say that this is a heroic assumption and only time will tell who is fooling whom.

The boundary between debt and equity is blurred largely because perpetuals are typically issued by banks from countries whose supervisory authorities consider these instruments—along with loans, bonds, and other debt—to be not only own capital (i.e., stock) but also a special type of equity whose cost (interest payment) is tax deductible.

In other words, perpetuals are not only a tax loophole, but also a loophole in BIS capital requirements regulations. Some banks hope to use them to improve their balance sheet. With the absence of equity-type obligations, they aim to better their free capital ratio, which is a metric of the relation between own capital (equity) and outside capital (bought money).

If, however, BIS, the Federal Reserve Board, the Bank of England, and other central banks recognize this new instrument as debt only and refuse to treat it as part of equity, the goal of improving the capital basis will be elusive. All told, the arguments surrounding perpetuals are far from over.

During the December 1988 meeting at the Bank for International Settlements in Basel, the supervisors appointed a committee to explore some of these issues, particularly that of equity. As a result, the then-scheduled sale of $400 million of such notes by Banque Nationale de Paris (BNP) was delayed.

Although the notes have been placed with Japanese investors, BNP (a state-owned bank) has reserved the right not to complete the sale and cancel the operation if the proceeds cannot be counted as Tier 1, or core capital. Meanwhile, the Royal Bank of Scotland, which appointed the Swiss Bank Corporation to arrange the sale of $500 million of such notes, did not seek to have the proceeds counted as core capital but as Tier 2, or supplementary capital.

Another example is provided by Banco Santander, Spain's fifth-largest commercial bank, which is selling $200 million of perpetuals with the proceeds to be counted as Tier 2. Placement of the Santander notes is being arranged by Shearson Lehman Brothers and Tokyo Lease, making it an issue of international collaboration.

The roots of the Tier 1/Tier 2 controversy lie in the fact that originally BIS placed no limit on how much core capital is made up of preferred stock. The peripheral factors were the attitude of a country's central bank and the receptiveness of markets to such issues. Many of the BIS supervisors want to use the discipline of the marketplace to force bank managers to focus more on profits and return on equity.

By improving performance, banks can force up the value of their shares to trade at a premium to book value rather than at discount. When this happens, banks will have every incentive to issue new stock.

In this sense, the subordinated perpetual notes are viewed as a gimmick designed to circumvent the need to improve performance, so that real equity may be sold. As a result, a core question supervisors must answer is whether the perpetual notes are the equivalent of noncumulative preference shares.

6. Using Technology to Magnify Financial Impact

It is common knowledge that the Japanese financial industry today is a global force. What is often forgotten is that as recently as 1980, none of the top five banks in the world were Japanese, and only one, Dai-Ichi Kangyo, ranked in the top ten. Ten years later, in 1990, the top nine are all Japanese and only one, Citibank, is American.

Size alone might not have made all that much difference if it were not for the fact that in 1985 the Japanese overtook the U.S. as the world's largest international lenders. Nomura Securities predicts that by 1995, the Japanese banks will have lent abroad over $1 trillion dollars.

Already the Japanese are the largest foreign lenders in the U.S., with an estimated 6 percent of total U.S. banking assets and almost 50 percent of the foreign sector's share. Japanese banks have been successful in gaining leadership in the commodity loan markets, in which price is more important than innovation; they have shown significant expertise in markets such as trust, securities underwriting, and trade finance.

Thus, the Japanese financial institutions have demonstrated that they are world-class contenders, as are the corporations they are financing. They are also focused in their investments.

In terms of globality of operations, there is a significant effort by banks from Japan (as well as Europe) to get a foothold in the U.S. market. Over the last few years there have been some major acquisitions suggesting that, despite the weakening dollar and the air of crisis in U.S. banking, the American financial market will preserve its attraction as a place for growth and diversification when compared with other national markets, which are viewed as virtually impregnable.

But while European banks make investments in the American financial market, the Japanese bet not only on money but also on technology. In banking, or in any financial services industry, technology facilitates financial innovation, cost control, and service quality; quality translates into customer service; and attention to service detail becomes synonymous with profitable business.

The Japanese financial institutions have spent considerably more than their European and even American counterparts on technological breakthroughs that can be used to achieve service and quality goals. They are actively experimenting with sophisticated solutions in an attempt to gain what they believe will be a competitive edge in the U.S. financial industry. Figure 4.3 shows the two main pillars on which rests the integrative applications environment of Japanese financial institutions—artificial intelligence (AI) and networks.

Today, most Japanese financial institutions have in operation fourth-generation networks.[7] Few American banks have a similar structure and none of the Europeans can make such a claim (most still relying on X.25 networks, which are slightly better than second generation). The gap is great, and

Figure 4.3 Pillars of an Integrated Application Environment

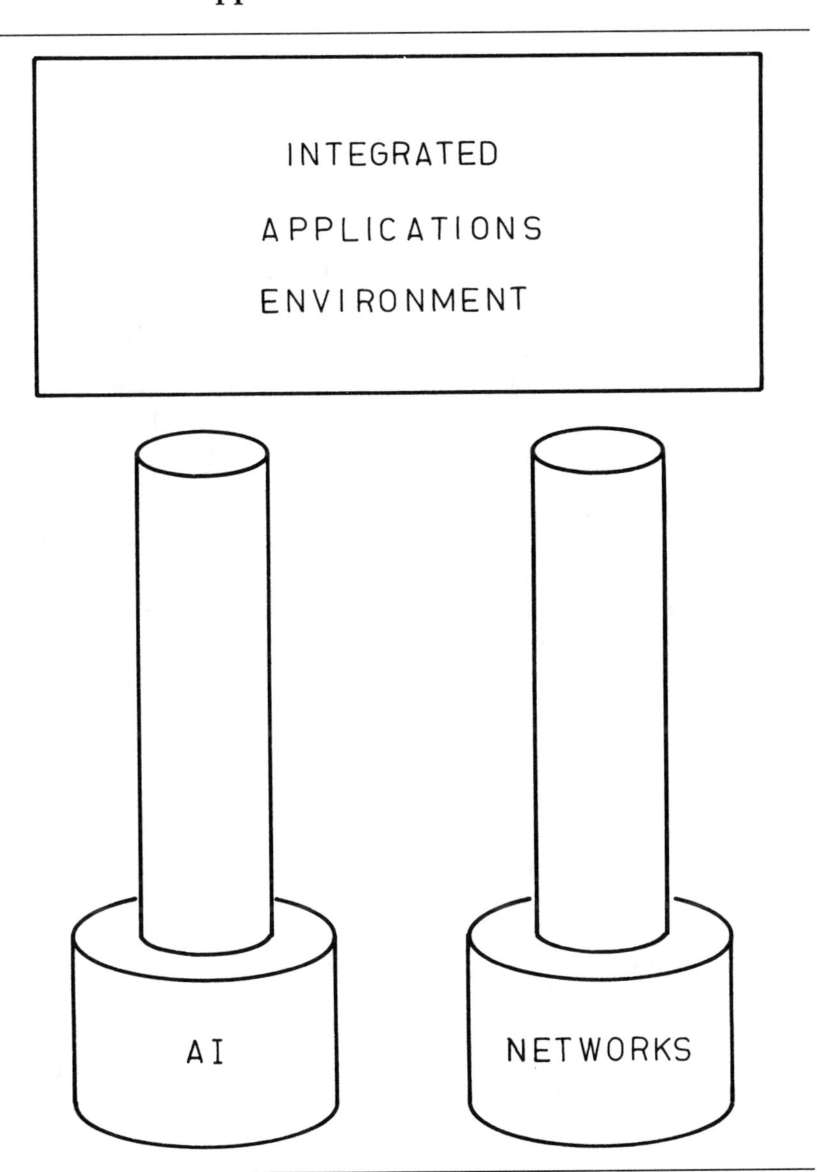

it is widening. Yet, while it is mainly Japanese securities houses that use the most advanced network structures, much of the associated expertise is easily transferred to retail banking and credit cards.

Also, Japanese securities houses are actively employing artificial intelligence.[8]

- All leading Japanese securities houses, as well as many banks, are today actively researching and developing the new-generation expert systems, which contain fuzzy sets and neural networks.
- Yamaichi Securities has a dozen major implementations of expert systems, from stock and bond trading to Forex. (These will be discussed in more detail.) It is also a user of supercomputers.
- Sanyo Securities has had a sophisticated AI-enriched information system, known as Sirnis, in operation since 1985. In the mid-1980s this was by far the most advanced securities trading system in existence; it remains one of the best in the world.
- Nikko Securities has a complex expert system for futures and options trading as well as other smaller AI-constructs, one of which lures low-net-worth clients away from savings accounts and into government bonds.
- Nomura Securities has implemented a retail portfolio analysis system, also based on artificial intelligence techniques, within Japan.

In contrast to European and U.S. securities firms, which have created a competitive battleground with incompatible technologies, Japanese securities houses have standardized their delivery vehicles and communications protocols. Nomura Securities has allocated over $1 billion dollars for a thorough overhaul of its technology and has retained a U.S.-based network consultancy to assist on the project.

After a few false starts, Japanese securities firms have developed what could be considered the leading integrated global communications systems. Nomura has its own Nomura Electronic Worldwide Total On-line Network, or Newton. This is an integrated high-capacity network that ties together over forty-thousand terminals worldwide.

Because Japanese securities firms have standardized much of their technology, American vendors have found that negotiating with one Japanese securities house often means that they are actually negotiating with three or four at the same time. Furthermore, a retail trading system delivered on a home-installed PC-based terminal—an arrangement considered the final frontier for American securities firms—has already been conquered by the Japanese. The aim is to use technology to magnify financial impact.

The architectural concept behind this approach is shown in Figure 4.4, and it is just as applicable in home banking as in an electronic banking implementation directed to client firms. For selling securities at home-banking level, Nomura uses Nintendo, a $90 PC with modem. By contrast, corporate connectivity is ensured through the use of polyvalent workstations, although approaches have their place.

Leadership in this field is important, because whether in Japan, the U.S., or Western Europe, an electronic marketplace will radically change or bypass most existing legislation as well as the exchanges. It will create new dimensions with global perspectives and widely fluctuating (but not necessarily well balanced) prices.

In economic theory, markets efficiently balance supply with demand by varying price; in the real world, this is complicated by a lack of perfect information and by the fact

Figure 4.4 Using Technology to Link with Customers and Markets Also to Amplify Financial Impact

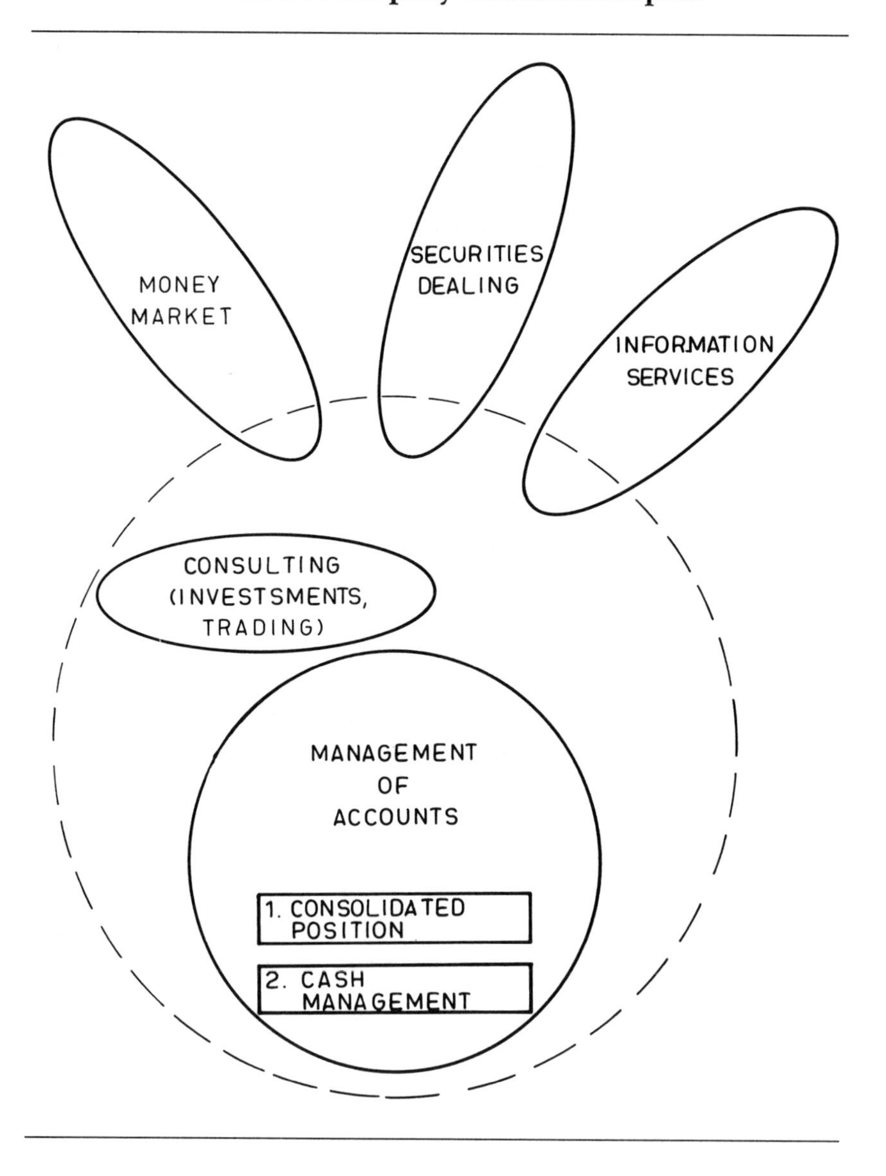

that in the short run people find posted prices convenient. As a result, there is often excess supply in one place and excess demand in another place, or vice versa. Intelligent networks make this apparent on a global scale while providing the means to do a balancing act; thus, they create a marketplace of dimensions never experienced before.

For many people, what is most significant about the global markets' gathering strength is that markets are able to act as the world's financial policemen. If any firm steps out of line, the markets tend to bring it back; nevertheless, this does not mean that markets can act as their own regulators.

Globalization will likely require a greater degree of regulatory conformity, at least among major financial markets. Technology will play a major role in this process. It is in everyone's interest to maintain a strong, stable system that protects consumers and institutions while allowing creativity to grow.

Newly built structures should be subject to continuous review and appropriate adjustment; and global rules should enhance, not impede, competition, while maintaining checks and balances. As well, they should draw on the input of central banks, monetary authorities, commercial banks, securities houses, and treasuries around the world. All these are critical partners in the financial process, and when the safety and soundness of the international monetary system is at stake, their own survival depends on its maintenance. Today financial institutions that do not compete aggressively for deposits, loans, forex, investment advice, and portfolio management are going to be left in the dust.

Endnotes

1. In product innovation, quality of customer service and cost control.

2. Capital requirements are discussed in Section 4. For greater detail on the work of the Cooke Committee of BIS, see D.N. Chorafas, *Bank Profitability* (London: Butterworths, 1988).

3. *Swiss Business,* January/February 1990.

4. *Time,* 30 January 1989.

5. For the definition of off-balance sheet activities, as well as the risks involved, see D. N. Chorafas, *Risk Management in Financial Institutions* (London: Butterworths, 1990).

6. See also an example with perpetuals in page 125.

7. See also D.N. Chorafas and H. Steinmann, *Implementing Networks in Banking and Financial Services* (London: Macmillan, 1988).

8. For specific implementation references, see D.N. Chorafas and H. Steinmann, *Expert Systems in Banking* (London: Macmillan, 1990).

Chapter 5

The Securities and Exchange Commission and Brokers

Chapter 5

The Securities and Exchange Commission and Brokers

1. Introduction

Offering and dealing in shares is subject to more statutory control in the U.S. than in Europe; the main relevant U.S. laws are the Securities Act of 1933 and the Securities Exchange Act of 1934. The principal regulatory authority is the Securities and Exchange Commission (SEC) which was created by the 1934 act and charged with the responsibility for administering both the 1933 and 1934 legislation.

The 1933 act is the first in a series of laws designed to protect the public from misinterpretation, manipulation, abuse, and other negative practices in connection with the purchase and sale of equities. Companies whose securities are to be listed and traded must register these securities under the 1933 act. This information is updated by means of annual and other periodic reports. Such registration statements and reports are public information and are available for inspection at the SEC and at the exchanges on which the company's securities are listed.

The 1933 act sets policies for disclosing financial and other information about both the securities offered for sale and their issuer. Disclosure is provided by means of a registration statement, which is a public document available for inspection by any person (though in certain situations portions of the document may be given nonpublic status).

The 1934 act vests the SEC, rather than the issuer of securities or the brokers or dealers, with the responsibility of protecting the public. While the 1933 act primarily addresses the initial distribution of securities, the 1934 legislation largely deals with the dissemination of information on securities traded on American securities exchanges or in the over-the-counter market; it also regulates the securities markets themselves, as well as the amount of credit used in these markets.

Aside from federal legislation, the fifty states of the U.S. each have their own securities laws, known as blue sky laws. These vary in content; therefore, any offer of securities must consider relevant state regulations as well as the federal laws.

Also, a foreign company that has registered shares in America is subject to further specific legislation, such as the Foreign Corrupt Practices Act. In addition to requiring companies to maintain high standards of internal accounting control, this act establishes penalties for bribery of foreign government politicians or other officials.

2. The Role of the Securities and Exchange Commission

The Securities and Exchange Commission exercises more control over the offering and trading of securities than any similar regulatory agency in Europe. It reviews prospectuses for new issues of shares, accept or rejects the documentation, and supervises the day-to-day operation of the securities markets.

Typically, a registration statement is filed with and cleared by SEC before securities may be offered for sale to investors. This is basically a two part document; Part I consists of a prospectus that includes information such as

1. the nature of the offering and a description of the securities to be registered (including voting rights for stocks, maturities for bonds, etc.);
2. details on the registrant's business, including what products it offers and which markets it is targeting;
3. the possible risks to be faced by potential investors, based on the nature of the industry and its operating history and liquidity;
4. the existing trading markets for the registrant's securities, as well as information on high and low sales prices, dividend policy, and shareholders;
5. financial statements and related disclosures, with fairly extensive references to be provided by the applicant (see Section 3);
6. a history of legal proceedings, including a description of any significant legal action involving the registrant or any of its subsidiaries.

SEC requirements for financial statements include audited and consolidated documentation. A balance sheet for the two most recent fiscal years; income statements for each of the three most recent fiscal years; and statements of changes in financial position and stockholders' equity for each of the three most recent fiscal years.

Financial information must also be submitted on subsidiaries not consolidated and 50-percent or less owned, if those units meet or exceed certain thresholds. The SEC also requires unaudited interim financial statements if the effective date of the registration is more than six months after the latest audited balance sheet date.

Part II includes information such as articles of incorporation, bylaws, and significant contracts. Its content is considered public, although, SEC does not view this supplementary data as essential to a prospective investor; consequently, it does not require it to be distributed with the prospectus.

Virtually all U.S. and non-U.S. initial registrations are reviewed, a process that starts upon receipt of the registration statement. The review team includes a financial analyst, an accountant, and a staffer with technical experience in the registrant's industry.

The SEC requires the applicant to file reports on an ongoing basis and to provide certain information to shareholders. This includes annual and interim reporting, with rules applicable to foreign registrants being more limited than those for domestic ones.

In 1982 the SEC adopted simplified rules for foreign issuers that modified a number of the accounting and reporting regulations previously regarded as incompatible with standard practice for many foreign companies. Also, in recent years, a growing number of foreign companies have taken advantage of having their equity traded in the United States in the form of American Depository Receipts (ADR). It is possible to trade in U.S. exchanges in a company's own shares; nevertheless, many foreign companies have converted some of their shares to ADR.

The existence of American Depository Receipts enables U.S. investors to trade in a dollar security while using forms, transaction methods, and costs that are familiar to them. The ADR depository bank will maintain the U.S. register and distribute the proceeds of rights issues that cannot be taken up directly by U.S. ADR investors.

3. Reporting Requirements for Financial Institutions

Since the early 1970s, the Securities and Exchange Commission has been issuing accounting series releases (ASR) as guides to filing registration statements. Banks subject to securities laws (i.e., those with assets in excess of $1 million and a class of equity held by 500 or more persons) in fulfilling the fundamental requirements set out by ASR, may find that these provide good guidelines around which to structure an internal accounting management information system (IAMIS). These requirements include

1. a listing of average balance sheets, as well as percentages of individual assets, liabilities, and components of stockholders' equity to their total assets, and averages of assets and liabilities attributable to foreign operations if such operations are significant;
2. a breakdown of investment securities by type and maturity range, including the weighted average yield for each range of maturities;
3. a breakdown of loans by type, maturity, number, and sensitivity to changes in interest rates (including nonperforming loans and the loss of interest therefrom);
4. a breakdown of the loan-loss reserve by type of loan;
5. a summary of loan-loss experience, including a description of the factors that helped manage-

ment to determine the provision for loan losses charged to operating expense;

6. a breakdown of domestic deposits, including a caption for certificates of deposit in amounts of $100,000 or more (plus maturity information), and deposits in foreign offices;
7. a listing of return on equity and assets and dividend payout rates;
8. a listing of interest rates earned and paid, average yield and average rate paid, and net interest differential;
9. a discussion of policy on commitments and lines of credit;
10. disclosure of foreign operations from which revenue exceeds 10 percent of consolidated total revenue or income (loss) before taxes, or foreign assets exceeding 10 percent of consolidated total average assets.

This disclosure would include details of assets and liabilities relating to foreign operations, as well as a breakdown of revenue and income by geographic area.

Some of these guidelines are so clear and management-oriented that, since the late 1970s, American banks have modified their information systems to provide the required data on a timely and ongoing basis, in the process using the distilled information for decision making. However, one provision, the required breakdown of the loan-loss reserve by type of loan, has created a 3-way controversy between banks, regulators, and the general public.

In the eyes of the American public, there are critical ways in which the market has not been properly regulated. Unease has been created by the market's volatility (which cannot be regulated), the criminal indictments on Wall Street (which have been processed with dilligence), untrustworthy brokers (no clear rules exist on this issue), and unease at the breakup of household-name businesses for the enrichment of a few operators.

One area the Securities and Exchange Commission does not evaluate is the individual company's global view of Profit and Loss (P and L), although, to financial institutions, this is vital. The Comptroller of the Currency and Federal Reserve Board, on the other hand, examines the health of financial institutions and decides whether or not to put them on the "sick list."

Profitability is a complex concept. Total income for a certain year may be running above or below the previous year's level. But, if return on expenditures for capital investments and equipment is considered, the picture changes.

As shown in Figure 5.1, a global view of P and L starts with the efficient integration of new technology, which is pivotal to cost-effective operations. Next come value-added innovation and product development, followed by production and distribution. For over thirty years, computer implementation has focused on data processing rather than on the effectiveness of the distribution system and control of risk.

Partly because a thorough quantitative and qualitative analysis of global risk is lacking, many financial institutions think that a descriptive narrative is sufficient to meet SEC requirements for information regarding risk and uncertainty.

This is not true. Firms must identify not only the various categories of loan loss reserves, but also the algorithmic approaches used to show provisions and analyses by loan category.

While a loan's ultimate collectibility may be subject to many factors, some of which are beyond the control of a lendor, management scrutiny and tight quality inspection are within reach. Interactive computational finance can provide

Figure 5.1 A Global View of Profit and Loss

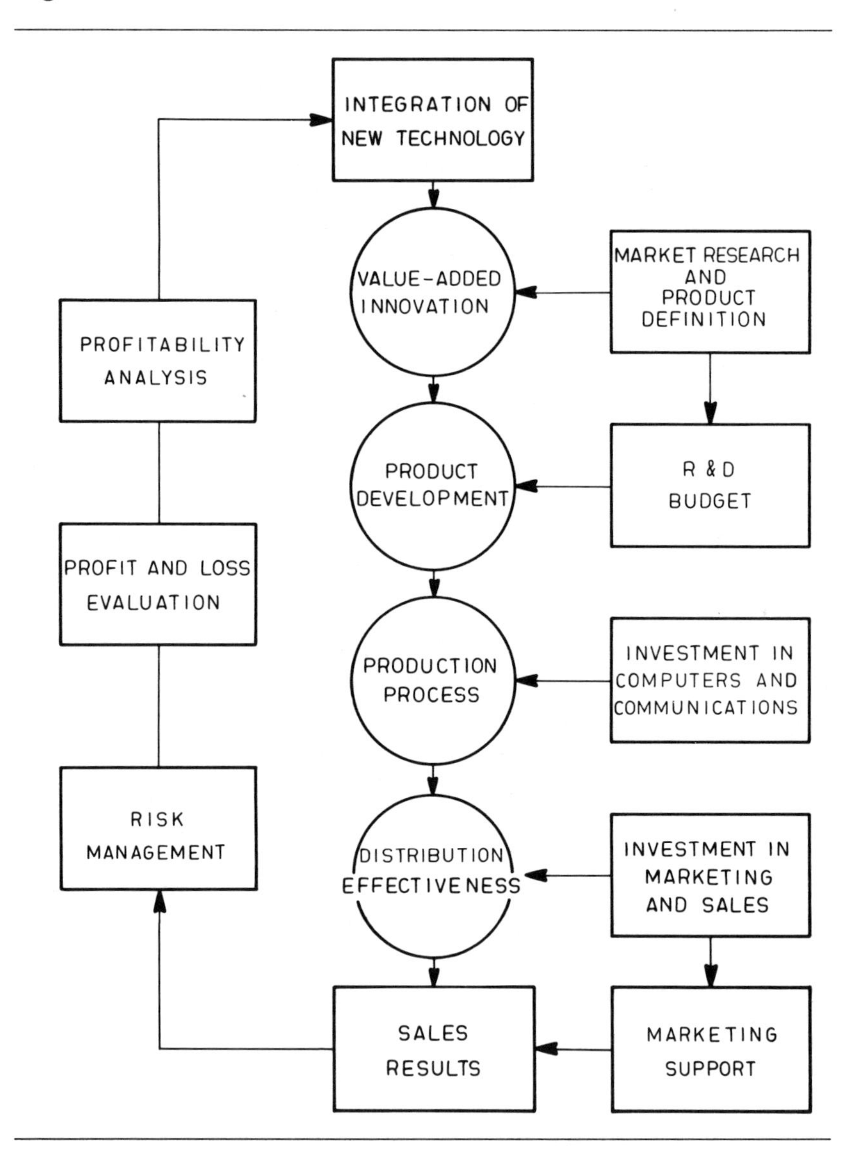

the tools necessary to sharpen management's judgment in this domain.

Streamlining of systems and procedures is also necessary. Because existing accounting systems are not geared to provide all of the necessary detail, disclosure requirements relating to foreign operations have, in the past, caused implementation difficulties.

Today, to obtain breakdowns of operations by geographic area, firms must work through a significant amount of assumptions, estimates, and internal allocations related to various income and expense items. Various financial institutions' reports are often incompatible with each other.

ASR 177, issued in September 1975, focused on this problem. Apart from quantitative reporting, it requires a narrative analysis of the results of operations. This analysis must give explanations for material changes in the amounts of revenue and expense between the most recent quarter and the immediately preceding quarter, and the most recent quarter and the same calendar quarter of the preceding year, as well as current year-to-date and prior-to-date comparative financial information.

To make the regulatory system work more efficient, the rules of the Securities and Exchange Commission specify a significant amount of detail. One regulation, which has frequently led to problems with brokers, prohibits short-selling in a declining stock. This uptick rule requires that the trade be marked on the order ticket as a short sale.

In a short sale, an investor, on the assumption that a stock's price will decline, sells borrowed stock, expecting to buy the shares later at a lower price and thereby make a profit. The uptick rule was adopted as part of the Securities Exchange Act of 1934 in response to abuses during the crash of 1929, when speculators circulated false rumors and short-sold shares as stocks tumbled.

In one of this rule's most recent applications, in May 1989, SEC censured Salomon Brothers and settled accusations that the firm illegally executed short sales of about $12.5 million of stock on October 19, 1987, the day the market crashed.

The SEC also charged that Salomon failed to promptly open its books and records for inspection by government officials. "I view both ends of this case as a warning to the securities industry that they comply with short sales rules," said Lawrence Iason, regional administrator of the agency's New York office. "They think they can violate these rules with impunity. That's simply not the case."

In settling the administrative action and agreeing to be censured, Salomon Brothers paid no fine, nor did it admit or deny the SEC's accusations. But the settlement did require the broker to assign a senior internal auditor who, in consultation with an outside accountant or lawyer, will make two semiannual reviews of the firm's short-sale procedures, even if they occur in an attempt to stave off mounting losses.

4. Control Action by the Exchanges

The Securities and Exchange Commission is not the only authority to supervise broker operations. The stock exchanges themselves have a policing action enhanced by research activities and often coordinated with the SEC. There is no alternative to steady vigilance.

One effective control NYSE has applied is Stockwatch, a computer-based system able to exploit large distributed databases. Once Stockwatch raises the alert, the NYSE orders all brokers that traded in the stock to turn over "blue sheets."

Blue sheets give, along with other information, the names, addresses, and social security numbers of the customers behind every trade. Since February 1989, NYSE has required brokerage firms to transmit these blue sheets on-line into its computer system.

Another monitor is Automated Search and Match, or ASAM. Upon receipt of information pertaining to suspect transactions, ASAM begins to match files. The system compares the names of the broker's customers (and any other data it already may have on them) with information on currency executives, investment bankers, and others with connections to the firm whose stock behaved oddly.

NYSE processes such information through a suspicion-ranking program. People who conduct the trading analysis at the various exchanges belong to what is called the Intermarket Surveillance Group (ISG). Its members get together periodically and share information, which sometimes uncovers a pattern of trades by someone whose buying or selling on a single exchange may not be ringing an alarm.

ISG automated its pooling of information to create a unified audit trail of stocks and options. This Intermarket Surveillance Information System Database contains historical trading information from all the exchanges. Computers manage the data, putting together, for example, a complete list of all company ABC trades done on the exchanges, with a listing of all the trades by time and by participants in the trading.

The SEC is encouraging stock exchanges to compile, upgrade and thoroughly exploit databases. Much of this work includes pattern recognition.

For example, the SEC investigates suspected cases of insider trading (brought to it by NYSE) by comparing the zip codes of people who bought company ABC stock. These may not be New Yorkers, but residents of Dallas, Sacramento or a foreign city, who may have got a tip to buy ABC even in casual conversation. Investigators suspect that leaks may come from insiders who also live in the same neighborhood.

When the blue sheets indicate suspicious trading in a stock, the exchange generally contacts the company and requests chronologies. A chronology is a list of people and events associated with a merger, acquisition, or other important activity that can move stock prices. This list generally includes management, lawyers, accountants, and investment banker(s).

The Securities and Exchange Commission recently used the pattern-recognition method to detect insider trading in the January 1990 acquisition of the U.S. drug company Rorer Group by France's Rhone-Poulen. The commission, having been tipped off by heavy trading in Rorer options, filed suits against investment groups in Switzerland, Monaco, Greece, and Lebanon.[1] France has launched a probe.

The automation of trading data and the NYSE's databases have made the SEC's enforcement job considerably easier. Ten or even five years ago all investigating had to be done by sorting through trading records by hand, a slow, difficult, and inefficient process.

SEC also monitors the exchanges by conducting periodic inspections of their systems. SEC surveillance people do periodic audits, review the exchanges' procedures, and look up enforcement files in order to ensure that their

1. parameters are reasonable;
2. inspections are well-documented;
3. internal audits are complete and timely;
4. sanctions are brought against violators.

It is now possible for an exchange to regulate the way trades are made. The Chicago Board of Trade's proposed master circuit breaker will apply to all trading relative to the Major Market Index (MMI) for futures contracts and will tighten the level at which trading is halted completely. (MMI is a 20-stock gauge designed to mimic the Dow Jones Industrial Average.)

Such measures are particularly important when initiated by the leading exchanges, and the Chicago Board of Trade is the largest commodity future in the world. Linked through satellites with the financial centers around the globe, CBOT wants to use this system to differentiate its offerings in a competitive market.

Subject to the approval by the U.S. Commodity Futures Trading Commission, the CBOT action enhances the ability of the exchange to respond to stock market volatility. The move is aimed at coordinating CBOT's circuit breakers with those of other exchanges.

Basket indexes are used often by program traders, but have come under criticism in some quarters as contributing to stock market volatility.

Under the market circuit breaker plan, if the price of the lead month of MMI futures falls 30 points below the previous day's settlement—roughly the equivalent of a 150-point drop in the Dow Jones industrials—trading may continue above but not below that point for the next sixty minutes. If the circuit-breaker goes into effect after 1:30 P.M. Chicago time, the restriction will extend until the trading day's 3:15 P.M. closing.

It is understandable that commodities exchanges are eager to keep a clean house. Sometimes even their own chief executives make uncomplimentary remarks. For example, Thomas F. Eagleton, who recently resigned from the Chicago Mercantile Exchange's board, negatively commented on the Merc's self-regulatory program; concurrently many outsiders as well are calling for more aggressive regulation of Chicago's booming futures markets. Whether a decision relates to trading procedures "or penalties for thievery," he wrote, "or, most recently, the Brian Monieson matter, the Merc decision is usually a non-Lincolnian decision of insiders by insiders and for insiders."

In London, the International Stock Exchange (ISE) develops expert systems to control compliance. It has established a well-staffed research unit known as the Division of Strategic Engineering. Dr. Peter Bennett, director of the division, says,

"The financial industry is rule-based and there is unlimited scope for the use of expert systems."

Current work focuses on embedded AI constructs in areas such as compliance and supervisory activities, diagnostics (learning from mistakes), filtering of incoming information, access to distributed databases, descriptive and advisory services, man-machine communication, and network Management (help-desk type).

ISE's research unit investigates and analyzes business and technical issues of concern to the members of the exchange. The unit's goal is to improve service and reduce financial industry costs by streamlining market structures, the supporting technology for market operations, and the business environment within which market operations and development take place.

The settlement of securities transactions is a problem in the UK and other exchanges; thus, automation, of both back-office operations following stock transactions and control and supervisory responsibilities, will have to take high priority.

5. Profit, Loss, and Individual Performance

Brokers' seem to have fairly mixed feelings about the developing market environment and its regulatory aspects. Globalization is a case in point.

For New York, London and Tokyo, the promise of around-the-clock trading in stocks and bonds seemed to preannounce a grand global market. From America, Europe, and Japan securities houses began actively pursuing business abroad, but many failed to establish a firm footing in overseas stock and bond centers. The majority not only sustained operating losses (which for some houses were severe), but also suffered from the October 1987 market crash.

In Tokyo all but six of forty-five foreign financial institutions reported losses in 1988; some dropped out altogether, while others cut back operations. While the Tokyo stock market survived the October 1987 crash better than the other major exchanges, the foreign firms paid a heavy price because they were ill-prepared to trade in Japan.

American and European brokers, for example, found that cutthroat competition caused profit margins on some securities deals to shrivel. Also, entrenched cultural barriers acted (and still act) to inhibit Japanese institutional customers from entrusting foreign brokers with their most important investments.

Past history leads Japanese firms to believe that since foreigners have no deep local roots, they cannot be expected to stay in the country for any significant length of time. No Japanese investor planning for the long term will work with a company that is expected to fold after a few years.

Foreign banks and securities houses had problems in other markets as well. In London, where the 1986 deregulation had thrown financial markets open to foreign competition, overseas investment firms reportedly lost more than $300 million in 1988. The result was that thousands of financial service employees were laid off.

On the other hand, investment houses that opened London offices before the Big Bang have done better. Morgan Stanley, for example, has been well-established in European markets since the 1970s and was thus able to grow during London's expansion phase. By using its international network to float stock and bond issues and arrange mergers, Morgan Stanley reportedly reaped a record $100 million in pretax profits in London in 1988.

Some Japanese firms have thrived as well. Nomura Securities had $100 million in pretax earnings in London in that same year; in 1989, it expanded the numbers of its employees in the British market.

Also, some newcomers, by taking the time to organize themselves properly, struck gold in their home base. When

Sears Roebuck entered the financial services business in 1981, industry wizards said it could not successfully diversify, or in Sears' words, sell everything "from socks to stocks." Yet Sears managed to make a lot more money on stocks than socks; Dean Witter, the financial-services arm of Sears has been thriving. In 1989, Sears' retail division earned just $647 million on revenues of $32 billion, while Dean Witter's financial services showed profits of $1.1 billion on revenues of $22 billion.

These results have not come about by accident, but from the use of tight cost controls and marketing savvy. The same is true of Sears' plastic money experiment, the Discover card, which is also paying off handsomely.

Figure 5.2 shows the sources of revenue for Shearson Lehman Brothers over nearly a ten-year period (prior to the acquisition of Hutton). Clearly evident is the shrinking role of commissions in terms of revenue.

This is not a universal trend. Other securities houses have made commissions and fees a focal point of their strategy. Over the same time frame, investment advisory services have grown as an income source, but not enough to compensate for the shrinking of commissions. Interest, principal transactions, and investment banking have all expanded as sources of income; this indicates a major shift of priorities, which has changed the profile of the securities house.

When it comes to advisory services and commissions, individual productivity is a useful performance metric. The averaged-out figures typically shown in an overall performance, can be most misleading; thus, securities houses should follow front-desk performance on a person-by-person basis.

The idea of individual performance measurement originated in the manufacturing industry with marketing quotas. Postmortem analysis can also be effective in evaluating the individual performance of investment advisors and account managers.

Table 5.1 comes from a study done by the authors some years ago for an electronics company. Its focal point is sales in dollars. In order to maintain the company's confidentiality, all figures have been scaled down by a factor; nevertheless, the ratios are real. Unearthing both individual performance and the great variation experienced during operations is instructive; as can be seen, individual performance varies by 1 to 72. Prior to this study, no researcher had identified such a great discrepancy.

High and low performers should be identified, because when hard times come, and it is necessary to reduce personnel, high performers may be penalized and low performers rewarded, with the firm's business suffering as a result.

6. The Brokers' View of Cultural Problems

Author Michael Lewis claims that anyone can prosper by conjuring up plausible explanations for why the market is up or down.[2] In his book Liar's Poker, Lewis describes how he plugged into several of the largest pools of money in Europe. "I had never managed money," he admits. "I had never made any real money....Yet I was holding myself out as a great expert on matters of finance." His crowning achievement was selling $86 million of previously unsalable bonds by convincing a French client that the bonds were so shunned by investors that they had to be a steal. The trade netted $2 million.

Unfortunately, such deals do not come along every day, and in the long run brokers prosper only through diligent effort. For this reason, analyses of individual performance (see Table 5.1) can be revealing. How do employees feel about the firm? "How can you speak of loyalty to the firm," Michael Lewis asks, "when the firm is an amalgam of small and large deceptions and riven with strife and discontent?"

Figure 5.2 Diversified Revenues by Shearson Lehman and Change in the Product Mix

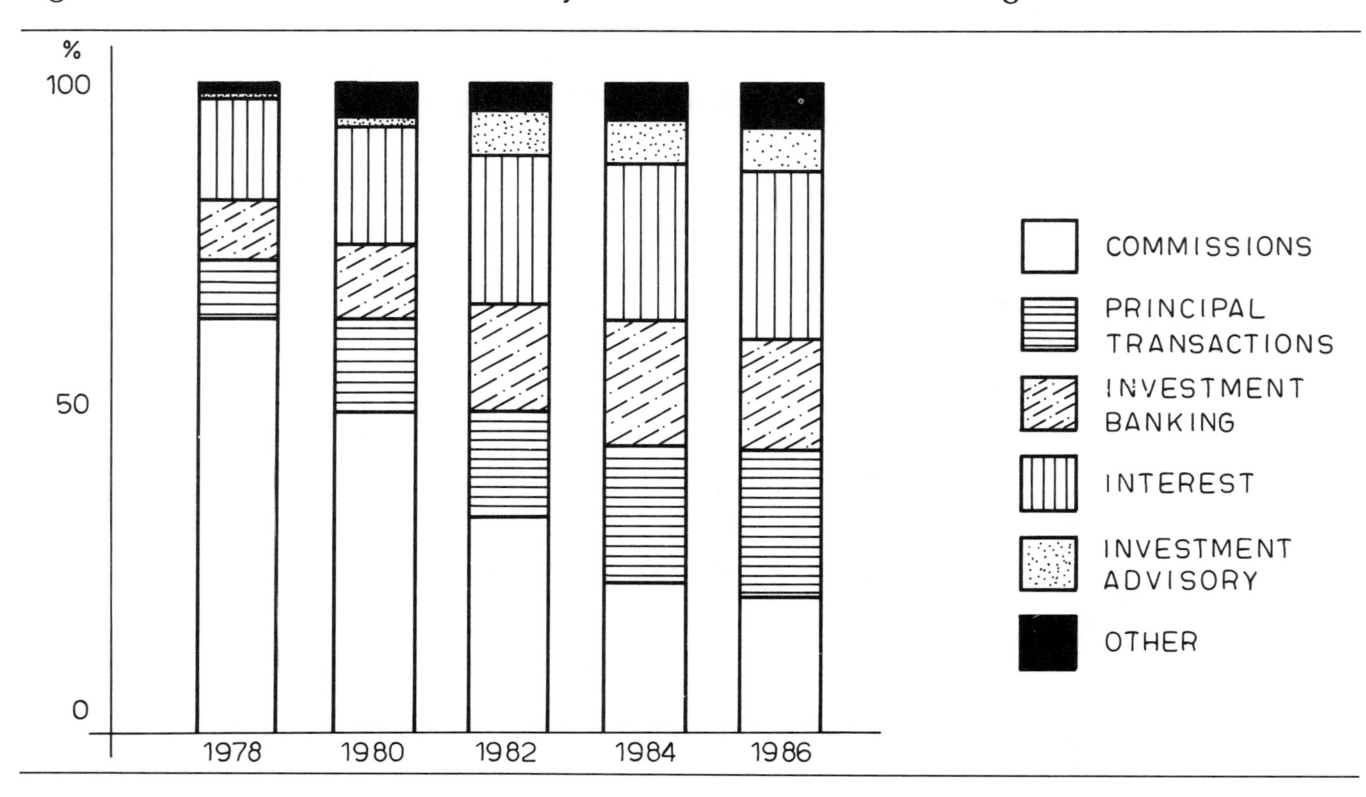

Table 5.1 Sales of Data Systems Technology by Salesperson

Sales-person	*$*	*Quantity in Units*	*Average Price*
A	1,800,000	38	47,368
B	504,000	63	8,000
C	248,000	12	20,666
D	847,000	93	9,107
E	24,000	8	3,000
F	300,000	27	11,111
G	97,000	6	16,166
H	255,000	20	12,750
I	687,000	35	19,628
J	258,000	19	13,578
	5,020,000	321	15,638

Average price per unit	15,638
Average units per salesperson	32
Average $ per salesperson/per year	502,000
Range/price per unit	3,000–47,368
Range/units per salesperson	6–93
Range/$ per salesperson, year	24,000–1,800,000

There is, of course, the other side of the coin. In Europe and in America, companies with few exceptions, feel that they do not get their money's worth from employees. "We see no real loyalty to the firm and no permanence in effort," says one senior executive. "Therefore employees should not be surprised when hard times bring survival into the front plane and we have to do layoffs."

The events of October 1987 caused a general retrenchment on the market. The international securities business was hit particularly hard; the first stocks investors sold were foreign ones. Despite these setbacks, few investment banks wanted to withdraw entirely from the international marketplace.

Thus, from the viewpoint of brokers, global trading is still viable, although most firms have discovered the hard way that cultural and other barriers exist in the markets. Nevertheless, cultural differences can be taught and, in some cases, new cultural elements adopted. The best approach to follow is what author Edwin Reischauer describes as the Japanese methodology:[3]

> The Japanese are determined to learn from each western country that in which it particularly excelled. For example they went to England to study the navy and merchant marine, to Germany for the army and medicine, to France, for local government and law, and to the U.S. for business methods....The world was one vast schoolroom for them, but they chose what and where they would learn and how they would use the knowledge to change life in Japan.

Note that the process is to learn, not copy. Copying does not pay, as the experience of the French Stock Exchange shows. In 1986, the Big Bang swept away many of the London stock market's obsolete practices. Two years later cut-throat competition forced many city brokers to drastically cut staff or close down altogether. The Paris stock exchange had an equivalent move in 1988 nicknamed "petit bang." French stockbrokers are now having the same troubles; rapidly rising costs, shrinking commissions, and inadequate management caused problems at several French brokerage firms in 1990. Many more are expected to run into difficulties in 1991.

Paris' first casualty was its most powerful independent, Tuffier, Ravier, Py. Unable to pay its bills, Tuffier was taken over in July 1990 by a Credit Lyonnais affiliate. Its 5,800 clients' accounts were frozen, and public prosecutors are investing allegations by the Commission des Operations de Bourse, the industry watchdog.[4]

Next to call for help was Giradet, in Lyons, one of France's fifteen provincial stockbrokers. It had run up losses of nearly FFr 200 million ($40 million). Then, in January 1991, bad news came from Ferri, one of the handful of Paris's forty-three brokers that is not controlled by a bank or an insurance company.

Faced with stiffer competition and rising costs, more French brokers will inevitably end up in the hands of banks. This worries the remaining independents who fear that if the stockmarket doldrums continue, their own businesses will be jeopardized.

7. Improving Market Performance

It is the job of the securities industry to evaluate the financial state of other businesses. But what is the state of the securities industry itself?

The statistics are telling: between 1980 and 1989, the American securities industry's pretax return on equity fell from 49 percent to 7 percent. The annual average amount of profit earned per industry employee has remained in the $5,000 to $23,000 bracket in the 1980s, while total average pay per employee doubled to around $80,000.

Costs are rising but commissions are not coming in. With daily trading volumes on the New York Stock Exchange averaging well below the daily turnover in the pre-1987 crash, there is little cause for optimism.

With barely any money stream from equities, junk bonds, leveraged buy-outs, mergers and acquisitions, risk arbitrage, property, or managing private investments, Wall Street now depends for survival on trading currencies, options, futures, and derivative securities.

In Tokyo, the big four security houses rely for half their revenues on Japan's fixed commissions for equity trading. With stock-market volume in 1990 a third lower than in 1989, and with a dearth of offerings of new shares, convertibles and warrant bonds, the squeeze is on the brokers. In one form or another, a similar scenario is happening in New York, London, Zurich, Frankfurt, Paris, and elsewhere.

Thus, brokers are becoming more selective about where they take their risks. In the 1980s many firms might have bid to trade a large block of shares; today few firms do. Also, brokers are committing fewer resources to risky markets. Cutting costs will be made easier by the intelligent use of computers, telecommunications, and knowledge engineering. This, however, requires a new culture in the brokerage house, one that uses solutions not based on data processing.[5]

One Dutch financial institution decided to use technology to reach three goals.

The first was to reduce error rate by an order of magnitude; the second, to cut by 50 percent general provision for losses; and the third, to eliminate 50 percent of the number of employees in the back-office—which stood at 55 percent of employment.

The management of this bank had thought that the error rate was 1 percent; this was considered acceptable. However, careful study showed that in securities the error rate was 4 percent, with all that this implied in terms of added costs for corrections. As a result, today even an order of magnitude reduction in errors can be seen as an intermediate step, not as a final goal.

The general provision for losses has been reduced through the able use of technology, but only by half the original goal. A second project is now looking after the difference. The toughest nut to crack has been personnnel reduction in the back-office. Yet, Sanyo, a Japanese sucurities house, has succeeded in this objective.

Another financial institution took the approach that technology can be used to ensure compliance to legal and cultural differences. Figure 5.3 shows how high technology has been used to reach that objective: it is an AI construct with six expert system modules that work interactively with market information, from equity valuation to advice given to traders and managers, including justification. Some of the modules in question vary by country of implementation to better reflect local market conditions and investors' culture.

Still another investment bank operates on the premise that control over risk factors must be enacted through artificial intelligence constructs operating on-line, interactively. The bank's chief executive officer says, "If we had had a system like that already in operation last year, our profit would have been 50 percent larger because we would have avoided severe loans losses."

In Tokyo, Sanyo Securities has used technology to enact a sharp personnel reduction in its back office. The firm (which has operated a sophisticated expert systems for securities trading since 1985) reached, within a year, the level of 0.5 back-office employees for every front desk. A comparison made at that time to a U.S. broker showed that the U.S. firm had 2 to 2.4 back-office employees for every front desk.

Figure 5.4 shows an integrated system for settlements and accounts that is adapted to fit the needs of a Western trading environment. This system works on-line, links to in-house operations as well as to the clearing houses, and connects to financial networks and the clients' own computer system.

It is important to remember, however, that with fast-advancing technology, even today's most efficient solution will not remain cost-effective for long. Also, successful implementation of computers, communications, and AI is not just matter of having technology.

Management must ensure that a firm handles fully on-line transactions, does client reporting by computer, and supports

Figure 5.3 Knowledge Engineering Modules for an Expert System in Securities

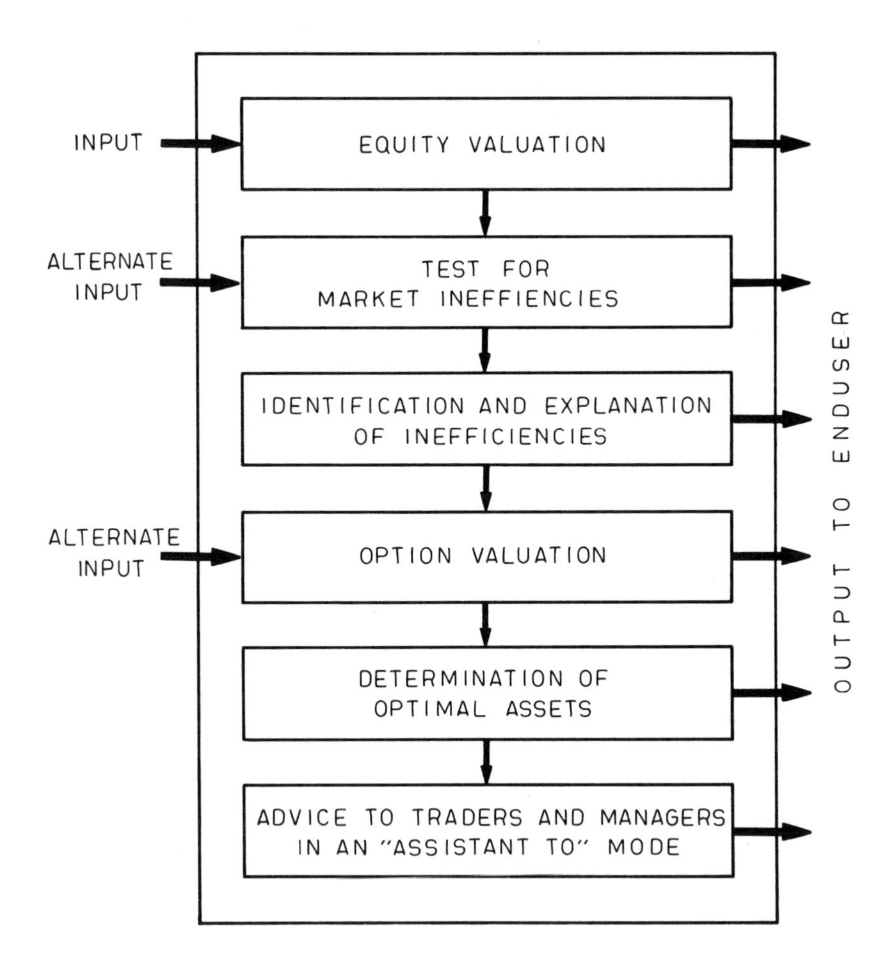

portfolio management through expert systems. AI constructs are able to track all decisions as well as compliance to them, and all archiving should be done automatically through imaging. Also, with efficient on-line authentication/authorization rules to provide security, clients must be able to input their transactions directly to the machine. Value-differentiation can also be offered, making it possible for sophisticated clients to simulate investment decisions prior to giving the bank an order.

8. Markets in which Brokers Can Thrive

Brokers can be wiped out if they stick to outmoded ways of thinking. For top firms, standard operational procedure has long been to corner the market on expertise and innovation.

Securities houses have always been vendors of specialized information and know-how. For more than a century, financial innovators, from J.P. Morgan to Lewis Ranieri, have thrived on knowing what to sell, to whom, and how to package it for greater appeal.

For example, in 1879 J.P. Morgan stunned the financial world by selling the largest block of stock ever publicly offered up to that time—250,000 shares of New York Central Railroad common stock—for $32.5 million, a huge sum 112 years ago.

A century later, during the decade of the 1980s, mortgage-backed financing (MBF) became the big money maker by collateralizing mortgage obligations. Proactive vendors also proceed with financial swaps and other market innovations. But financial products can die fast. Today many instruments of the 1980s have become a low-margin, commodity-type business.

Nevertheless, if companies can move quickly in a changing market, they will prosper. By the late 1970s, for example, despite generally poor performances throughout most of that decade, mutual fund and brokerage houses capitalized on

Figure 5.4 Component Parts of a Solution for Settlements and Accounts

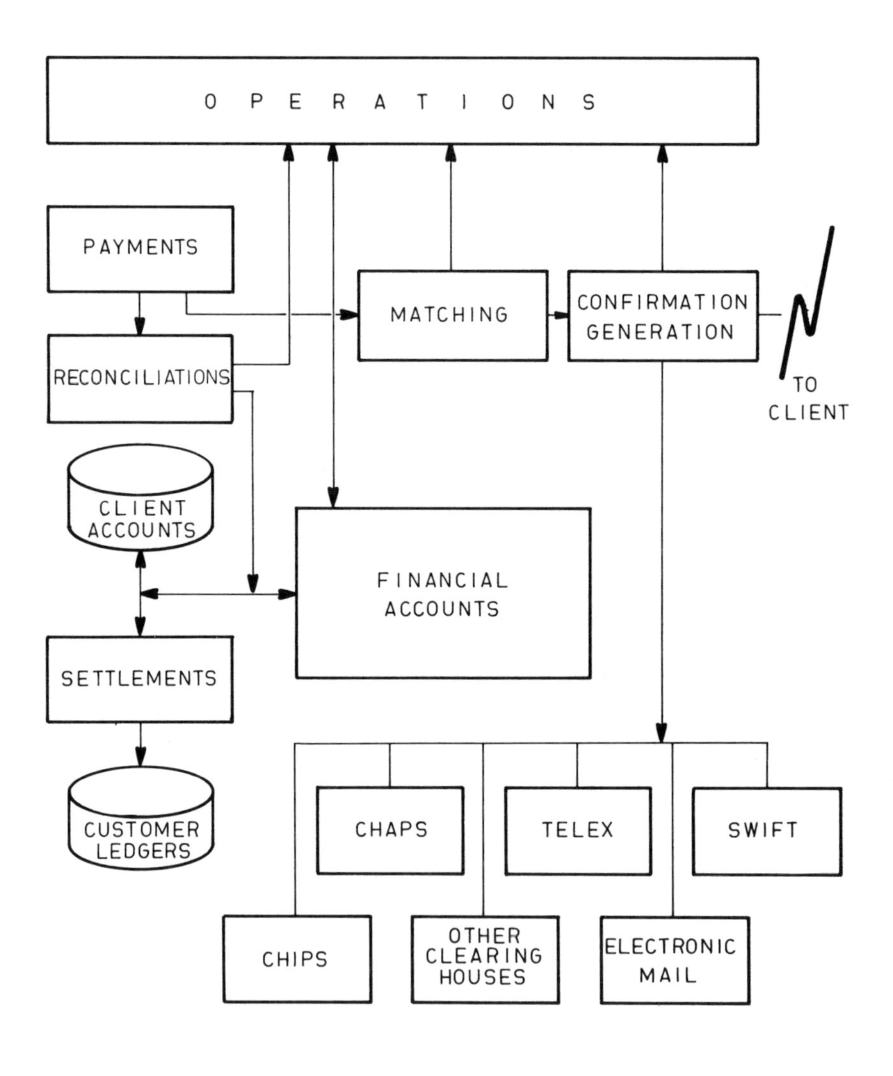

high interest rates, developing strategies to keep new customers even when interest rates dropped. The money-market fund, a liquid, high-yield, variable-rate product, offered what wealthy and sophisticated consumers wanted.

The money market involves short-term securities with a maturity of less than a year, including ninety-day bank bills and certificates of deposit (CD). Compared with property and equities, however, money markets and fixed-interest securities are not well understood by private investors, who are sometimes confused by terms such as rediscount rates, yields to maturity, bullet bonds and inscribed stocks.

This is unfortunate given that the fixed-interest market is a vital part of any financial system and is subject to trends and events that can affect investors' decisions in a more general sense.[6] There are two types of fixed interest securities, categorized according to the issuer and maturity of the instruments traded.

Any interest-earning investment can come under the fixed interest heading, insofar as the interest rate is fixed for a day, a year, a decade or other time frame. But in practice, the market applies the term to securities for which the coupon is fixed at the time of issue and the maturity is longer than one year. This includes bonds or notes issued by sovereign nations, quasi-official and local government authorities, supranationals, utility companies, manufacturing and distribution firms, banks, and other finance companies.

Wise investors hedge their holdings in order to keep the proper mix between equities, bonds, the money market, and, for example, precious metals. When the stock market is in the doldrums, most fund managers have to keep about 40 percent of their portfolios in fixed-interest and money-market securities.

Proper hedging is the essence of investment, and while the ratios may vary from one time (or one market) to another, brokerage and mutual fund industries count on their ability to convince consumers that the equities, bonds, commodities, or other products that the firms are offering will be desirable in different economic conditions.

Typically, a fixed interest security may be defined by

1. its face value, that is, the loan amount to be repaid on maturity;
2. the coupon rate, which is fixed at the time of issue;
3. the maturity, or period to repayment of the principal;
4. the yield, which is the return if held to maturity, expressed in annual percentage terms, including the coupon and capital gain or loss.

During the 1980s, investors developed a taste for short-term and long-term bonds as well as for transaction accounts that they can turn to for withdrawals. For customers who equally prize the safety of capital and yield, U.S. Treasuries offered for many years a timely combination of both, thanks to the wide gap in the U.S. federal budget.

Interest on the securities is exempt from state and local taxes, and investors daunted by the $10,000 minimum-purchase requirement for T-bills can buy longer-term Treasury notes and bonds in face amounts of $1,000 and $5,000. Treasuries mature in two to thirty years. They offer a good rate of interest without event risk (in which a prime company's bonds can turn overnight into junk bonds due to a leveraged buyout).

In the U.S., some small investors buy Treasuries by withdrawing money from accounts in banks or savings and loans. Customers can save the $25 to $50 commissions that brokers and commercial banks charge on Treasury sales by purchasing these securities directly from the government at a federal reserve bank.

For brokers serious about success, policies are as important as products, as the example of Credit Suisse First Boston (CSFB) shows. The Euromarkets are now the second largest source of capital in the world, close behind the U.S. market. Not surprisingly, this has attracted the Japanese. In 1987, Nomura Securities took the lead in managing new issues, the first time in a decade that CSFB has not been at the top in this market.

In Eurodollar issues, CSFB had a 15-percent market share, more than double the share of the number-two investment bank, Morgan Stanley. In the floating rate note sector, CSFB held 23 percent, again more than double its nearest competitor. In the smaller but highly profitable market for convertible debt issues, CSFB had 33 percent, four times the market share of the number two bank.

For a bank with such clout, CSFB is a relatively small institution, with fewer than 800 staff. But other statistics, too, are significant. The average CSFB banker is twenty-eight years old and has worked for the firm for 1.9 years. In the tough dynamic environment of the Euromarkets, personnel matters. It is essential for a financial institution to attract good people to work with it.

In 1977, Hans-Joerg Rudloff, general manager of Credit Suisse, invented the bought deal in Eurobonds, in which a bank agrees on a fixed price with a borrower for a new issue. In doing so, the bank incurs the risk that interest rates, and thus prices, will move adversely before the bonds can be sold. This technique has transformed the Eurobond market by causing it to become dominated by the few banks large and enterprising enough to take such a risk.

In bought deals, lead managers of bond issues give borrowers a single all-in price for the entire issue. The managers then have to syndicate out pieces of the issue to other banks and sell their own allotment of bonds to retail investors. Thus, the lead managers put their own capital and credibility at risk.

The potential for loss is great. But if the lead manager has a good instinct for the direction the market is headed, and also has the placing power, the potential for profit is even more impressive.

Salesmanship is a major part of Eurobonds transactions, from selling the bank know-how to the borrower, to persuading other banks to join in a syndicate, to selling bonds to investors.

The best salesmen become the stars of a brokerage house. Coordination, management, accounting and systems all take a back seat to being out on the road getting business and cutting deals.

The bought deal has other prerequisites. It demands new levels of speed in getting a deal out into the marketplace. A few hours can make the difference between a million-dollar profit and a million-dollar loss. People must work day and night, and they must be supported through first class on-line information systems with interactive capabilities.

Management policy should be governed not by grand ambitions of growth, but by a short-term, market-sensitive search for profitability. "When a firm tries to be everything at the same time," Hans-Joerg Rudloff explains, "it blows up its balance sheet, inevitably loses control, and the return on capital goes down. I am happy to be smaller but more profitable."

In a highly competitive financial environment, the right approach to the market is typically based on the vision of one person in charge. Consensus decision making is often the way to lose business; policies and procedures must be such that the firm can move fast and be aggressive.

Brokers consider derivative securities as possible products—including futures, options, mortgage-backed bonds, and financial products based on various stock indexes. They are expected to be star performers in the 1990s. Current surveys predict an international explosion in issuing and trading them.

Of 403 international money managers and traders who participated in a survey on changing global investment patterns done by *The Wall Street Journal,* a majority predicted that over the coming years their activity in traditional investments, stocks, bonds and currencies, would increase slightly from current levels, but their use of derivative instruments would soar. (In 1990, 80 percent of the interviewed financial executives expected this to happen, up from 63 percent in 1989.)

Also, 65 percent said they will be investing in stock indexes or baskets of stocks, up from 44 percent who do so today. Furthermore, 62 percent (compared with 43 percent in 1990) expect to be dealing with securitized products, such as bonds backed by mortgages or other receivable assets, in the coming years.[7]

Significantly, this study predicts that nearly a quarter of the trading volume accounted for by major financial institutions will involve foreign securities. That is up from about 14 percent currently.

The increase in the number of international money managers dealing in derivative securities is, in itself, an important signal. The same is true of globalization's aftermaths; as a percentage of their overall activity, the U.S. traders' international trading volume is expected to triple in the next five years.

Securities need to be sold quickly, but registering public securities with SEC at the outset of an LBO or other acquisition slows the process. Some investment banks therefore do private placements, with rights to register them as public securities later.

In the private placement market, securities are promoted to institutions, but not publicly sold. Prudential, Metropolitan

Life, CIGNA, and other huge insurance companies, as well as institutional investors, are directly soliciting new corporate issues.

Prudential Insurance directly purchased $3.9 billion in private placements in 1989, up from $700 million in 1984. Though the company still uses investment houses to buy private placements ($5.6 billion in 1989), direct transactions are closing the gap.

Wall Street has been affected by Prudential's unwillingness to be a passive buyer. In 1989, the firm sold some $1 billion in private placements to twenty-six other institutional investors; in that same year, Metropolitan Life tried to buy a $100 million public debt offering of Carolina Power and Light; it bid against four securities firms. (Met Life lost that bid.)

There are disadvantages to private placement. One is that the practice narrows the market of buyers; for example, most mutual funds buy only public securities. The procedure is also more expensive to the issuer; because privately placed securities are not supposed to be traded, buyers demand a higher yield or other favors as compensation for the lack of liquidity.

For placement, as for the marketing of other products described in this chapter, success depends on the ingenuity of management; but fundamentally, are bottom-line driven, moving from client to client, country to country, institution to institution, with an overriding sense of performance. The lightly regulated, multinational, multicurrency, and multi-instrument Euromarkets are an ideal environment in which to pursue such a strategy.

Endnotes

1. *Business Week*, 6 February 1990.

2. *Liar's Poker: Rising Through the Wreckage on Wall Street.* (New York: Norton, 1989).

3. Edwin Reischauer, Japan: *The Story of a Nation*

4. *Business Week*, 19 November, 1990.

5. See also D.N. Chorafas, *Simulation, Optimization and Expert Systems: How Technology is Revolutionizing the Way Securities are Underwritten, Analyzed and Traded* (Chicago: Probus, 1992).

6. Not only brokers should be making money market instruments more comprehensive to investors, but also the investors themselves should be able to learn about them in order to protect their interest.

7. *The Wall Street Journal*, 24 and 25 November, 1990.

Chapter 6

The Money Managers

Chapter 6

The Money Managers

1. Introduction

"One of the sad things about money managers," said a *Business Week* review of John Train's, *The New Money Masters,* "is that few of them can ever become truly distinguished. Their goal, after all, is to beat the market, and it has been true for some time that money managers are the market."[1] Another common assumption about this profession is that human money managers are increasingly being replaced by machines. Is this true?

The answer is that they are not being replaced, but assisted. Computers now perform routine functions that formerly used up managers' time rather than contributing to their professionality. For example, massively parallel computers are particularly suited to searching for patterns in mountains of data.

Money managers try to beat the market in order to bring wealth to the investors whose accounts they administer. The trick to getting rich in the securities market is correctly assessing supply and demand, thus making it possible to identify investment opportunities. As will be discussed in this chapter, brokers can be assisted in this endeavor by investment theory regarding equities and debt, and this theory can be tested through AI and computers.

When buying, says John Train, astute money managers look for stock groups that are out of favor in the market. Experts in the field provide insights into subjects such as, selling discipline; that is, when to buy into a particular equity or bond, and when to let it go—a thorny matter for investors.

There is so much intuition involved in this activity that a computer cannot outperform an expert player. Nevertheless, with an underlying infrastructure in investment theory and some first-class interactive expert systems at their disposal, even experts can improve their performance.

Thus, Morgan Stanley, after a couple of years' experience with a minisupercomputer (Alliant), has installed a Cray supercomputer; Bear Stearns now uses three Floating Point supercomputers. These firms know that, if the new technology is used, it is possible to beat the market—on a consistent basis.

2. Money and Risk

Successful money managers and investment advisors do not treat the financial market as a game of chance. They plan their moves, look for opportunities, and carefully position themselves in the ever-changing market landscape.

Unsuccessful brokers, on the other hand, are those who cannot explain where they are going and why they think they will succeed. Everyone makes mistakes in judgment, but it is crucial to be right more than once in a while. Even a broken watch is "right" two times a day.

A money manager should have a valid investment theory to put into practice. In order to understand the business he or she is in, and what goals to pursue, a broker must understand the essence of money. As discussed in Chapter 2, money is the raw material for the banking industry: a means of exchange and transacting business; a store of value (the oversupply of which makes it worthless, as seen in times of hyperinflation); and a unit of measurement that makes it possible to have metrics, evaluations, and reference points. This is the basis of accounting.

The management of money involves risk. Figure 6.1 shows a matrix of the major risk classes in financial intermediation.[2] Of these, credit risk can sometimes be controlled through overnight and interday limits; interest-rate risk is particularly important in unmatched positions; and sales-condition risk can be partly controlled through limits.

The common denominator of the last three classes shown in the matrix is liquidity risk. Of these, fulfillment risk is reflected into margins, and follow-the-sun overdraft calls for redefining financial responsibility. A question inherent to these three types of risk is, when the counterparty will be called to face its obligations, will it be liquid and, therefore, able to do so?

Not all activities (transactions, positions, settlements) or all actions by entities (clients, traders, managers) involve every one of these ten types of risk; but in many cases, several of them are present in greater or lesser amounts (the latter indicated in the risk matrix by a cross within parenthesis). The compound effect can often be severe; thus, the financial institution has to be extra careful in controlling such risk.

The management of money is never static. The financial markets constitute a dynamic entity that must be steadily watched and its changes anticipated. The market accepts no half-truths, evasion, or stubborness; it penalizes each one of them with financial losses. Sometimes it is not difficult to foresee what is coming.

In late 1988, for example, prior to the great savings and loans bailout, about 500 insolvent thrifts were losing money

Figure 6.1 Matrix of Major Risk Classes, and Risk Involved in Each of Them by Type of Operation

	TRADERS, TRANSACTIONS	INVENTORY OF POSITIONS	CLIENTS	SETTLEMENTS	
POSITION RISK	X	X			
CREDIT RISK			X	X	LIMITS - OVERNIGHT - INTERDAY
INVESTMENT RISK		X	X		
INTEREST RATE RISK	X	X			UNMATCHED POSITION
CURRENCY RISK	X	X			
COUNTRY RISK	X	X	X	(X)	
SALES CONDITION RISK	X		X		LIMITS
FULFILLMENT RISK			X	X	MARGINS
TRANSACTION RISK	(X)			X	
FOLLOW-THE-SUN OVERDRAFT	X		X	X	FINANCIAL RESPONSIBILITY

at the rate of almost $17 billion per year; and since the government did not want to see the fabric of the financial industry torn apart, it imposed a sugar-coated form of nationalization, called "thrift bailout." In the early 1980s, the same happened with Continental Illinois. In other cases, forecasting is not so simple.

In 1954, with the nascent computer business still unsettled, IBM projected that it would sell perhaps fifty of its model 650 data processors to clients and priced it accordingly. The 650 became the workhorse of its time and sold thousands of units, producing a bonanza for IBM as well as for the investors who rode on the IBM stock.

In the mid-1980s, on the other hand, IBM did not think that the optical disk market would become a major player in the future. But as prices dropped sharply, the optical disk reached the workstation level at an affordable cost; it has since become quite popular.

Likewise, in the financial industry, no two securities analysts or brokers will have exactly the same opinion about which direction the market is taking. The financial market represents a cumulative community intelligence, and while eventually some of forecasters will win, others will not be as "lucky" (Luck being a combination of preparation and opportunity)—nobody can afford an unlucky money manager.

Investment experts' experience helps them to foresee coming events. This experience is typically composed of three kinds of knowledge: factual, judgmental, and procedural.

Each may be encoded separately but they operate together, fired by incoming information that may or may not satisfy trigger conditions.

Factual knowledge allows one to make assertions about market movements and individual securities as well as the relationships among them. Causality lies at its roots. Judgmental knowledge is based on experience; conditions are compared with conditions that appeared in the past; and adjustments are made, as no two market opportunities are precisely the same. Procedural knowledge allows one to reap benefits when a business opportunity is located, while avoiding the wrong move.

The investment expert makes a portfolio design for the holdings of each client and for all of them by specific position. As the market changes, he or she may construct a new portfolio, revamp an old one, or make switches that enrich a portfolio's content.

A careful investment administrator will do periodic assessment and reevaluation of a client's portfolio. Each such assessment is short-term management; nevertheless, it should be done from a medium- to long-term perspective.

A good money manager will have a basic theory by which to trade and manage a client's portfolio. His theory should assess the short- and long-term views and orient investment decisions accordingly.

Each portfolio manager has an individual decision profile. Some money managers are chartists, who make their buy, hold, or sell decisions by carefully watching the developing pattern on a time series chart. Others are quants, whose choices are based largely on the results of a thorough quantitative analysis of market trends and underlying factors.

Still others base their judgment on profit-and-loss evaluations and return-on-equity measures, which are applied to companies in which they invest or plan to invest. One of these is William P. Frankenhoff, whose investment policy is one not of forecasting the economy, interest rates, or the stock market, but one of buying stocks as if he were buying businesses for clients.[3] Rather than quick trading profits, he focuses on the longer term.

"Companies don't enter a business to get out of it in six months," Frankenhoff says. "Investors shouldn't do it either." For his investments, he requires that a company has at least 20-percent annual growth in earnings per share and 20-percent return on equity, little or no debt, a proprietary position, or niche, and a focused product line, not diversified, disparate businesses.

Companies whose products face import competition or risk obsolescence don't make Frankenhoff's list. He also frowns on companies that are interest-rate sensitive. Not surprisingly, he rarely holds more than eighteen stocks and estimates that there are only sixty companies at NYSE that meet his criteria.

Not every money manager thinks in the same terms, nor is this the only prescription for being a successful investor. Nevertheless, Frankenhoff's approach is a good example of how having a basic investment theory helps, from filtering candidate work horses to periodically scrutinizing them to assure that they are in line with basic criteria that have been spelled out in advance.

Every valid money manager has an investment theory and set of criteria by which he or she abides; thus, it is not hard to decide which way to go when evaluating each situation. The fact that these theories diverge and the criteria are not necessarily compatible is precisely what makes the market. The relationship between gains and risk lies at the heart of the money manager's and the banker's art, which is why the financial business is so dynamic.

3. Stockbrokers and Small Investors

A stockbroker, advises Woody Allen, is someone who takes your money and invests it until it is all gone. A survey commissioned by the American Stock Exchange suggests that ordinary investors think Allen may be right.

A retired air force major named James Eunice followed his broker's advice and sank $155,000 of his savings into Gateway Medical Systems in 1986 and 1987. The securities analyst at his brokerage (Memphis-based Morgan Keegan) had said in a report that Gateway's "aggressive acquisition program will provide tremendous growth in revenue and earnings for the next several years."

What Eunice did not know was that the analyst had a strong incentive to be bullish. He stood to realize a 2.5 percent share in the commissions Morgan Keegan received from sales of the nineteen stocks he was recommending—even if they went under, as Gateway did a few months later.[4] This experience illustrates one of the hidden pitfalls facing small investors. Securities analysts often have a direct financial stake—sometimes up to 50 percent of their compensation—in the commissions generated on the stocks they follow.

"It is the nature of the business," says Thomas G. Rosencrants, research director at Interstate/Johnson Lane, a North Carolina brokerage. "If we don't generate business, we don't get paid." But it is also a conflict of interest as well as a highly counterproductive practice, which kills, in the long run, the market on which securities houses depend for their business.

Small investors are vital to the securities business. They keep the market liquid, reduce volatility, and keep commissions flowing. Thus, it is important that the industry come to grips with the fact that small investors are leaving the stock market and often not returning.

Statistics show that noninstitutional investors have been leaving the market steadily for years. These departures accelerated in the late 1980s, even as the market was recovering from the October 1987 crash, and no segment of the securities industry was more strongly affected than discount brokerages by the dearth of individual investors.

Discount brokerages are at the mercy of small-investor sentiment. Commissions make up three-fifths of their revenues; the rest comes mainly from interest charged to customers. As a result, the decline in the number of individual investors has seriously affected the brokerages' bottom line.

At the New York Stock Exchange, the percentage of volume attributable to trading by individuals is believed to be as little as 10 percent and shrinking. The stock market is virtually monopolized by the institutional investors. Why is this happening?

A group of investors, most of them professionals, was polled in mid-1989 by AmEx. The typical interviewee was fifty-five years old, had a university degree, and was head of a home with an annual income of $80,000; he or she also understood options, zero-coupon bonds, and stock-index funds, and was more interested in preserving capital than in trying to make a killing. Interestingly, while more than four-fifths of the investors in the survey described themselves as risk-averse conservatives, two-thirds of the brokers described themselves as risk-oriented.

This difference in strategic orientation goes to the heart of the matter. Investors like blue-chip shares but prefer safer forms of investment; they equate share-buying with gambling. Brokers, who work on commission, want their clients to trade often and to plunge their money into flashy stocks that typically fail to deliver. As a result, many investors, having been burnt, become demoralized and eventually leave the stock market.

Cases of fraud magnify the recently acquired distaste by individual investors for stock investments. For instance, for years Walter F. Curran was thought to be a high-flying stockbroker. He pulled down commissions of up to $170,000 a year from his employer, Dean Witter Reynolds. But in February 1989, the U.S. attorney in Boston said Curran will be charged with bank and mail fraud.[5]

According to the government, Curran not only took $2.6 million in cash from four investors while promising extraordinarily high returns, but also claimed falsely that he was investing the money in his personal account at Dean Witter, and to keep clients happy, prepared false monthly statements showing how well the firm was doing.

This is not an isolated case. Every year another horror story emerges. While these stories have many twists, most describe a broker who exploited investors' hopes of making extraordinary profits.

Charles Ponzi, Robert Vesco, and Michele Sindona are all well-known cases of abuse and therefore do not require repeating. Others, though they never really caught the headlines, have been just as damaging to the brokerage industry. One of the most recent concerns Juan Carlos Schidlowski.[6]

The losses inflicted on ordinary investors by Schidlowski, and the thousands like him who ply the penny-stock trade, are big. While some $3 billion was raised in America in legitimate venture-capital channels during 1988 alone, state securities regulators estimate that another $2 billion was squandered on phony penny-stock schemes that same year.

The number of new penny-stock investigations opened by state officials doubled to 737 in 1988; as of 1989, the pace has quickened, says John C. Baldwin, Utah's securities director. He calls the epidemic "the number-one threat facing the small investor today."

SEC has paid penny stocks scant attention, especially in comparison with the resources it has poured into more glamorous areas, such as insider trading; yet, penny stocks have been propelled from a crude cottage industry into a world-class con scheme—one that turns affluent investors, capital-hungry entrepreneurs, and low-net worth-individuals into victims of sophisticated, multibillion-dollar securities frauds.

As its name implies, a penny stock trades for pennies; it typically belongs to a start-up company, which finds it to be a cheap way to raise capital. One example of a start-up is Neobionics, a company founded in 1979 to develop home pregnancy-test kits.

While such products are now common on pharmacy shelves, Neobionics investors are not sharing in the profits. The company ditched the project in 1984 and later merged with another lab, practically disappearing from existence. Originally, the stock came out at $.50 and went as high as $1.37, but it no longer trades in the market, and its certificates have become worthless.

Most often penny stocks are peddled from door to door, which does not mean that securities houses are totally blameless; losses inflicted on investors, whether they are a result of lack of care or of sloppy management control, do not constitute a commentable reference. The business of lending securities is another example.

Since early 1990, the U.S. government has been investigating Wall Street's stock-loan business, in which firms lend stock to their institutional customers and to each other. Critics charge that such activities are rife with corruption and kickbacks.[7]

The brokerage business reaps millions of dollars every year in interest by lending their customers' securities without sharing the profits with the securities' owners. And the lending business is rocketing. As of mid-1989, loans outstanding amounted to $32.6 billion, versus $6.6 billion at the end of 1980.

Lending stocks owned by customers is not an illegal practice. The borrowers are often short-sellers. When traders want to speculate that a stock's price will fall, they sell the stock with the idea of buying it back at a lower price; but since they do not have the stock in hand, they must borrow it.

Brokerages that hold the stock in customers' margin accounts can lend it to them, with the lending broker keeping the interest fee earned for the loan. This is part of the standard margin agreement between brokers and customers.

Most brokers have an unpublicized stock-loan department, whose activities are frequently not reported to the front office.

The absence of strict controls over this department makes it easy for its clerks to siphon off funds that should flow back to the firm; also, the intermediaries, known as finders, are not regulated by the SEC because technically they are not arranging for the stocks to be borrowed.

But brokers are regulated, and over the past several years, SEC has brought a number of charges of securities-law violations against stock-loan departments. For instance, in 1983, the SEC censured Merrill Lynch and two regional brokerage firms, Advest and McDonald, for failure to supervise three employees in their stock-loan departments. In 1987, Shearson was censured for unauthorized use of customer securities.

The news of these occurrences tarnishes stockbrokers' image, particularly among individual investors. Whether rightly or wrongly, investors begin to associate the brokerage business with a con game, with the result being that the retail market thins out. An industry that cannot police itself properly has bleak prospects, because having the confidence of consumers is, after all, a prerequisite to doing business.

4. Two Issues for Big Investors: Venture Capital and Downsizing

Investors and people who manage investment funds want to know whether to buy stocks or bonds and when to sell them. They examine the dynamics of a company from the outside. But, a venture capitalist is primarily interested in inside information, such as the potential of the product the company sells; how management runs the company; how it solves the problems of growth and faces the issues of competition; and whether it can meet the challenges posed by technological change.

The modern venture capital industry was started in 1946, when General Georges Doriot, the father of the venture capital funds concept, raised $3 million to invest in start-up companies, especially high-technology spinoffs of MIT. American Research and Development (ARD) was the first of these funds in the U.S. Some of Doriot's investments have since become the stuff of legend in the high technology industry.

One of them, High-Voltage Engineering, at the end of December 1946, received a check for $200,000, making it the first venture-capital-financed company in modern America. Another, Digital Equipment Corporation, is perhaps the most famous venture capital investment of all time; the $67,000 ARD invested in this firm grew to $600 million, an increase of five orders of magnitude, in slightly over twenty years.

Today the venture-capital industry comprises about 500 firms, with over 2,000 or so professional venture capitalists managing a total pool of more than $30 billion. For the past few years, the annual flow of new money into venture capital funds has been an estimated $3 to $4 billion.

How well have venture capital funds performed? The answer is not easy to determine, because the industry abounds with hype. The compound annual rate of return, of 100 percent to 150 percent, is spectacular. Nevertheless, even with as spectacular an investment as Digital Equipment Corporation in its portfolio, ARD's annualized rate of return for the first two decades of its existence was only 14 percent. Subsequently, return-on-investment ratios have fallen to single digits, one of the main reasons being that the supply of venture capital exceeds the availability of good deals to invest in.

There are also market ups and downs. Venture capital was popular during the bullish years of the late 1960s, but the catastrophic bear market from 1973 to 1974 dried up the supply of fresh ventures in the United States. There was little incentive to put up seed capital for new companies; thus till the end of the 1970s, venture capital was a rather stagnant, unglamorous niche of the financial world, funded mostly with money committed by investors before the 1973 market break.

This illiquidity proved to be a blessing in disguise, because in contrast to the booming years of the 1960s, venture capitalists encountered very little competition in finding new technology companies to fund. In fact, venture funding was so scarce that Gene Amdahl had to find capital in Japan when he started the Amdahl Corporation.

Investors should not be discouraged, however. They merely need to overcome the habit of looking at a business from the outside, that is, examining a company's five- or ten-year track record and its ratios.

The difference between investing in stock and engaging in the financing of new ventures is significant, because when looking from the inside, questions must be asked about market demand, cost factors, volume relationships, competitive positioning, and the financial resources needed to maintain staying power. In other words, future potential, not past results, must be examined. (Up to a point, the venture capital boom of the early 1980s bears a resemblance to the leveraged buy-out (LBO) movement; what worked well on a modest scale with new ventures, however, became risky as it expanded with the LBO.)

There are a number of varieties of risk capital. Venture nurturing involves managerial assistance from the investing corporation as well as cash; sometimes marketing, manufacturing, and even additional research, are also included.

Venture spin-offs are usually the by-product of a large corporation's own R and D effort. A new business is created if management feels that the project does not fit too well within the firm's mainstream activity. Venture merging is a term used to describe a deliberate attempt to piece together various approaches to technological venturing.

Joint ventures are the result of large and small companies developing projects together. The small firm provides ideas, entrepreneurial enthusiasm, and flexibility; the big firm provides capital as well as worldwide marketing and service backup.

Internal ventures occur when a corporation sets up a separate "greenhouse" division to develop radically new products or to enter different markets. The firm counts on this approach providing small-company conditions, with ideas incubating and growing before having to stand on their own feet.

Internal ventures have polyvalent aspects; one of them is known as demassing, or the creation of independent business units. Some boards are willing to make deep cuts in their organization's size, provided these can be made without major disruptions. The reason for independent business units is to promote innovative ability by releasing the management of the unit from the constraint of central planners.

Not only is planned downsizing a sustainable alternative to large centralized organizations, but it may well be the way of the future; it

1. helps reduce management layers significantly;
2. bends the curve in the proliferation of staff experts and central planners;
3. makes the management of the independent business unit reliant on its own forces and more responsive to market demand;
4. lays the groundwork for a type of federated management.

Independent business units generally have a quicker response to competitors' actions, faster diffusion of new ideas, less distorted internal and external communications, higher morale, greater ability to respond to customer needs, and straightforward pinpointing of individual responsibility as well as accountability.

Downsizing is a good way of attacking excess management, as well as dethroning entitlement processes, which typically suffers from bureaucratic arthritis. The two main characteristics of corporate arthritis are that nothing can be made to happen in a firm, and everyone seems to have the power of veto over every decision.

In the 1980s, the promotion of an entrepreneurial spirit has done much to eliminate bureaucratic ossification. In 1987, a Conference Board study was done on U.S. industry; this study concluded that in the eight years which preceded it, more than a million managers and staff professionals lost their jobs because of restructuring, that is, downsizing and the institution of entrepreneurial solutions.

Nevertheless, the process of descaling cannot be done in a haphazard manner; thus, while consulting companies get much of the related business, there are also opportunities for investment banks. In fact, to judge from Wall Street's increasing number of Mergers and Acquisitions boutiques (which involve a considerable amount of capital), the investment banking sector itself is descaling. "These are the new professionals," says author Charles Hardy, "who want their names to be as well-known as their roles, who see themselves as partners in the enterprise, and want to be recognized as colleagues, not subordinates."[8]

Whether based on venture capital or evolving through descaling, the successful organization of the future will be one that is able to create and sustain a culture built around the talents of professionals, not traditional management layers. This is restructuring in the style of a federal organization.

Corporate federalism seeks to make it big by combining autonomy with organization. Any of the venture-capital alternatives discussed, as well as intrapreneurial approaches and independent business units, will fit this description.

In Chapter 11 we will discuss workouts, a new and lucrative line of business for investment banks. Workouts and downsizing have much in common, but there is also a significant difference; while downsizing typically starts before top management is forced to restructure by the course of events, workouts are done after a catastrophy has occurred.

As with new ventures, a federally organized corporation, utilizes leadership of ideas and know-how, not a chain of command. Such a company has many professionals and few managers. To use Dr. Peter Drucker's analogy, it resembles an orchestra with 100 professional musicians but one conductor.

An orchestra does not have sub-conductors and sub-sub-conductors, as do industrial and financial organizations; it does, however, have a first violinist, a professional distinguished from other professionals by being a virtuoso. One of these virtuosi will be the investment banker. Like the other professionals, he or she will have to rely increasingly on leadership and conviction rather than on formal authority or absolute power.

5. The New Capitalists: Pension Funds and Other Institutional Investors

A major challenge for financial institutions all over the globe has been steady and sound management. Too often, senior executives have favored bigness for bigness' sake. The few banks that have been run with solid earnings rather than size as prime criterion, stand out, and their shares trade at a premium to net asset value.

This is also true of mutual funds, pension funds, and other institutional investors. Many have become overly big in too short a time to allow for management skill to build up. This can have severe aftermaths in the financial markets, because the making or breaking of these markets increasingly depends on the response of institutional investors, and tiny steps in improving the level of know-how and administrative skills are less and less significant.

The money managers of institutional investors and other financial organizations know this. They are the people who ran investment portfolios for insurance companies, public and private pension funds, mutual funds, college endowments, securities companies, commercial banks, thrifts, and different offshore institutions. And they are the people who have the capital.

Led by large public-employee pension funds in New York, California, and Wisconsin, institutions say they have little choice but to own the shares of the biggest U.S. companies. The Association of Retired People (AARP) has 15 million members who, through their pension-fund holding, represent the largest single block of ownership in the American industry.

Yet, in spite of the securities specialists and their technology, as well as the assistance they get from investment banks, institutional investors find it difficult, if not impossible, to outperform the market. As a result, they have abandoned the costly and relatively inefficient game of outguessing the stock market in favor of indexing, or buying a basket of shares to follow widely accepted market indices.

This practice has had significant effects on securities houses. In 1980 institutions held 33 percent of all publicly quoted American shares. As of 1990, they own 45 percent.

In England, institutional holdings have risen from 47 percent of shares in 1975 to 63 percent in 1990. Even more significant, such holdings have been concentrated in fewer hands, chiefly pension funds. These alone own 25 percent of American shares.[9] Hence, through their pension funds and mutual funds, employees have become the new capitalists.

Pension funds are a good case study in money management. They are a growth industry and represent one of the best hopes for decent retirement for millions of working people; but as they have grown rich, they have also become a target for a number of people, from leveraged buy-out addicts to corporate raiders and legislators.

American pension funds today constitute the largest pool of investible capital in the world. At the end of 1989, this capital stood at $2.6 trillion in assets, which is half the gross national product (GNP) of the United States, and equal to the GNP of Japan. In the opinion of investment analysts, U.S. pension funds fueled the economic surge of the 1980s, and made possible the stock-market boom.

These funds are also thought to be behind the explosion of hostile takeovers, management buy-outs, employee stock-ownership plans, and venture capital. Having tripled in size since 1979 and with their return on investment alone reaching $340 billion in 1989, pension plans, according to some accounts, are operating at a surplus of $600 billion.

Out of $2.6 trillion in assets, $600 billion represents less than 25 percent. It may seem to be an impressive figure, but it is really no more than a comfortable margin, particularly when the risk involved in financial markets is considered.

Most of the assets under the control of pension-fund money managers are invested in the stock market, and October 1987 should be a reminder that stock markets are not always bullish. A crash may in one day wipe out most of this 25-percent margin. Another large chunk of pension-fund money is in junk bonds—the result of a move that, while it produced a high return on investment, was a mistake, as is evident from what took place in January 1990 in the junk-bond market.

Could this enormous money machine be the victim of its own success? Some people are fighting to siphon off pension funds' riches for reasons that often have little to do with providing retirement of the work force. Corporations are dismantling plans, creaming off their surpluses, and leaving retirees with bare annuities; the government is looking at taxing their trading gains; and fund managers are now meddling with corporate policy and sinking money into risky buy-outs and low-return projects.

In a radical and regrettable change of policy, organizations as well as individuals are gambling with the future by pitting pension money against immediate problems. One of the first cases to come to the public's attention was that of the municipal unions that bought New York City securities during its mid-1970s fiscal crisis, helping save the city from bankruptcy. This, unfortunately, set a bad precedent.

By law, only the pension plan's surplus can be recaptured by management, a process known as a reversion. The amount needed to pay beneficiaries remains earmarked for them. Because there are loopholes, however, corporations have circumvented this stipulation.

When the Tengelmann Group took over the ailing Great Atlantic & Pacific Tea Company in 1982, it used the pension fund's $200 million surplus to finance A&P's turnaround; Carl C. Icahn followed a similar strategy when he bought Ozark Air Lines to add to his Trans World Airlines (TWA) holdings, as did Charles E. Hurwitz in his buy-out of Pacific Lumber, a century-old logging concern in Northern California. Furthermore, when Texaco bought Getty Oil in 1986, it used $250 million from the target's fund to buy annuities for Getty employees.

Pension funds raiders have come into the scene as fortunes changed from underfunding (with funds being unable to afford their projected payouts) to overfunding (as the bull market of the 1980s provided plenty of opportunities to create surpluses).

Today, not only is some pension fund money directed to causes that have little or nothing to do with pensions, but also there seems to be a lack of clear policy on what is and what is not acceptable practice. Many companies want their own pension funds to score big in the market, and that includes takeover plays. Some, however, actually punish their pension managers for failing to vote for antitakeover proposals that hold down another company's stock price.

Thus, the role of pension funds in financial and social issues is far from being resolved. There are many money managers with conflicts of interest who see big amounts of available money as a sleeping giant and want to push it into action, even if this action happens to be outside the original aims of a pension fund.

At the same time, declining federal aid has spurred calls for greater "social investing" by pension plans. The Housing & Urban Development department is examining whether pension funds should invest in low- and moderate-income housing, where returns are poor; also, the House Ways & Means Committee is investigating the idea of allowing companies to use pension surpluses to pay for retiree health benefits, an expense that is getting out of control.

These are by no means the only issues whose resolution rests on an unstable base. Legislation and regulation may have the best of intentions behind them, but sometimes the aftermath either becomes counterproductive or shows that the measures were based on wishful thinking rather than on a solid foundation. As the U.S. Congress is now laboring to revamp the law regulating pension funds, it is hoped that the lessons will not be forgotten.

Also, there is an assortment of financial organizations, loosely affiliated with the U.S. federal government, who when in financial trouble have issued more than $700 billion in debt and securities. This extravagance could come back to haunt taxpayers; working people's pensions should not suffer the same fate.

The Treasury has never formally promised to make good on the paper of the different government-sponsored enterprises, anymore than it did on the promises of the Federal Savings & Loan Insurance Corporation when it provided the funding for salvaging the Savings and Loans. But the markets assume that if worst came to worst, Uncle Sam would be there to bail out the Federal National Mortgage Association (also known as Fannie Mae); the Federal Home Loan Mortgage Corporation (instituted in July 1970 and nicknamed Freddie Mac); the Student Loan Marketing Association; the Farm Credit System, and an assortment of smaller operators.

All of these corporations were established for a purpose, whether it be to create a secondary market for mortgages, provide liquidity for student loans, or lend farmers money to buy land. Nevertheless, their borrowing does not require congressional approval; their debt does not count against the federal budget deficit; and their spending is not subject to the Gramm-Rudman Act.

Between 1970 and 1989, the outstanding debt and securities of these five enterprises soared from $37 billion to about $800 billion; thus, the potential danger of their collapse is enormous. In the meantime, Congress continues to create new welfare-financing businesses.

The money for the S and L bailout will be raised by the off-budget Resolution Funding Corporation, which as of January 1990 was having difficulty selling its bonds. The question is will the huge off-budget government debts of the future be handled in a similar manner, or will the funding of pensions become problematic because different governments have tapped their resources as the boomers reach retirement?

6. The Roles of Information Technology and Organization

The future of pension funds is very important, both because they represent a valuable contribution to society and because their impact in the financial markets can be tremendous. This has both positive and negative aspects. Yamaichi Securities forecasts that by the mid-1990s more than half of the business of a securities house will come from pension funds; this being the case, any major crisis in the pension funds sector can snowball into a major market panic.

When dealing with security trades that entail millions of dollars in each transaction, investors need confidence that some sort of continuity will prevail. Computers, communications, and artificial intelligence constructs can do nothing to increase investor confidence in the financial markets. This is a political issue and should be handled by legislators and the federal administration.

Technology can and should be used to ensure that information is available to financial managers, whose job requires that ad hoc queries be answered in real time and the inventory of securities be updated on-line for every equity or bond that is bought or sold.

Every transaction should be completed with information such as security type, identification numbers, transaction code, account traded for, and delivery instructions. For bonds, face amount, purchase price, maturity date, callable or bullet, interest rate, and so on are needed.

Solutions should accommodate all types of credit instruments, including all government securities (interest and discount), all governmental agencies' issues, world bank, export/import bank, foreign securities of the major financial centers, commercial paper, bank holding paper, certificates of deposit, and banker's acceptances. Customer accounts should be updated in real time, and risk resulting from customer transactions should be established on-line, with the appropriate files updated.

In most securities houses, data processing takes place at the completion of the day's business. This is not a good idea. It is better that multiple files be concurrently updated in real space in order to both control risk and allow for ad hoc questions being asked at any time of day. The system can be used to produce a complete and detailed list of any security inventory requested. This list should include the exact denomination of each security certificate.

Other jobs include maintaining detailed stock records, maintaining steadily updated customer files, calculating all transactions on-line, upkeeping pending files as transactions roll in, sending all customer confirmations, if possible, through networking, transmitting database to database, and producing interactively the required operational and management reports.

These reports—stock record/inventory details, trade recaps, trade transaction summaries and details, cash sheet summaries and associated details, purchases and sales journals, bank loan balances, daily purchases outstanding, securities pending, profit-and-loss reports, government dealer reports and fail reports—should all be handled interactively on-line.

Despite these information-technology-oriented activities, the greatest difficulty for a firm is not running computers but maintaining organization. There will be parallels between the disorganization that prevails in managing a securities inventory and that which is to be found in the administration of a company's own property, such as real estate.

Despite the fact that real estate usually accounts for at least one-third of a firm's assets, and sometimes more than that, many companies are quite careless in managing their own property.

Surveys showing the extent of the problem have been conducted by the Massachussetts Institute of Technology in 1987; and, another by Reading University for the account of the Royal Institution of Chartered Surveyors. Of the companies that participated in these studies, 25 percent in the U.S. and 30 percent in Britain do not keep full inventories of their property holdings, know where their property is, have accounts on what taxes they pay on property, or know how large the floor space is or who its occupants are.

In fact, these surveys showed that half of the British participants organizations, and two-thirds of the American ones, have no property-management information systems at all. Typically, they do not know the running costs of a building, its market value, its annual repair costs, or alternative possibilities.

Often, rather than looking for savings on costs or investment potential, companies manage property on the basis of what is most convenient. The majority of companies interviewed admit that they do not even charge company departments rent for use of property owned by the organization, much less a fair market price.

On the other hand, top-tier securities firms have really taken care to merge professional know-how and technology into one unified system. And, these institutions recognize that the wave of change has added many new strategies to the money manager's arsenal. These include tactical asset allocation, portfolio insurance, program trading, electronic order crossing, real-time portfolio performance evaluation, multicurrency swaps, and more.

Figure 6.2 shows an integrative solution adopted by a leading financial institution in the aftermath of thorough reorganization. This approach brings together all of the bank's operating systems (channels of business) at the senior management level, with the application of the appropriate financial controls.

Note the emphasis placed on asset management as well as the proximity of long-range planning functions to those of the short-term financial plan (budget). An AI-enriched profitability and performance subsystem contributes to the forecasting function which, in turn, provides input to the planning premises. This subsystem also interacts with evaluation routines that focus on profit center performance, product line profits, customer profitability, and cost-center performance.

The Bank Operating Systems box operates in real time and depends on efficient networking more than any of the other components of the overall system.

The goal of programs in this box is to closely follow the flow of funds, not only by monitoring electronic funds transfers, but also by simulating in real time the way these flows affect the Treasury. A similar interactive evaluation is done of current assets and liabilities, particularly those items sensitive to stock-market movements.

This firm's solution is not only computationally efficient, but it also allows operators to develop hybrid operations that incorporate new AI modules with existing DP-type programs. The system integrates front-office and back-office sites and supports both analogical and numerical reasoning.

Figure 6.3 shows a front-line operating system that divides transaction processing into three major groups—operating channel, market orientation, and accounting and control. This solution, which runs worldwide in real space, is a good example of how networks and financial products can come together. The financial institution that developed it evidently capitalized on the proliferation of broadband communications facilities. The changes financial markets are undergoing was a consideration in many company decisions.

In other words, the company recognized that in the 1990s, networks will be the franchise and customer information will be the product; the combination of franchise and product will become the market opportunity, and the market opportunity is global.

With this perspective, securities houses, banks, and other financial institutions will increasingly pursue customers and markets across geographic and political boundaries, while companies in other industries will use their networks and customer data to invade traditional financial markets. The better organized corporation is the one more favored to win.

Figure 6.2 An Integrative Approach to Financial Controls with Focus on Profitability

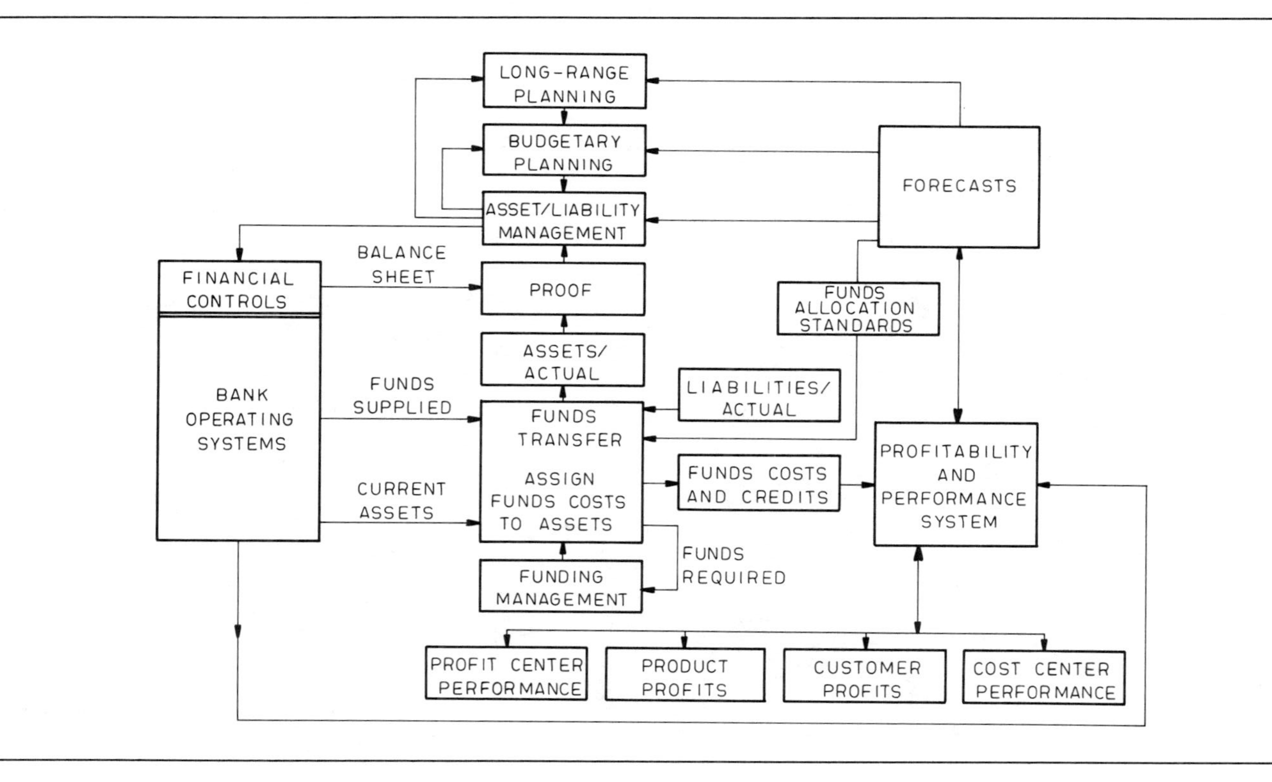

7. Two Top Agendas: Risk Management and Cost Control

In Section 2 of this chapter, it was noted that securities transactions and the securities business at large are confonted with ten types of risk. Risk management is a domain of vital interest, because risk is a process imbedded in every policy and in every transaction.

Author Gary Hector, having examined the unwise risks that brought the Bank of America to its knees, divides the blame between Samuel Armacost (chairman in the early 1980s) and A.W. "Tom" Clausen (who both preceded and succeeded him). Hector faults Clausen for promoting fixed-rate home mortgages on a gamble that interest rates would fall (a move that eventually cost B of A $3.5 billion) and for failing to build a solid management team and for failing to invest in new technology.[10]

Sometimes risks are taken and failures happen because a gamble turns out to have been poorly calculated or an outright long shot. Often the risk factors involved have not been thoroughly researched. Some have even been ignored without an attempt being made to understand what they meant.

At the same time, individual decisions can be no better than the information money managers have at their disposal. Lack of information, or worse, misinformation, is a major cause of investors, fund managers, and companies finding themselves with negative assets. Even more important than information is knowledge; but, knowledge needs reliable and timely information in order to operate effectively.

Knowledgeable securities analysts appreciate that risk is a qualitative and quantitative notion that reflects the variability of assets against expected return. To assess risk, analysts examine the relationship of assets to liabilities.

Sometimes however, in an effort to optimize assets versus liabilities, analysts may forget to take the proverbial "long, hard look" at risk. This involves examining the opportunities

Figure 6.3 Major Groups Constituting Transaction Processing and Back-Office Operations

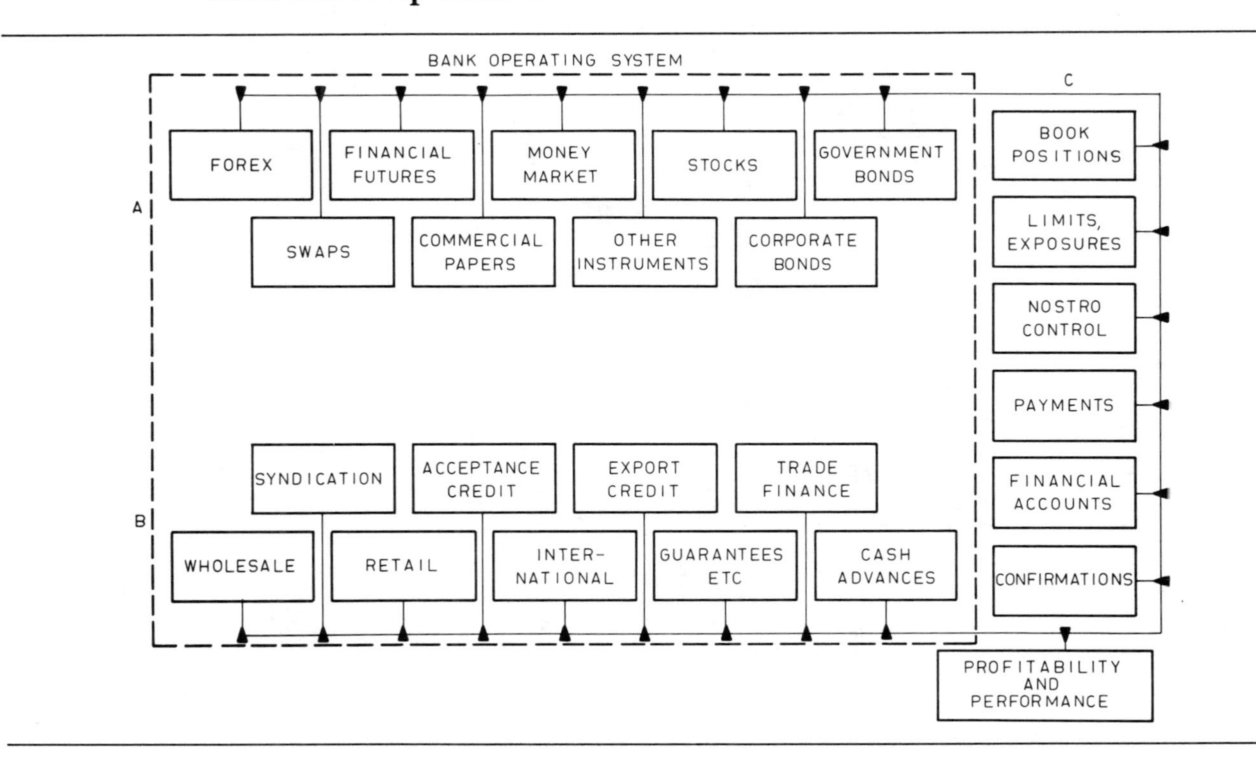

that are available, the risks that are being taken, and the most likely profitability of a certain action.

In other words, risk management should aim to provide accurate answers to focused questions, such as What are the company's options? How much will cost to optimize assets versus liabilities? What is the probability of success of the plan developed to reach a certain goal?

Analysts should develop simulators and AI constructs (preferably run on supercomputers) that can respond to these queries in the way a high-grade professional would answer them. Subsequently, the system should allow senior management to constantly monitor and periodically redefine, evaluate, and coordinate overall financial objectives and the strategies chosen to achieve the desired results.

The focus should be on domains, (see Figure 6.3) not on general, abstract terms. Constantly changing market movements as well as rules for competition will probably alter the approaches that might have been chosen. A plan that is adequate one year may be invalid the next year. This is particularly true in a dynamic economy where the management of risk becomes synonymous with good administrative practice.

Foreign exchange markets continually operate under risky conditions. Even when stock markets are bullish, risks do not disappear; economic uncertainties lead to a larger gap between opportunities and failures. Since continued uncertainty is the rule, it is necessary to have a balanced, well-planned investment portfolio; furthermore, this portfolio should be supported through networks, databases, supercomputers, and expert systems. Technology can also be used to face always high labor costs.

Next to market beatings and account losses due to failure in focusing on global risk, overhead is the greatest threat to a securities firm's profits.

Integrative approaches are instrumental in swamping costs (see Figure 6.4). The nervous system of an investment bank is its international network. On the applications side, emphasis is placed on the market data filter, hedging, trader's assistant, expert systems, arbitrage, Forex, telex parser and analyzer, tax advice, legal help, portfolio management, error diagnostics, and so on. From management's viewpoint, the high points are global risk, customer assistance, planning premises, access to distributed databases, subsecond response time, and cost control.

The facts are, in the typical financial institution, that staff constitutes the bulk of operating costs; thus, cost-conscious managers should reduce their numbers wherever possible. Most personnel reduction can be done within the armies of support staff. But how much reduction is enough?

In London's securities industry, the number of support staff has dropped, from forty thousand at the industry's peak just prior to the October 1987 crash, to about thirty-five thousand. Still, *The Economist* estimated that to earn a decent 20-percent-plus return on equity in a brokerage, the staff and capital employed in the trading of British equities will each need to fall by about one-third.[11]

It is perhaps best never to have excessive staff in the first place. Bear Stearns and Morgan Stanley are two publicly quoted Wall Street firms that continue to report good returns on equity (In 1989, Bear Stearns and Morgan Stanley returned 18 and 26 percent, respectively), yet have avoided layoffs. Both adhere to a basic management discipline too often ignored by financial institutions—they never pay more than 50 percent of revenue in salaries and bonuses.

Nevertheless, financial institutions should remember that there are two sides to the cost-income equation—cutting costs and boosting earnings. With fast-advancing technology, and given that the competitors also try harder to control staff costs, it is no longer sufficient to make the system run a little

Figure 6.4 Nervous System of an Investment Bank and Link to the Exchanges

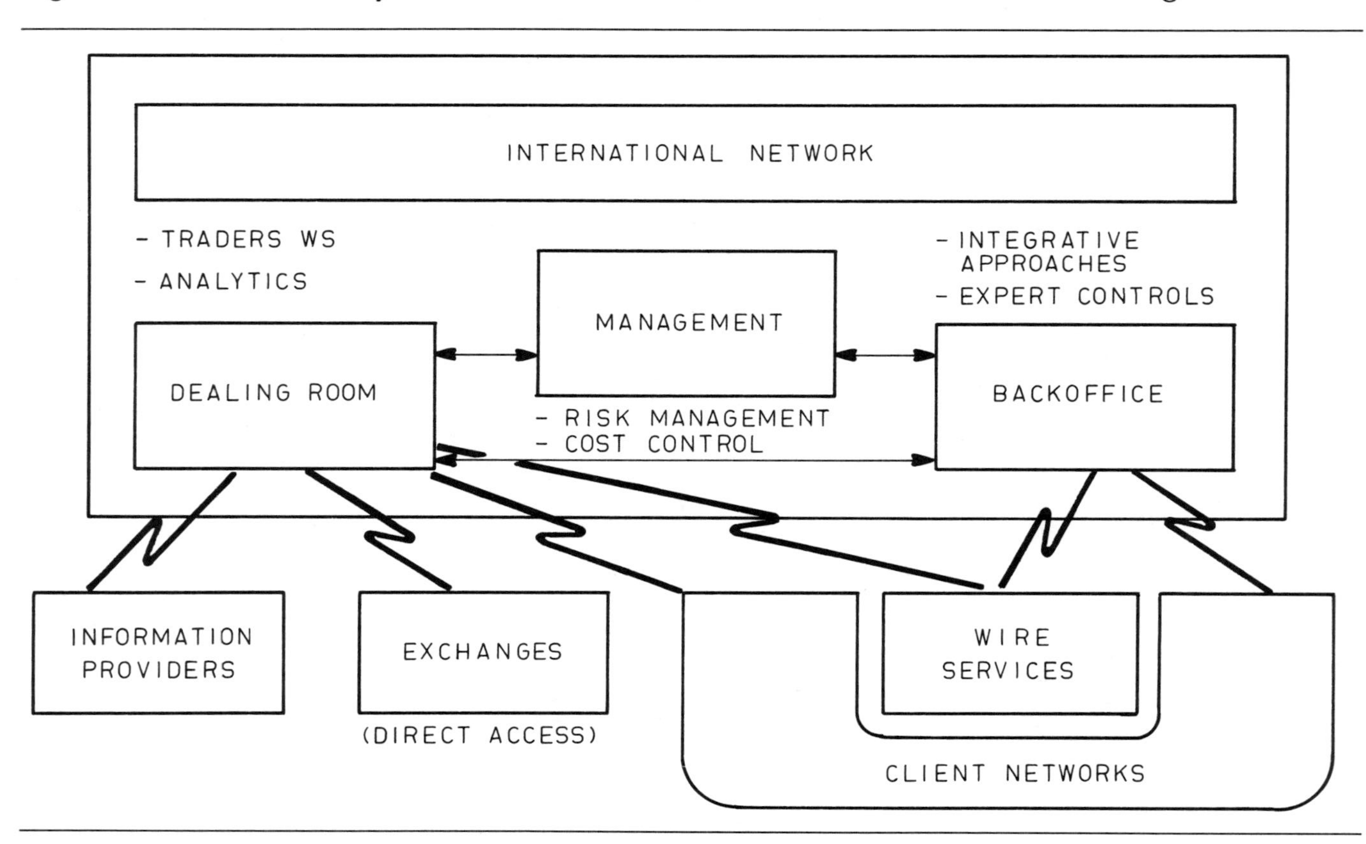

more efficiently. Only broader structural reforms can give results.

Endnotes

1. John Train, *The New Money Masters* (New York: Harper and Row, 1989).

2. See also D.N. Chorafas, *Risk Management in Financial Institutions* (London: Butterworths, 1990).

3. *Business Week,* 26 September, 1988.

4. *Business Week,* 18 December, 1989.

5. *Business Week,* 6 March, 1989.

6. *Business Week,* 20 November, 1989.

7. *Business Week,* 8 January, 1990.

8. Charles Hardy, *The Age of Unreason* (London: Arrow Books, 1989).

9. *The Economist,* 12 January, 1991.

10. Gary Hector, *Breaking the Bank. The Decline of Bank America* (Boston: Little Brown, 1988).

11. *The Economist,* 25 November, 1989.

Chapter 7

Portfolio Management

Chapter 7

Portfolio Management

1. Introduction

Throughout the 1970s and early 1980s, I worked as personal consultant to Dr. Carlo Pesenti, chairman of a large financial group. He was more concerned that his immediate assistants—the presidents of his banks—be focused on the subject they were handling than that they make the "right" decision. This showed me that portfolio management is above all a process of making focused evaluations and decisions. This entails not permitting precedents and generalizations to influence thinking without subjecting them to a rigorous examination in relation to the particular conditions prevailing at any given moment.

The portfolio manager uses investment theory (and the models through which it can be applied) in conjunction with real-time information on markets, prices, and trends to clearly define the market sector being addressed. Unambiguous goals involving buying or selling can then be set for the investments that are made.

Portfolio management should not be confused with portfolio accounting, though the latter is part of the former. Portfolio accounting is a more limited and mechanical process than portfolio management. Among other things, it includes (in a computer-oriented sense) automatically generating dividends, making coupon payments, calculating maturities and expirations (options), handling data affecting processing, updating client accounts, upkeeping the bank's account, and so on.

When it comes to investments, the best management is specialized, and that specialization is based in part on client needs and in part on the market's drives and wants. Figure 7.1 shows a Dutch financial institution's investment management characteristics.

Three major classes exist in portfolio handling—discretionary powers, cooperative solutions, and broker-level activity. The one involving the smallest number of clients yet generating the most profits is broker-level activity. Institutional investors prefer brokerage proper and holding positions. But at the same time, neither discretionary powers nor cooperative solutions can be discounted.

What the portfolio manager needs is clear vision, enabling technology, and the determination not to let statistics take the place of reasoning. This will connect him or her to the pulse of the market for years to come.

2. The Responsible Management of a Portfolio

Here we define a portfolio as commercial paper (including effects and promissory notes) and financial paper (stocks and bonds) belonging to a bank or to an investor.

A portfolio must be managed continually and efficiently. Shares and bonds are for buying and selling, not for buying and forgetting. A financial market is dynamic; thus, one can expect a great deal stock volatility.

Figure 7.1 A Dutch Example of Investment Management in Percents of Clients and Profits

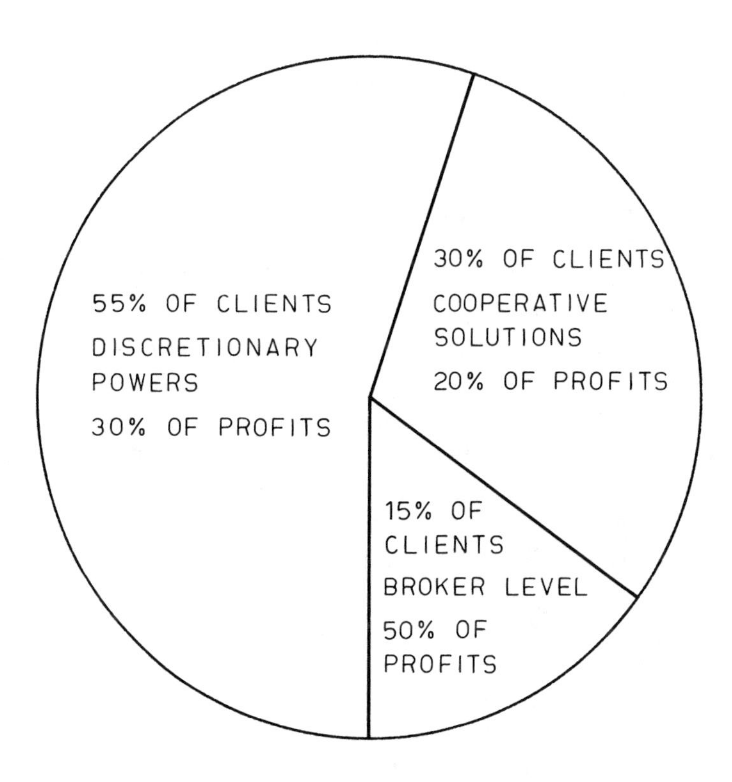

INSTITUTIONAL INVESTORS PREFER BROKERAGE LEVEL USAGE. IT INVOLVES:

- BROKERAGE PROPER
- KEEPING POSITIONS

Market prices depend, to a large exten,t on sentiment, which may be bearish or bullish. They also depend on

1. the state of the economy as well as those economies with which the first economy interacts and upon which it depends;
2. the state of a particular segment of industry within an economy;
3. how well a certain company is performing within its segment of industry.

A company's success is a function of management, products and services, prices, market appeal, production and distribution systems, information technology, and cost control. Company profits are not an abstract notion or a coincidence. All of the factors just mentioned contribute to profits.

Are corporate profits next year going to be improved? Will the market strengthen or ease? Will the gross national product show good growth, taper off, or decline? Can one forecast the most likely dividends? These queries lead to answers that can help financial analysts to anticipate market volatility as well as the more likely market trends.

Following up on such projections, portfolio managers try to determine dangers, opportunities, and trends. The job of investment advisors is not easy. While they receive input from the research department of their bank and other sources, the final advice to clients is their own. Also, they know that serious investors regularly monitor their own investments, some weekly.

Thus, investment advisors, knowing that even the best shares have spells in the doldrums, must watch for a share to start losing ground against its peers and against the market in general. This is known as a deteriorating relative performance and could signal a major downward rerating for the shares of a certain firm. At this point, without getting emotional, the portfolio manager has to advise the investor whether or not to do some switching.

Sophisticated investors hedge among not only different kinds of portfolio investments, but also among different currencies. Figure 7.2 shows an example of this.

Every country has its currency, and with flexible exchange rates, parities change all the time. A group of countries with sound currency presents the opportunity of investing in a basket of currencies but, for each individual investor, one of these currencies should be chosen as the reference or base currency in which profits and losses will be calculated.

In this way, overall portfolio performance can be measured by accounting not only for fluctuations in exchange rates, but also for stockmarket variations, which can be projected and evaluated in investment terms.

The predictions about market behavior are often based on the assumptions that investor responsibility, market rationality, efficacy of information, and financial accountability can all be taken for granted.

In fact, investor responsibility often gives way to lust and greed; sometimes this can take on epidemic proportions. Market rationality is more or less an illusion, though the argument about market efficiency is a favored one in college textbooks. The sophistication of the information system varies substantially by investment bank, even if most are heavily engaged in the technology race. Financial accountability is a factor that cannot be dissociated from the liquidity prevailing in the markets.

Forward-looking financial analysts, in making decision models, have replaced these four standard assumptions with six key factors—currency, debt, equity, risk, return, and liquidity.

These factors, when arranged in matrix form (see Table 7.1), constitute the base decision matrix in portfolio management.

Figure 7.2 Hedging Investments and Currencies for Sophisticated Investors

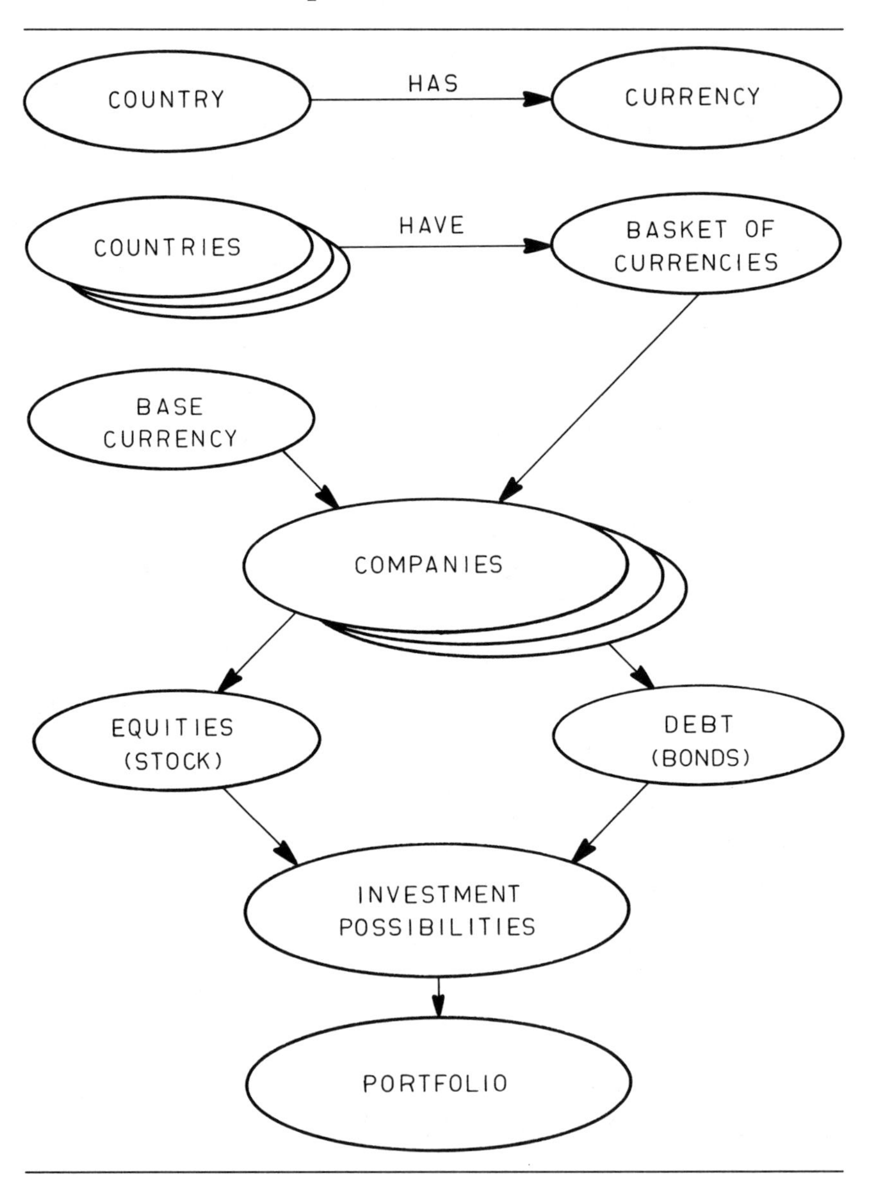

Table 7.1 Factors Influencing Portfolio Management

	Types of Investment		
Day X	*Currency*	*Debt*	*Equity*
Risk			
Return			
Liquidity			

While it is still important to assess factors concerning the economy as a whole, the industry within the economy, and the individual company, the base matrix focuses attention on those issues that need to be quantified and qualified when an investment evaluation is done on Day X.

3. Investment Risk

There is no investment without risk, but investment risk that cannot be avoided can be managed. An investor holding a portfolio of international stocks and bonds faces at least four specific types of risk.

Market risk, also known as systematic risk, is caused by overall market movements (such as the October 1987 crash). Investment theory, as well as some practitioners, suggests that market risk might be reduced if during bull markets (upswings) investors seek to maximize gains by acquiring high beta growth stocks, or aggressive growth mutual funds investing primarily in such stocks. Then, during major bear markets, investors could switch to conservative or defensive investments such as fixed-income and money market funds, as well as utilities stocks.

This is a good theory. In real life, unfortunately, no investor really knows the market and the exact timing of its upswings or downswings. If any investor does claim to know how the market will go, that investor is likely the person most exposed to market movements, and, therefore, a sure loser.

There are various factors to be considered in risk management. These include

1. the state of the global (worldwide) market;
2. the principal market to be invested in;
3. the currency in which investments are being made;
4. the amount of industry risk within the principal market(s);
5. the specific stock (or bond) to be invested in;
6. the expected dividend (or interest rate);
7. carry (the cost of leverage to hold a position).

These factors add many dimensions to the decisions made on buy and sell, hence on trading operations. Hedging requires a global market viewpoint as well as consideration of trends in currencies and in industry sectors. With few exceptions, most people find it difficult to map the whole market into their mind. With the use of supercomputers and artificial intelligence, however, (plus associated tools permitting experimentation and evaluation) this job is easily done.

Many investors diversify their portfolio to hedge from adverse fluctuations in the value of stocks or bonds of a specific company or industry. Risk diversification can be minimized by investing no more than 5 percent of assets in one company, and no more than 10 to 15 percent of assets in one industry. Some mutual funds and unit trusts are doing so with a reasonable degree of success.

Diversification risk is increased if there are too many investment vehicles. For example, it is nearly impossible for a portfolio manager or individual investor to put 1 percent of portfolio assets into each of a hundred different companies and then attempt to follow all of them.

Overdiversification sometimes happens because investors take too much advice from non-experts who claim to be well-informed but quite often just guess. It is sound policy not to buy shares over the telephone, or as a response to rumors or informal chats.

Various investment banks' executives spend time developing relationships and organizing presentations to investors and potential investors—a practice commonly referred to as doing a road show. These are designed to publicize the securities company and its products and prospects.

All market offerings require a considerable amount of senior financial analysts' time and attention. Able choices need not be made randomly. Investment banks can provide the professional advice of securities analysts, accountants, lawyers, and bankers.

Interest-rate risk can significantly affect the value of bonds; it also has aftermaths in the stock market. Generally speaking, the longer the maturity, the greater the risk an investor takes with bonds. Fluctuation in interest rates impacts on bond prices as well as on the prices of interest-sensitive stocks such as banks, utilities, and financial-service companies.

Interest-rate risk can be minimized by avoiding interest-sensitive stocks and long-term bonds during inflationary periods, when interest rates are apt to rise rapidly. Here again, it is best to be suspicious of the dubious reference regards anyone's ability to forecast long-term market movements; no one can really outguess the market.

Because forecasts are only tentative at best, and change with market conditions as they develop, serious investors closely watch asset-allocation relationships, and ask themselves questions such as, are these relationships positive or negative for equities or for bonds? Does market weakness offset the increase in short- and long-term interest rates? Does the market follow a yo-yo pattern of ups and downs? Are there conflicting economic reports? Have there been recently headline-grabbing deals? What would bring a sustained stock market growth or decline?

With the wave of leveraged buyouts (LBO) in the U.S., particularly during the mid- to late-1980s, there is another interest-rate risk, known as event risk, that should be brought into perspective. Since LBOs are usually done with junk bonds, there is a risk that bonds purchased as AAA or AA may turn overnight into BB and B bonds.

Currency exchange risk comes into play whenever an investor buys stocks or bonds denominated in a foreign currency. One way to minimize exchange risk is to diversify among different key currencies, such as dollars, pounds, yen, deutschemarks, and Swiss francs, without overextending oneself. Another is to invest in foreign markets through professional portfolio managers that employ currency hedging techniques. Before doing this, the portfolio manager (and high-net-worth individuals) should learn the tricks of the Forex game, in order to be able to speak with the specialized foreign exchange experts in meaningful terms.

The point is, investments require management, and a number of factors (shown in Fig. 7.3) come into play in managing investments. These include the risk strategies an investor chooses to follow, the portfolio profile selected, the liquidity requirements, the base currency and other currencies used, and investment preferences.

Figure 7.3 Factors Coming Into Play in Managing a Client's Investments

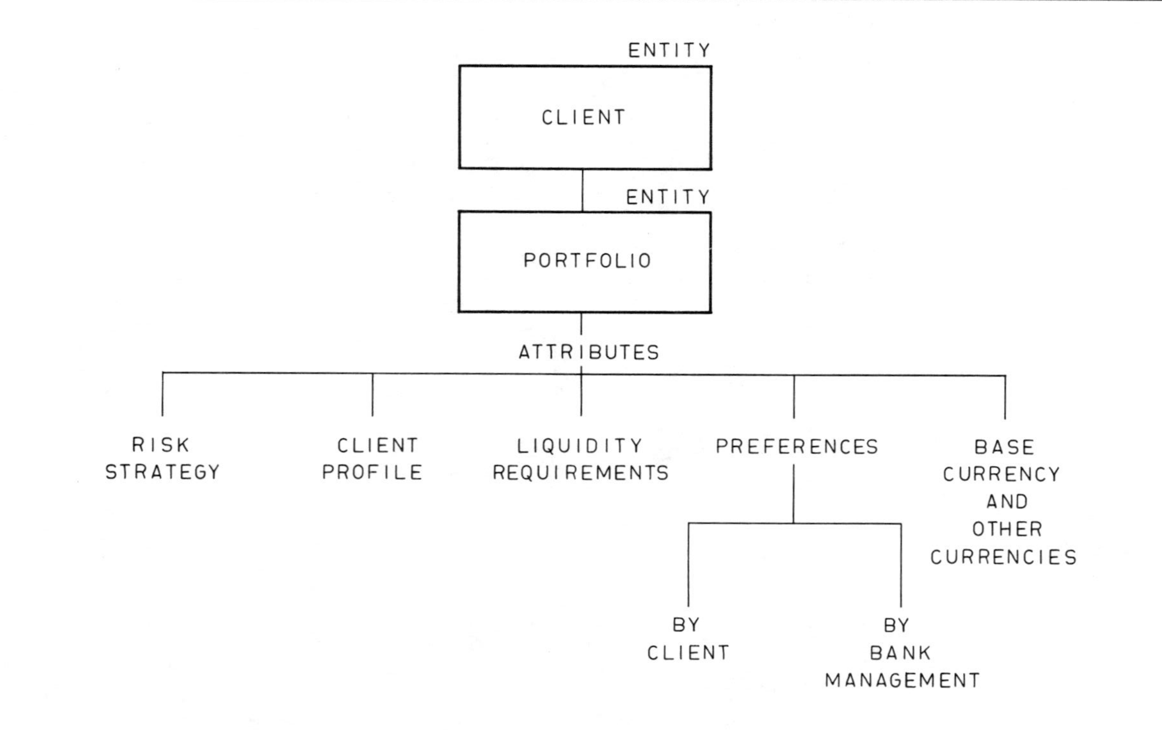

A financial institution should consider not only its own investment preferences, but also those of each client. It should also be aware of the level of risk each client is willing to accept. A portfolio strategy can be developed on these premises.

4. Global Asset Valuation

Globalization adds an important dimension to asset allocation decisions made in a financial industries environment. The traditional concept of allocating money among financial products, such as stocks, bonds, and cash-equivalents, remains a key investment directive. However, when investment alternatives are expanded to include diverse assets from major financial powers, whether in Europe, Asia, or North America, the complexity of the allocation task increases—and so do opportunity and risk.

Twenty or even ten years ago, the globalization of investments was an issue that concerned only money-center banks and major investment houses. Today, this is a globalization option for every high-net-worth individual, as well as corporations.

Globalization has added to the number of allocation choices by heightening their interdependence. Political, economic, and currency risks must be integrated into the equation in order to produce a valid global strategy.

In principle, investors and firms that use a global asset-allocation process do not decide in any absolute sense if a particular asset is valuable or not. Instead, by examining the expected rate of return from individual assets, then choosing a set of portfolio weights maximizing expected return, while minimizing risk, they compare the relative attraction of one asset with another.

Figure 7.4 shows some of the crucial factors that enter into this equation. These range from the cost of the investment

Figure 7.4 Critical Factors Concerning Return on Investment in a Client's Portfolio

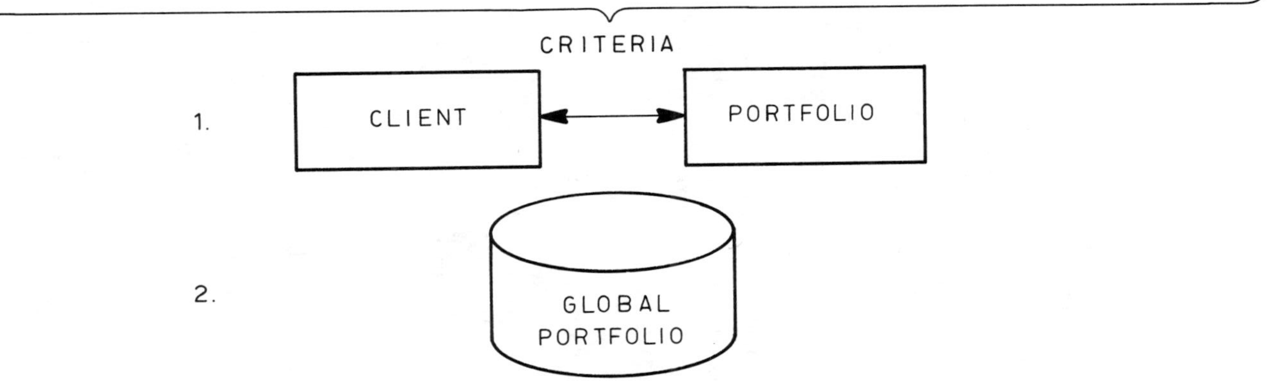

and its current appreciation, to its valuation further on. Investment management must look at this picture from the dual perspective of the client portfolio, with its entity relationships, and the global portfolio, that is, from an overall management perspective.

In a risk/reward framework, superior performance is defined not only by percentage return, but also by the risk necessary to achieve that return. In a global asset-evaluation model, a given portfolio outperforms or dominates another by exhibiting one of higher return at lower risk (best case), higher return at comparable risk, or comparable return at lower risk.

Financial analyses have demonstrated that with careful assumptions and the right tools valid allocation strategies can be derived from taking optimally weighted local markets, individual equities, bonds, and moneys, and measuring their effect on global portfolios. This is done by examining the expected rate of return of representative financial instruments, taking into account cash-equivalents, fixed income and equity spread across different countries' financial markets.

Once funds are allocated across asset classes and geographical regions, an investment model is able to maximize return while minimizing that portion of risk that is not rewarded, whether it be country risk, political risk, or exchange-rate risk.

A properly conceived investment model will typically have many and diverse duties to perform in connection with investment strategy. In addition to providing sound business advice, it can help in identifying differences between markets and investment tools. It can also assist in evaluating the accounting principles followed by various companies and relating them to the accounting principles of the investor to permit the preparation of the bridging statements.

In evaluating and choosing a portfolio, the selection of appropriate factors and values is crucial. The following factors are taken from the global asset evaluation done by a Paine Webber model.

Expected rate of return for cash-equivalents data represents the coupon-equivalent yield of discount rates on three-month Treasury Bills; *expected rate of return for government bonds* focuses on the yield from central bank securities with maturities of ten years; *expected rate of return for U.S. equities* is based upon historic forecasts of expected normalized earnings, dividend, and earnings growth rate. This factor is calculated as

$$P = \sum \frac{D\,(1 + g)}{(1 + R)}$$

where
P = current price
R = expected rate of return
D = current normalized dividend, and
g = secular long-term growth rate

Another Paine Webber criterion is *expected rate of return of foreign equities*. This is based upon a proxy for the foregoing formula using historical forecasts of the secular growth rate and actual dividend yields, where *d* stands for the prevailing dividend yield on the foreign market.

$$R = g + [(1 + g) \cdot d]$$

Through the examination of these measures of return rates expected by the investor, the premium expected return from one instrument versus another is being determined.

The Paine Webber model further considers the difference between two rates. The current difference, or *risk premium*, is compared with average normal levels (and the range about the average) in order to determine the relative attraction of one financial instrument and another in the final allocation decision.

Asset weightings are calculated by placing constraints on the weights which may be assumed by individual assets. For instance, within the global equity and fixed income models, each asset is constrained to be between one-third and three times its relative percentage of total market capitalization. Similar assumptions are made for other factors.

Along this line of reasoning, an excellent application has been done in Japan by Sanyo Securities. In 1986, Sanyo introduced the Radar Chart as an integral part of its expert systems structure in investment management and securities trading. (As previously discussed, Sirnis is the largest and most sophisticated AI construct in the financial industry, and still remains one of the best.) Since then, many financial industries have developed and applied radar charts.

Yamaichi Securities, also in Tokyo, improved upon Sanyo's invention by creating multi-layered three-dimensional structures enhanced through a process of visualization and assisted by number-crunching through supercomputers.

Figure 7.5 shows a radar chart. It is an experimental model designed by the author, in collaboration with Riada Securities in Dublin, as part of a design review of the Esprit project EQUUS. This radar chart focuses on the gilts (government securities) market in Ireland.

One crucial dimension in this radar chart is oil prices, which significantly influence the financial market in non-oil producing countries such as Ireland and Japan. Experts often associate fluctuations in oil prices with changes in export outlays and inflation.

Another important dimension in this radar chart is government funding in terms of public debt. The same is true of capital momentum. If there is a large but negative capital momentum, then small stocks are more likely to do better than big company stocks—or at least that is what security analysts say.

Figure 7.5 Radar Chart for Gilts Market (Government Bonds) in Ireland

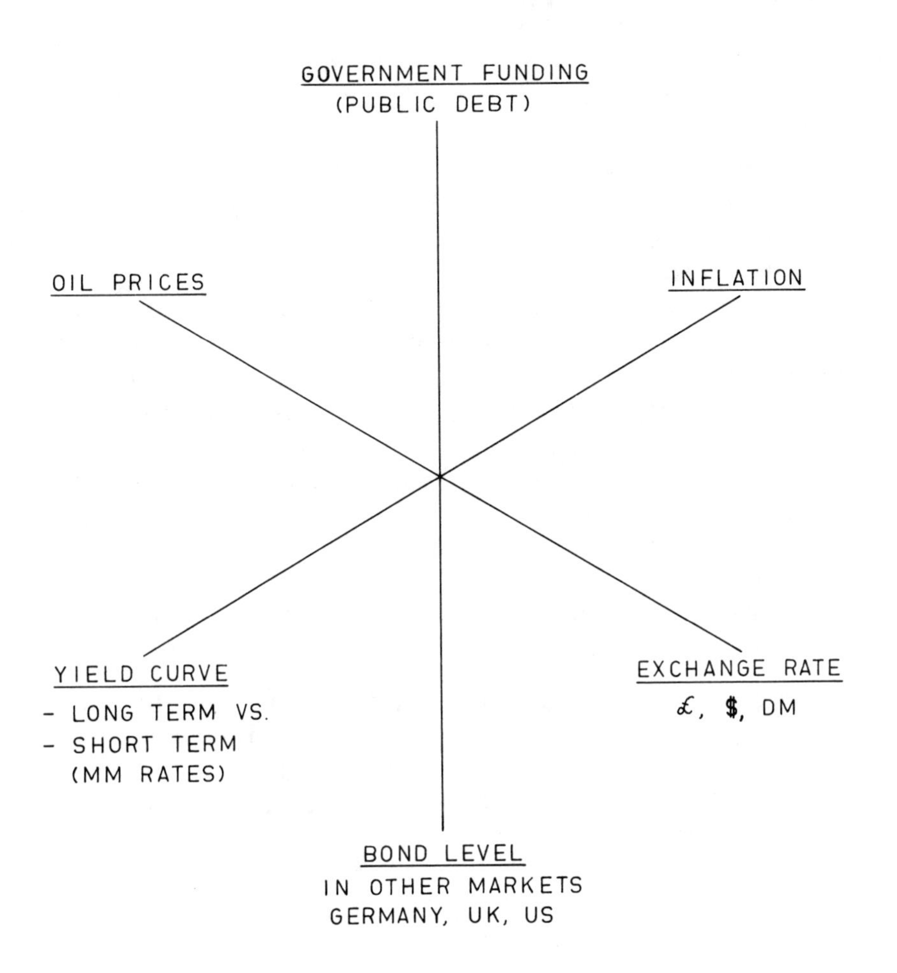

The Irish pound is part of the Common Market snake of moneys, but all member currencies can vary within range. Hence, still another factor is the exchange value of the pound against Ireland's trading partners including the United Kingdom, Germany, and the United States. A similar reference is valid regarding bond prices in other markets, as well as the predominant yield curve. In a radar chart, only the top factors should be reflected.

These and similar tools are necessary both for trading and for portfolio management, as the investment scene is becoming very sophisticated; and complexity can be expected to increase in the future.

Not only knowledgeable investors but also big funds and their managers are attracted toward financial institutions whose advice they can trust. The fine grain of such advice is an example of what is meant by value-differentiation; this advice typically goes beyond the level of portfolio administration into a sales-oriented research approach that can unearth hidden values.

5. Evaluating a Company Position for Investment Purposes

An investment manager concentrates on maintaining a balance between equities, bonds, cash and precious metals through buying and selling. Equities often have similarities to each other; thus, theoretically, a passive recall of a past deal might aid the expert in evaluating a current equity, and particularly in positioning it within a given market pattern.

In practice, however, a number of financial research projects have documented that judgments of similarity in financial trading are often tenuous in nature, and that an expert will accept a similarity between one target and a past case, while not accepting the similarity between another apparently similar target and the past case.

In other words, some reasons for a given deal remain implicit in the context in which that deal has been made. But not all reasons fall under this class. This means that designing a computer-supported analogical system, even for equity deals, can be complicated. This approach is useful, however, because it can reveal market trends and drives.

A basic ingredient in an analogical system is the assumption that all things are equal. This may not always be the case; for that reason, investment houses do a thorough analysis of companies in which they are considering investing.

The analogical approach emphasizes similarities on which investment analysis can capitalize. A thorough company-by-company examination can show the reasoning behind an investment choice, often documenting it in a factual manner. For instance, in August 1989, having done a thorough evaluation of Microsoft (the personal computer software company) the Technology group of Paine Webber presented this as a summary:

> *Positives.* Strong momentum. Applications business (especially on Macintosh) zooming; grip on systems software still tight; company investing heavily in R&D. Applications (software) could soon be 50 percent of revenue.
>
> *Negatives.* OS/2 has been OK for IBM, but a dud for Microsoft. Operating systems growth slows as result of industry slowdown and competitive factors.
>
> *Valuation.* 3 times projected $1 billion for fiscal year 1990 revenues, 15 times projected $3.80 fiscal year 1990 EPS. Apple's copyright infringement lawsuit puts cloud over Microsoft's future growth rate.
>
> *Overall.* While Court ruling [Apple Computers vs. Microsoft] reduces Microsoft's litigation risk somewhat, odds of losing rights to Windows/Presentation Manager still considerable; consequences of losing could be severe.

As a result of this valuation, the one-word assessment of Microsoft stock was *unattractive*; yet this company has a number of positives. For several years, Microsoft has led the PC software industry in size, profitability, influence, and control of key PC technologies such as the DOS operating system.

If Paine Webber had not made a thorough examination of the potential of Microsoft stock, the average investor would have bought in to the firm because of its past accomplishments, which include developing strong products in the areas of operating systems, word processing, and spreadsheets. But to the trained eye, Microsoft seems to have become a victim of its success. In mid-1989 Microsoft lowered expectations for fiscal 1990 earnings. Also, its management projected that its volume of unit shipments might grow only 10 percent from that of fiscal 1989; prior expectations had been of 15 percent to 20 percent growth.

Securities experts had reason to believe that these lowered estimates were consistent with a downward trend in buying intentions by PC users, particularly in the operating systems business. Also, as IBM gained share, especially with its PS/2 Model 30 at the low end, it hurt Microsoft's business because the mainframe does not pay royalties. Piracy and a competitive clone that was introduced in 1988, were also putting pressure on revenues. And there was another major cloud: the Apple lawsuit that was a potential financial burden.

By projecting future earnings, the type of analysis done by Paine Webber can be of significant value to a portfolio manager. For example, there is evidence that because of the uncertainty it creates, ongoing litigation can inhibit product development.

Of the factors that influence investors' success in the market, the three main ones are in order of importance, timing, market sector, and the selection of each security.

For a securities analyst, one major challenge is that of determining what the future health of a whole industry will be in light of market demand and international competition. Another challenge is that of identifying anomalies and establishing a dynamic methodology for following minute movements around expected values. Investors, whether dealing in money (Forex) or debt and equities (securities) want to know the downside risk of a given company, market sector, or stock exchange.

The trader needs tools capable not only of detecting business opportunities, but also of providing the possibility of experimenting on possible outcomes prior to making a financial commitment. Thus, the development of artificial intelligence constructs is important because while such experimentation is not necessarily quantitative, it always has major qualitative elements. In essence, AI operates in the same way that a human mind does; therefore, heuristics can be of significant assistance.

Traders must do more, however, than evaluate companies and assist clients; they must also produce results, that is, process customer orders quickly and at low cost. As well, their actions should be well documented. This calls for rules and methods that allow brokers to maintain uniform efficiency.

6. Executing the Trades

Portfolio managers have been trying for some time to find ways to avoid judgmental pitfalls and to sharpen their sense of timing. Trust departments, in their experiments with technical and fundamental factors, dollar-cost averaging, index funds, and matrices of common funds or collective investments, have been in the forefront of this ongoing search.

There are several investment techniques designed to take some of the guesswork out of investing; one is that of instituting automatic action triggers related to complex fundamental or technical analyses. On the sell side, procedures often involve one or more liquidation methods. For example, if a security has a liquidation method indicated, this method will override ad hoc solutions that may be closer to a client's or investment advisor's thinking. This approach is normally used to simplify the liquidation of options and futures in high-volume situations. In the same way a clearing house or broker would, the user sets an option or a future to liquidate on a FIFO (first in, first out) basis.

Other computer programs available for automatic execution allow the selection of liquidation methods by the user as well as an override by type of security. The most basic ones are LIFO (last in, last out); the high-cost method, in which the highest-cost purchase lot is selected for sale; the average-cost method, in which a portion of each purchased lot is liquidated by a sale, and the low-tax method, in which a purchased lot is liquidated based on a scale that indicates the least tax being generated. (Each position has an associated tax code, which gives the tax rates being assumed and the holding period for long-term gains either in terms of months or as a percentage.

There is currently a revival of a portfolio management technique known as formula investing, a concept that was relatively stylish (and partly successful) in a bygone fiduciary era. In formula investing, every portfolio is divided into two parts—conservative and aggressive. In the days of non-competitive trust investing, the conservative portion consisted of high-grade bonds, whose liquidity was unquestioned and price volatility infrequent and inconsequential. In today's environment, the conservative portfolio will largely consist of T-Bills, short Treasury Notes, commercial paper or CD, and money-market funds.

The aggressive portfolio is open to everything else acceptable. In addition to deep discount bonds, such portfolios might accommodate emerging technology companies, interest rate futures, and call options. The ground rule may presume the acceptance of higher risk and volatility in the aggressive portfolio and the retention of liquidity as a prime criterion in the conservative one.

Both accounting and market data are important for portfolio modeling. The user should be able to create the model definitions and have the system generate the transactions accordingly. Every support should be provided for experimentation.

In executing the processes involved in liquidation methods, formula investing, and more, computers and communications are indispensable tools (see also Chapter 9). Because of their capacity for performing higher data resolutions (a term that originated in the oil industry), supercomputers have resources that are extensive enough both to develop complex financial instruments and to provide experimental base that is necessary for improved accuracy in portfolio management.

Supercomputers have proven to be dramatically faster than conventional mainframes. In a recent project in which the author took part, a mainframe took about seven minutes, to turn around a complex portfolio; after some reworking, the same program ran in less than thirty seconds on a minisupercomputer.

Furthermore, supercomputers allow securities firms to do things they could not accomplish otherwise, such as analyzing and assembling more complex portfolios and trading them globally in real time (see also Chapter 16). Supercomputers can also operate through parallel processing thus providing networked workstations with significant number-crunching power. This will become increasingly necessary as the securities market becomes more competitive.

7. Global Custody

Seeking ways of attracting commissions from the sale and purchase of securities, brokerage houses have entered the global custody domain, which until recently had been dominated by banks. This makes sense in terms of vertical integration; a broker aims to sell products as well as to receive fees and commissions, and a bank or trust company seeks to have custody of third-party assets.

Bankers have been involved in securities custody since the days when shares were pieces of paper stored in vaults. These vaults have been replaced by warehouses of safety boxes with cranes commanded by computers; computers and networks have assumed the functions of brokerage, clearance, and settlement. (In the opinion of the author, traders' and bankers' jobs can complement one another, and as soon as the restrictions of the Glass-Steagall act are lifted, bankers will likely agree.)

The job of the custodian or trustee is to keep account of each individual portfolio on behalf of its customers. This job involves issuing corporate notifications, handling tax reclamations, and settling trades. In well-organized institutions, the related information is kept in deductive distributed databases with notifications of changes delivered on-line through the financial company's global communications network.

Major American securities houses are using twenty-four-hour trading to launch global telecommunications networks, on which they then piggy-back custody operations. Morgan Stanley, Merrill Lynch, and Goldman Sachs are among the investment banks who have done this during the past few years.

Trust services are typically provided through subsidiaries such as Morgan Stanley Trust, Goldman Sachs Trust, who handle the custody function.

Not surprisingly, brokers plan to use global custody as a sales tool to increase their market share in securities trading. Given the administrative chores involved, however, significant expenses are incurred in establishing global custody systems.

The subsidiary trust company links the counterparties, clearing agencies, and subcustodians through its computers and communications network. Emphasis is placed on quality of service and product control, both of which can be key competitive advantages.

Product quality has much to do with normalization. The Group of Thirty, an influencial industry watchdog panel comprising officials of financial institutions worldwide, has recommended the standardization of global securities settlement procedures. It also advocates measures aimed at making the world's securities markets more efficient and less risky.

The panel has recommended the adoption of a delivery-versus-payment rule, which would ensure simultaneous receipt of payment when securities are delivered, thus eliminating any exposure arising from the delayed delivery of a counterparty.

Another recommendation is for the implementation of a global securities numbering system. Currently, securities are numbered by their domestic numbering agencies, which creates discrepancies between assigned members who do securities trading in a multicountry setting.

Since technology can be instrumental in increasing the quality of custody while swamping costs, both commercial banks and securities houses are investing heavily in computers and software that can handle inventories and produce unified reports of customers' worldwide assets.

The challenge is to implement the best system in the shortest time, thus gaining competitive advantages. These go well beyond safekeeping to include the tracking of investments in a global portfolio management sense.

Advanced solutions are important, particularly because sophisticated clients, which are a bank's or broker's most lucrative market, are steadily increasing their investment overseas. They do so in an attempt to diversify their portfolio. Some estimates suggest that the international investments of large U.S. firms now constitute 10 percent of the compound portfolio; this is an order of magnitude more than the 1 percent that they represented in 1985.

Is there money to be made in global custody as competition heats up? The answer is, at best, elusive. Because competition is growing, fees are declining. Some players estimate that fees for Western European capital markets have declined by half in the past ten years.

This is bad news for securities houses that are seeking new sources of income not only for better redeployment of expensive assets, but also as another source of income or to replace lost revenue sources. Brokers know, however, that their survival depends on taking business risks. "During the first period of a man's life the greatest danger is not to take the risk," wrote Soren Kierkegaard, a Danish philosopher, in 1850. This should also be the operating principle behind any company that intends to remain innovative.

8. Automating the Administrative Chores

There is plenty of administrative work associated with the securities business at large in general, and with portfolio management in particular. Such administrative work is typically done at the back office. It is voluminous, paper-intense, error-prone, and costly. The best that can be done is to automate it to the fullest extent.

Among the administrative and accounting operations involved, portfolio management, coupon payment, principal paydowns and maturities, expirations (options), exercises (futures and options), debit/credit to client accounts, and credit/debit to the general ledger can all be automated.

Computer programs can define multiple-step capital changes and automatically generate transactions to process them. These programs will handle bonds, stocks, options, and futures, with all processing affecting data being table-driven. Also available should be software that can handle less-common securities, such as zero coupons, perpetuals, floating rate notes, and odd-paying bonds, and amortize bonds with the constant or straight-line method of calculating interest.

One vital operation in securities is pricing. Multiple price sources can be handled with customization; retention of prices must be determined by the user on a security-by-security basis; as well, it should be possible to create user-defined indices.

Accounting software must reflect considerable detail by client level. Each client may have multiple accounts differentiated by manager, product line, or tax incentives. Accounts may need to be gathered into multiple consolidations, and in every case, presentation formats should be simple as well as comprehensive.

Computer software should be on hand to display the accounts, their average daily balance during the from and to periods, the amount of income to be distributed, and the cash equivalents in the cash balance. Intelligent software available not only allows experimentation, but is also capable learning its user's profile and shaping its presentation accordingly.

Particular attention should be paid to futures. The purchase of a future, while it will create a holding, will not necessarily update cash with its purchase cost—unless the user wants to keep a double balance. By contrast, the sale of a future should liquidate the holding and book the net amount of the difference (positive or negative).

The purchase of options should create a holding and update cash with the cost of the holding. A sale of an option should liquidate the holding and book the net amount. The programming product should ensure that at any time that the option is in the money, the system will assume the option has been exercised.

Software solutions typically parallel the broker's course of action. Computers can provide interactive on-line queries regarding clients, accounts, chapters in accounts, trade or settlement date basis, specified date ranges, and consolidation perspectives.

Queries regarding positions may focus on current or past holdings, and should be detailed by account, security type, or other criteria. The queries may reflect the position of cash and focus on current cash in user defined buckets, such as principal, income, accrued dividends, bought/sold coupons, and so on. Queries may also concern transactions focusing on gain/loss and tax lot (realized or unrealized), income (actual or projected), broker commissions (budget versus actual), and so on.

Queries based on transaction processing can cover a wide domain, including cash and holdings maintained on a trade and settlement-date basis, input from a trade support system, and observance of client restrictions (whether generic or specific). Accounting queries will typically involve accrued interest, current yield, yield to maturity, yield to call and put, and credit/debit by currency.

The last of these is particularly important, as transactions may be booked in multiple currencies, with conversion rates provided for each transaction. With a given client, the system should allow cash rebalancing across accounts.

The system should also spread cash-equivalent trades and income across accounts according to average cash balances for a specified period, maintain tax lots with original and tax cost, and hold other relevant management-accounting information.

Queries should cover high-cost, average-cost, low-cost, taxation, LIFO, FIFO, and selected-lot liquidation options. The system should handle "as of" trades by updating all holdings and cash records between the "as of" date and current date with the effect of the trade.

Other queries may reflect on commission information at a detail transaction level and on a broker/purpose level, tracking actual commissions being paid. Still others could address a wide range of accrual broker budget, capital events, cash distribution, cash transactions, collateral, current holdings, dividend history (domestic and foreign), gain/loss, holdings by account, holdings by specific class, index value entries, loan entries, loan repricing, loan payments, portfolio comparison, transaction entries, projected transactions, and statistical references.

Statistics may involve average maturity, quality, duration, and so on. An effective approach would provide a companywide standard on statistical presentation but also permit different clients, as well as company executives, traders, and accountants, to specify their own statistical visualization, which would enhance decision making.

Chapter 8

Securitization

Chapter 8

Securitization

1. Introduction

Securitization is the wave of the future. In the 1990s, financial markets will trade securitized products from mortgages to corporate and other liabilities. Nevertheless, traders and buyers will be cautious buyers. No amount of hype will sell an inferior, unsecured, or overpriced financial product.

Many people think that securitized products are a development of the 1980s. In fact, the appearance of a secondary market dates back to the 1930s, when the first packages of mortgages were sold; however, this market did not really start moving till the 1970s, when the Government National Mortgage Association (GNMA, Ginnie Mae) came into being.

Ginnie Mae is guaranteed by the Federal Housing Administration (FHA) and the Veterans Administration (VA). Another player in the secondary market is the Federal National Mortgage Association (FNMA, Fannie Mae), which is guaranteed by FHA, VA, and the Farmers Home Administration

(FHDA). A third organization is the Federal Home Loan Mortgage Corporation (FHLMC, Freddie Mac).

Ginnie Mae started offering packetized loans around 1975; Fannie Mae, in 1982. By 1983, Freddie Mac was doing the same, and among them, the three agencies created a securitized market for home mortgages. This market stood at a little over $200 billion, or somewhat less than 10 percent of the estimated $3 trillion involved in home mortgages in America. Subsequently, mortgage-backed financing grew between 30 and 40 percent per year, to $1 trillion. The securitized market for commercial paper has not yet been touched, but it may be coming.

Given that the boom years started after 1980, it may be said that securitization was reinvented in the 1982-to-1983 time frame. Subsequently, securitization has become one of the major forces in the world's financial markets. It is increasingly displacing the more traditional forms of intermediation on which the Euromarkets were founded only a few decades ago.

Securitization has precedents; one is the Euronote, a means of funding a medium-term loan by the issue of short-term debt. The structural characteristics of note-issuance facilities (NIF) and revolving underwriting facilities (RUF) give guidelines to pricing and placement methods, as well as the types of borrowers and investors in the market. Another precedent is provided by the development, prospects, and techniques of the Eurocommercial paper market.

The United States government has become involved with securitization in its present form, offering fixed-income instruments through the Defense Security Assistance Agency. This agency repackages Defense Department loans to U.S. allies, and sells them at a premium over Treasury Bonds. The objective is that of reducing the national deficit.

Because of securitization, commercial and industrial companies have less need for intermediaries (i.e., commercial banks); at the same time their desire to buy and sell securities has grown. Thus, in reality, the role of financial intermediary appears to have been assumed by investment banks.

2. The Process of Repackaging Debt and Allocating Assets

For investment bankers, the key to survival is having innovative products. Investment banks profit when their product offerings make the market dynamic, which in turn provides business opportunity to everybody.

In 1982, Salomon Brothers created a security that stripped the interest payments from U.S. Treasury bonds and put the proceeds into a series of notes, which then withheld interest until the maturity date. The idea behind these zero-coupon bonds was to trade the body of the bond and its coupons separately.

Such transactions produced tax benefits, because stripped treasuries are newly created financial instruments with no tax laws regulating them. As a result, by the early 1980s, zero-coupon treasury bonds (the corpus) and the coupons themselves (or strips) had become a multibillion-dollar business. The boom only began to dwindle when, with the tax equity and fiscal responsibility act (Tefra), tax law became more precise.

Nevertheless, new financial products continued to flood the market. In 1983, First Boston's research team engineered the first collateralized mortgage obligation (CMO). This was followed by a series of securities backed by computer leases, car loans, and credit card receivables. The coup of the early 1980s, though was Salomon Brothers' industrialization of mortgage-backed financing. Lewis Ranieri built a $1 trillion market by packaging residential mortgages into securities and persuading institutional investors to buy them.

All these are examples of securitization, or the business of repackaging and selling debt. Using sophisticated computer programming, banks restructure traditional loans and convert them into securities. The new instruments are then bought and sold in the credit marketplace in the same way that conventional bonds are.

In only a few years, the technique has proven to be a boon to banks and consumers, as it has brought with it fresh infusions of money for mortgages and car loans. Also, securitization guarantees banks their fees and allows them to do more lending. On the other hand, the loans that remain in banking hands are of steadily decreasing quality especially those made in areas such as oil-related business, farming, real estate, and Third-World debt.

Nevertheless, financial institutions have embraced securitization because they are feeling the effects of disintermediation; with deregulation, commercial and industrial firms rely less on intermediation through banks and more on securities bought and sold in the financial markets. As a result, commercial and industrial debt is rising rapidly, and much lucrative business is being placed in the hands of the investment banks who are the issuers and traders of corporate securities. (Commercial banks are not locked out of all markets, however. While American and Japanese banks are limited, the "Big Bang" allowed British commercial banks to trade in securities; German and Swiss banks are unrestricted.

Today, the hot securitization field is mortgages; tomorrow it may well be corporates (corporate bonds). Investment firms buy multimillion-dollar chunks of mortgage portfolios from banks and thrifts, and repackage them in bond-size units of $1,000 to $100,000. After the securities are issued, the bank that originated the mortgage typically continues to service it; this service includes collecting payments and hounding delinquent debtors. For this the bank earns a fee.

While it is relatively easy to understand the concept of securitized loans, constructing them is a complex affair. The investment bank sets a uniform, profitable interest rate and ensures that it is based on many different underlying mortgages. It establishes terms, interest rates, and payment schedules that may vary substantially from one offer to another, depending on the underlying debt. Adding to the complexity is the polyvalent evaluation and real-time execution of securitization offers, as well as the range of debt instruments that can be securitized (and quickly turned into billion-dollar markets).

Securitization has undergone exponential market growth, Figure 8.1 shows U.S. statistics on the early years of securitization of auto loans, credit card receivables and computer leases. Not only are auto loans securitized, but also the financing divisions of Detroit's major automakers have increasingly been able to offer below-market interest rates (sometimes as low as 2.9 percent) to prospective auto buyers, thanks in part to investment bank repackaging of car loans as securities.

The growth of securitization is drastically changing the way that more than $6 trillion worth of non-government credit is and can be channeled through the American economy. Investment banks cannot afford to stay out of that market, but many prerequisites have to be fulfilled to get control of it.

As it becomes evident that the rules of banking are changing, old-fashioned bank methods seem to be losing the investment instruments contest. John Dawson, the executive in charge of the retail division at Lloyds Bank, says, "Our Strategy is to address the changing nature of the personal savings market." You hear a lot about the securitization of lending to large corporations, but you could also argue that we are at the front end of the securitization of the savings market.[1]

Lloyds is one of the first banks to introduce a current account that includes asset management. The competitive advantage of this account is that it is so systems-reliant that it cannot easily be copied. Swept by computer daily in exact accordance with the customer's instructions, this service has

Figure 8.1 The Formative Years Growth Curve of Securitized Offerings

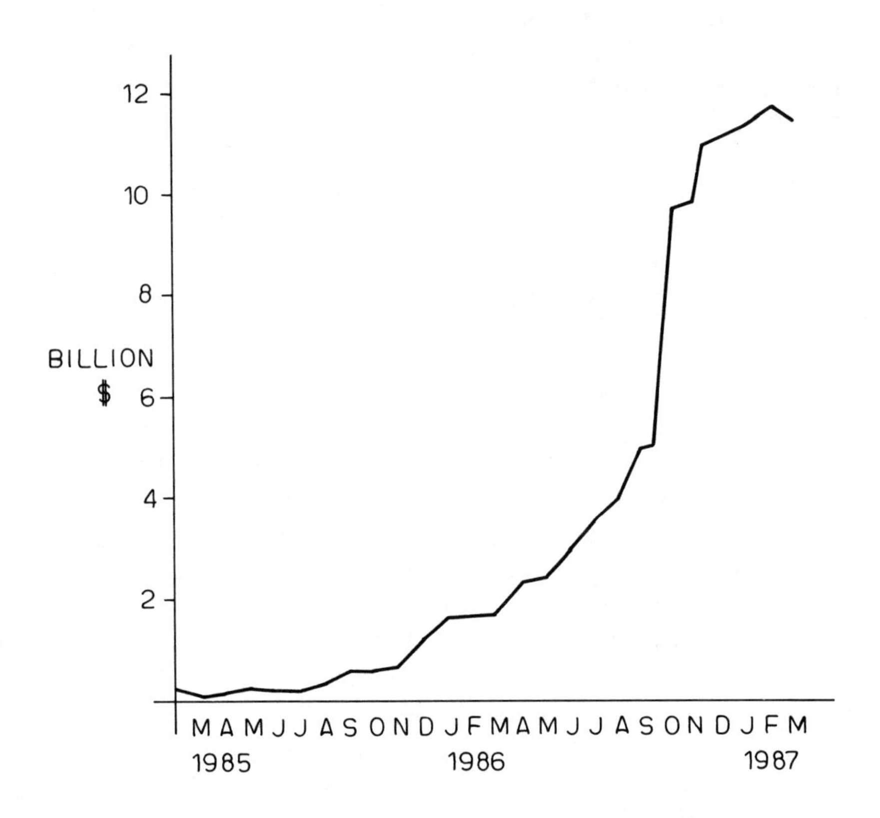

US CUMULATIVE OFFERING OF SECURITIES BACKED BY AUTO LOANS, CREDIT-CARD RECEIVABLES, AND COMPUTER LEASES

been drawing in customers at the rate of more than 500 a month.

Repackaged financial products provide convenience to those who are prepared to pay a premium for it. Thus, the bank can use them to broaden its customer base, (although it must also take care to hold costs down so as to maintain margins). With this in mind, banks are introducing private banking services for people who have sizeable portfolios. For example, British banks, following the lead of Swiss banks, now attach an individual account manager to each customer.

One major new financial product is Tactical Asset Allocation (TAA) (see also Chapter 11); this practice allows investors to move money back and forth among stocks, bonds, and cash. This is done on a short-term basis so that the investor may not only profit from market anomalies, but also make the largest profit possible with the least amount of risk. Within a couple of years from the product's introduction, TAA managers controlled $20 billion, and the money is coming in fast.

As with securitization, the principle behind TAA is relatively simple. The most critical decision is not whether to buy DEC, IBM, Ford, or General Motors, but whether to invest in stocks, bonds, or other instruments. This simplification of the process leads to successful asset management.

Institutional investors such as pension funds are among the best clients of securitized products, but they also practice some form of asset allocation. Both form part of their strategy for meeting future cash needs.

In order to determine how much cash will be necessary to care for their members in the future, funds develop long-term guidelines (based on the age of employees, the number of retirees, and projected salary levels) for the amount of stocks, bonds, and other assets that they should own.

In a strategic plan, the mix of assets may not change for years but swings are always possible. Since there are many random events for which to account, Monte Carlo techniques, and to a lesser degree heuristics, are favored analytical methods.

Through computer-based models enriched with expert systems, money managers may move funds as often as necessary. They can estimate what the returns will be from various stocks, bonds, cash, and metals, then buy or sell, allocating the bulk of funds to those assets that their computers predict will do well over the short run. This system levels off the impact of emotional reactions.

Experience shows that at least 80 percent of the returns that investors earn come not from choosing individual securities, but from properly allocating funds among asset categories. Thus, money managers use quantitative, computer-driven models to divide funds among stocks, bonds, and money-market instruments; or, they diversify even more by using foreign stocks, foreign bonds, precious metals, and real estate. Finally, they invest in securitized products with known option against spread (OAS), which permits them to be fairly accurate in their calculations and optimization.

Louis Lowenstein estimates that less than 10 percent of stock trading reflects long-term judgments about companies and industries.[2] Most investors behave more like traders than owners and care only about short-term fluctuations in the price of stock. As a result, stock prices often bear little relationship to the actual circumstances and prospects of a company or an industry; nevertheless, market transactions do send some useful signals to corporate managers. This trend has been magnified by the rapid growth of indexing, which encompasses 30 to 40 percent of all institutional stock investments, and by futures and options (see also Chapter 11).

From securitization to TAA, the newer investment methods expressly eschew underlying business values. "The availability of money is determining the desire to buy," says Tully M. Friedman, a partner in San Francisco-based investment banking boutique Hellman and Friedman.[3] This desire can be cultivated, and by securities traders.

3. Creditworthiness in Securitized Instruments

In early 1987, Standard & Poor's rated Bank of America's conventional debt a low BBB; at the same time, the bank's credit-card issue won a top-flight AAA rating. What made the difference is that the credit-card issue was backed not by the bank itself, but by the creditworthiness of the cardholders. Also, investors were at least partially protected against consumer defaults by a reserve fund and a letter of credit from Union Bank of Switzerland.

As with other financial institutions, Bank of America has been eager to differentiate its offerings from those of the mounting competition. After turning $1.25 billion in auto loans into securities, it planned another $1 billion in consumer and even corporate loans. Such feats involving securitization are examples of a financial instrument with the potential to revolutionize the way companies raise cash and, at the same time, displace the issuing of traditional debt securities. Securitization accomplishes this by getting investors to lend directly by buying the repackaged instruments rather than via deposits in the banking system.

In a wave of change sweeping the international financial market, modern financial instruments like floating rate notes, currency swaps, and zero-coupon bonds are becoming increasingly popular. This has forced a change in the thinking of reserve banks, who at one time rejected the use of these instruments, because they felt that the new types of financial intermediation blurred the clarity-of-choice and transparency needed in a soundly run financial system.

In fact, this more liberal approach to financial services makes ideas, skills, and jobs more dynamic. This is true all over business and industry from public transport to internal air services, the professions, telecommunications, broadcasting, the insurance business, and the banking system. The new instruments lead to new forms of employment and provide for growth in the economy; they also thrust themselves against vested interests.

But while deregulation is instrumental in knocking down the walls that protect the old structures, creditworthiness is crucial in selling the new financial products to the public. For this reason, management auditing should be continual and commensurate with the amount of risk involved (see Figure 8.2). Short of this type of assurance, there will be no market really worth exploiting because the bank will find no takers for its products.

One way to judge the creditworthiness of the securitized market is to examine how investors respond to it. As of late 1989, for instance, according to credit market analysts, Japanese investors have been beefing up their holdings of U.S. mortgage-backed securities, mainly by using money they no longer care to invest in the volatile U.S. corporate-bond market.

This switch may reflect the increased confidence of Japanese investors in mortgage-backed products, which offer higher yields than those of Treasury notes and bonds with similar maturity dates, but carry comparable credit ratings. Market analysts now expect the amount of Japanese funds flowing into mortgage backed financing products to expand between 20 percent and 40 percent per year during the next few years.

The majority of securities analysts do not expect this trend to be reversed even when corporate bonds lose their present instability (created by the LBO risk). Nevertheless, mortgage-backed securities do have some drawbacks. One of these is that if interest rates fall, homeowners are likely to pay off their mortgage loans ahead of schedule. This will cause a quicker

Figure 8.2 Question of Balance: Audit Costs versus Risks

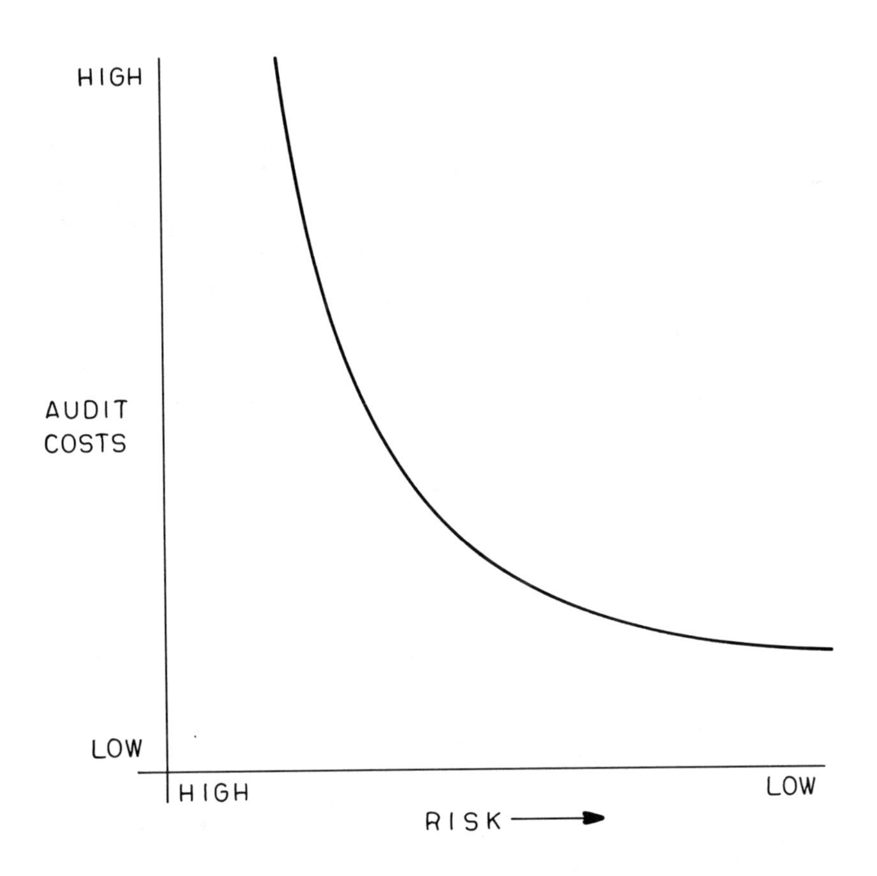

return of principal to lenders, in this case the holders of the mortgage-backed instruments.

Although investors do not lose money as a result of prepayments, they may find themselves with fewer funds invested at a time when interest rates are falling and high yields are therefore harder to find. Furthermore, cash-flow projections will have been made based on these assets still being in the portfolio.

The last item is particularly unsettling to institutional investors such as pension funds, which depend on projected cash flows for their pensions. In the absence of these they must hedge through other market instruments. As discussed in Section 2, the solution to these problems lies in computer-intensive studies of mortgage-backed financing. Processed interactively on supercomputers, AI-enriched computational models make it possible to

1. examine in significant detail different prepayment hypotheses;
2. study their distribution under the assumptions of steady, increasing, or declining interest rates;
3. compare the cash flow that will be generated with cash-flow requirements;
4. calculate option against spread (OAS) and assure the dependability of the financial product.

Analytical studies have become inseparable from the creation of a secondary market for loans and other similar financial paper commodities. Mathematical methods such as Monte Carlo, multiple regression analysis, binomial lattices, and heuristics help in evaluating prepayment risk and limiting much of its impact. All of them facilitate a better packaging of mortgage-backed securities in the form of collateralized obligations.

All these methods are part of a process called loan liquification; through this process a commercial bank, investment bank, or securities house becomes the banker to other banks. The underlying principle is that rather than keeping the loan for years, the financial institution ensures the loan's creditworthiness and then distributes it. Fundamentaly, this process involves three steps—origination, underwriting, and distribution—for which the bank gets a fee.

This process imposes demands on the financial experts and the information scientists of the financial institution. The computers and communications architecture to be chosen must be capable of relaying information quickly and reliably to originators, underwriters, and distributors; it must also ensure timely access to databases, no timezone barriers, no geographical limitations, and uninterrupted availability of communications, databasing, and computing resources.

Loan liquification has eroded the boundaries between commercial and investment banking, thus giving financial institutions a chance to break out of the retail business. Nevertheless, if banks are not careful, securitization will pass them by, much in the way that commercial paper did. In the U.S., when $300 billion in commercial paper debt was outstanding, companies with new financial products took the top business, leaving commercial banks floundering with problem loans to Silicon Valley firms, energy companies, farmers, and ailing Latin American economies.

When a new and promising product comes to the market, competition soon becomes cutthroat. In the commercial paper case, some banks, on behalf of their corporate customers, even offered to pay the legal costs of setting up a financial program. Banks need to realize that corporate treasurers are increasingly aware of opportunities presented to them. After all, many of these corporate treasurers are ex-bankers and know very well the secrets of the banking trade.

At some large companies, the treasurers claim that they can raise funds very cheaply by borrowing in the right money market; for example, they may borrow in continental Europe and subsequently convert the proceeds to dollars or to sterling in the foreign exchange market, if this is the currency they need. To compete with that, sterling commercial paper, which involves extra administrative and legal costs and takes up more management time, needs to offer more attractive rates—or capitalize on innovation.

4. The Growth of Competition in the Financial Market

Leading companies are nowadays as likely to want to issue commercial paper and swap the proceeds into dollars, pounds, deutsche marks, Swiss francs, or yen as they are to borrow a straightforward loan. Banks must be able to offer multinational clients a palette of possible transactions, or risk losing these clients' business.[4]

Figure 8.3 shows an integrated approach to this marketing perspective. Each of the five interdependent building blocks can be computer-assisted, particularly if expert systems are employed. The marketing services covered by these building blocks are oriented to the finance industry; therefore they should be fully interactive.

The more focus is put on product orientation, the more it is necessary to have constant diagnosis of a firm's own faults and those of competitor institutions. Whether in the manufacturing or in the service industry, any product is bound to have faults; in the financial sector of the economy, however, such faults can be rapidly magnified and dispersed; hence, they have to be handled (and corrected) in real time.

At first glance, this reference to market analysis and to price/feature evaluation may sound strange, but there is a good reason to consider these factors. Normally interest-bearing securities such as bonds have a fairly straightforward

Figure 8.3 Basic Component Parts of a Marketing Policy

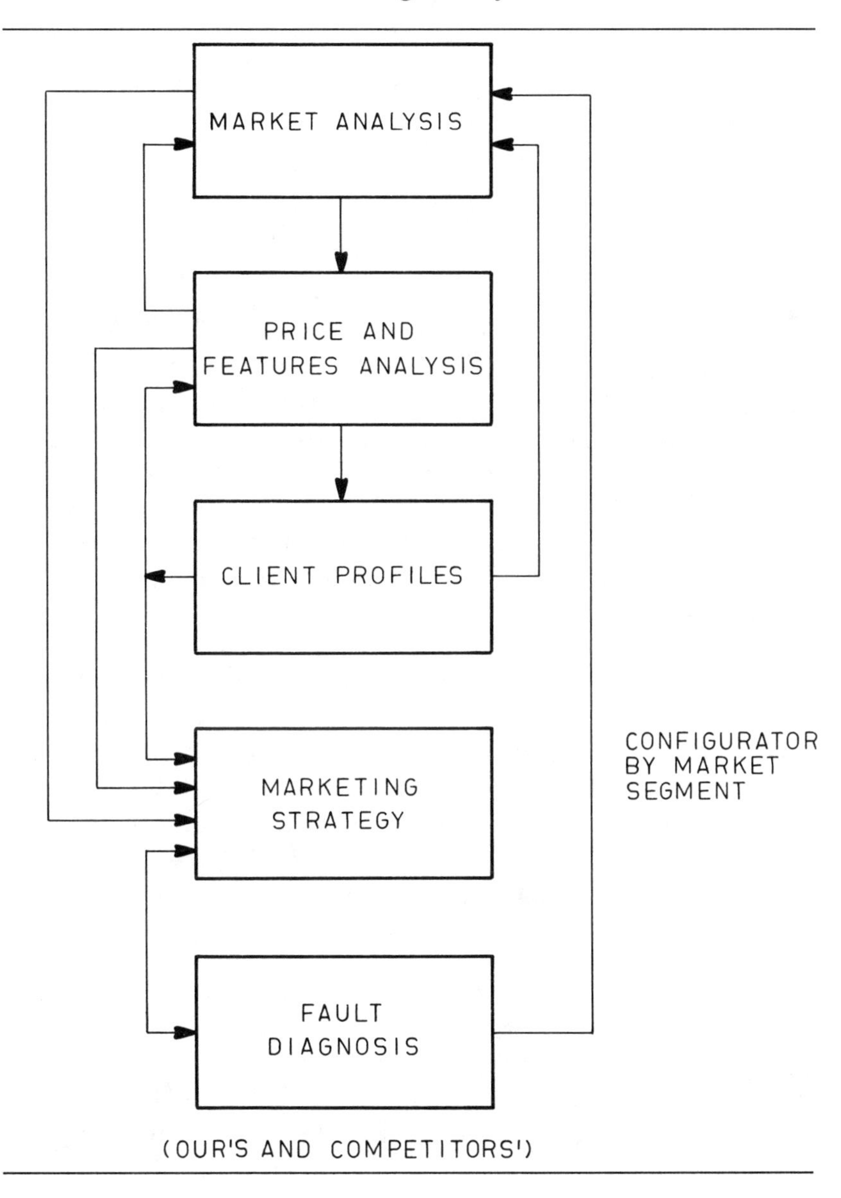

relationship with interest rates. If rates go up, the bond certificates' market value declines; if rates decline, the certificates' market value rises.

Loans-backed securities are a little different. Since these investments are based on pools of debt, investors get back a portion of their principal along with their interest payments. This is because some types of loans, like mortgages, are amortized. For instance, homeowners pay both interest and principal when making a mortgage payment.

A key feature of modern finance is the shift away from bank lending with banks as intermediaries between lender and borrower toward direct lending by investors (in the form of notes and bonds). The reason for this shift is that during the 1980s, competition and the need to bolster reserves against bad loans drove up the cost of bank funds. With the help of investment bankers, corporations and governments found it cheaper to issue their own paper.

Big companies in America now meet upwards of 25 percent of their financing needs by selling commercial paper directly to investors. The Euromarket note issuance facilities (i.e., issues of tradeable short-term paper) have also become increasingly popular. These are substitutes for bank loans.

Interest-rate swaps and other financial instruments are also becoming tradeable. By transforming assets into securities, companies can obtain long-term financing at less cost than they could obtain traditional bank loans.

Institutional investors are evidently interested in this process; pension managers are using a variety of new strategies to improve cash management and hedge fund assets against swings in interest rates or stock prices. In mid-1984, Chrysler Corporation put its entire pension fund into bonds. Using a computer program created by Salomon Brothers, Chrysler built a $1.1 billion dedicated portfolio that carefully matched the interest income from the bonds with future benefit payments. The deal proved to be well-crafted, profitable, and timely. After a steady decline in interest rates over the next two and a half years, the value of the fund's assets doubled to $2.1 billion.[5]

Mortgages have also been securitized to fit developing market needs. As savings banks and commercial banks limited their funds for mortgage lending, many needs were not met. The creation of mortgage-backed securities allowed retail mortgages to be packaged for wholesale consumption. Investment bankers created a number of new ways to refinance borrowers or meet credit requirements; at the same time, pools of savings available in insurance companies and pension funds were pulled into the market.

Today, many institutions are turning to Eurobonds, zero-coupon bonds, junk bonds, and other securities as ways of increasing yields. The message to traders should be that securitization is nothing more than a new financial instrument which has to be marketed properly.

In order to grow and reap profits, banks and securities firms constantly invent new kinds of financing vehicles, each of which is designed to appeal to a particular class of borrowers and lenders. Among these are new types of securities offerings, leveraged buy-outs, venture capital, and highly targeted mutual funds.

The business community should recognize that the new approach represented by these products is permanent. If these products die out, newer ones will take their place. Furthermore, this is as much a communications revolution as it is a financial one; for this reason, new financing vehicles are never owned by one firm for long. With the advent of global communications, a new approach or financial tool can become well-known around the world in a matter of hours. Running on supercomputers and interconnected through intelligent networks, expert systems ensure that a banking product is immediately value-differentiated, further enriched, restructured and repackaged, and aggressively marketed. This is causing a fundamental transformation in the way financial business is conducted.

From the consumer's standpoint, the benefits of new financial products and globalization of the markets may not represent real advances. The fact is, many innovations are designed to help the financial industry interact more efficiently with itself.

If investment banks and securities companies succeed in wholesale securitizing of loan portfolios, distinctions between financial institutions will fade even further. The system will come closer to being one big capital market. As a result, those banks which find it difficult or impossible to move to the new financial instruments will be subject to market erosion, diminishing business, and considerably less profits.

5. The Securitization of Mortgages

Almost all loans with a predictable cash flow can be packaged as securities and sold to investors; this allows investment bankers to charge a sizable fee for their help. As discussed, however, any company that securitizes its loans is giving up long-term interest income stream for up-front profit.

Generally the most easily marketable loans are those that have the lowest risk; hence, there is always interest in home mortgages. There are three ways for individuals to invest in mortgage-backed securities—via pass-throughs, builder bonds, and collateralized mortgage obligations (CMO).

Pass-through securities are created when home mortgages are gathered into a pool and interest in the pool is sold. The cash flow from the underlying mortgages is passed on to holders of the securities in the form of monthly payments of interest and principal.

Most pass-throughs have a stated maturity of thirty years, but with prepayments of principal, pass throughs have an average life (ranging from twelve to eighteen years on the average) that is actually shorter than the final stated maturity.

Builder bonds are mortgage-backed securities issued by some of the nation's largest home builders. Their average life, though estimated to be twelve years, actually varies based on how rapidly homeowners repay their mortgages.

Builder bonds provide investors with interest in the form of a steady stream of monthly payments. Principal payments, including any prepayments, are deposited into a special redemption account and are not directly returned to the investor.

Collateralized Mortgage Obligations, introduced to the market in July 1983, are multiclass mortgage-backed securities that are available in $1,000 denominations. They are unique because, while backed by a common collateral pool, each issue is divided into separate classes.

The cash flow from the collateral pool is directed to each class in specific order, creating investments with various average lives. CMO provides interest income to all interest-paying classes, but principal to only one class at a time. There are two types of CMO classes—coupon/interest bonds and accrual/deferred interest bonds.

The sequential payment structure enables an investor to select a CMO that closely meets his or her maturity preferences, making it possible to address personal income objectives in the process. Cash proceeds from the sale of the CMO permit a financial institution to fund new mortgages at prevailing rates and generate commitment fees on jumbo loan production. If all goes well, as more CMOs are issued, the bank has the potential to increase gradually the rate of return on its equity.

Interest and principal payments on the CMO are often payable solely from the principal and interest payments on the underlying agency securities or mortgage loans. The latter collateralize the public debt security, plus any amount of collateral needed to secure a top credit rating. In addition, there is a small amount of earnings from the investment of the monthly flow of payments on the underlying collateral, while the payments on CMO are only made quarterly.

Some institutions are willing to pay a higher price—that is, accept a lower yield—for CMO than for mortgages or agency securities because the former are tailored to maturity and yield requirements established by management. They also represent a diversified pool with spread-out risk.

As discussed in the beginning of this chapter, the same is true of credit-card receivables, auto loans, and computer leases. Even utilities' nuclear-fuel and equipment leases now support short-term commercial paper, while inventive investment bankers securitize vacation time-share payments, pleasure-boat loans, and life-insurance contracts. Thus, consumer debt is a major type of easily securitized asset that may become a large, lucrative market in the 1990s.

Asset-backed debt instruments are structured much like mortgage-backed securities. A pool of receivables is segregated into a specially created subsidiary or trust, and investors buy shares in the subsidiary or in the pooled assets. In return, they receive principal and interest payments (minus servicing fees and other costs) as the receivables are paid off.

The biggest buyers of asset-backed securities are pension funds, money managers, bank trust departments, and savings and loans (who in 1986 took advantage of Congress' decision to sell as marketable securities federal loans with a face value of $7 billion).

The U.S. government has also become a buyer, through federal agencies such as Eximbank and Farmers Home Administration (FHDA). Highly rated companies, such as General Motors Acceptance Corporation, find asset-backed financing attractive because they can increase loan volume, and therefore auto sales, without boosting leverage. Eventually, more such securities are apt to come from retailers, as the new U.S.

tax law is phasing out the ability to defer taxes on installment sales; hence, companies have less reason to hold onto receivables.

Eager to package and sell new kinds of paper, Wall Street investment bankers are hoping that securitized loans, whether private or federal, will keep on growing. They expect that the market's valuation will ensure that management and servicing become more efficient, thus increasing the weight of fees in the yearly profits. At the same time, they understand that securitization is technology-based, and product planning is too complex to be done without computers. (Financial, legal, and computer programming work can take up to nine months to prepare, perhaps less if artificial intelligence constructs are used for prototype development.)

Some bankers are concerned that as securitization becomes more common and competitive, banks will make less money from originating loans. If this happens, they may have to try position trading in the secondary market—and not all banks can make that leap for reasons of know-how and of technology.

6. Why New Products Fail

A "new" product may be a brand new idea, an old one that has been rediscovered and restructured, or an ongoing financial service addressed to new markets.

Each of these alternatives has its own R and D and marketing requirements. Unfortunately, in many financial institutions the R-and-D function is new or practically nonexistent. As a result, research in financial products may not be properly structured within the investment bank itself, or in relation to the environment in which the institution operates.

Virtually every manufacturing company knows that when a product comes out of the laboratory it has to be test-marketed. But even before this, products of a certain complexity, such as computers and software, undergo alpha and beta tests[6] (not to be confused with the alpha and beta factors in banking).

In 1988, at Shearson Lehman Hutton, a new financial product in the making was dubbed The Manhattan Project, in reference to the secret efforts by American scientists, in World War II, to create the atom bomb.

Shearson's project provides a good example of a new idea for a financial product that went astray for lack of in-depth research and market analysis.

For nearly eleven months, a team of Shearson staffers worked in strict secrecy to generate a new financial instrument that they said could change the structure of public ownership of corporations. Lawyers, bankers, and publicists worked on the project, which was the brainchild of Shearson's new-product department. The new product, unveiled in December 1988, was called unbundled stock units (USU).

The USU breaks down into three components—a bond, a share or preferred stock, and an equity appreciation certificate (EAC). These pieces can be traded as a bundle or be unbundled and offered separately. The basic idea was to split a share of stock and sell rights both to a dividend stream and to a future share. Thus, current dividend was turned into interest on a bond, and an option was made out of the capital appreciation. USU represented a new security that would give investors the right to future dividend increases.

It was thought that investors with three separate instruments to trade might be able to squeeze more value from a share of stock. It was as also projected that in this way, corporations would have a way to cut taxes and increase earnings. If such a product were successful, the project's developers said, it could easily bring multimillion-dollar fees to Shearson. At the time Shearson announced the new product, American Express, Dow Chemical, Pfizer, and Sara Lee all said that they would exchange $5.6 billion in common shares—or up to 20 percent of their shares outstanding—for a package of unbundled stock unit.

If Shearson and the issuing companies were right, the new trio of securities could be worth more than the common share of stock which it replaced. But big money institutions reacted coolly. While developing the new product in secrecy, the developers failed to do market analysis and product testing.

What the designers of the new financial instrument failed to perceive is that it takes an enormous selling effort to win a permanent place on Wall Street's menu of offerings. The unbundling of the stock was basically a good idea. Investors do buy stock in order to reap current dividends, dividend growth, and capital appreciation. And the new package created three securities that try to match those objectives.

Nevertheless, to make the USU swaps work, Shearson and its company clients had to persuade tax-exempt institutional investors, such as pension funds, to tender their stock for the new securities. And it was quite foreseeable that since the swap would be subject to capital-gains taxes, it would not be attractive to many individual shareholders, particularly in the domain where the market might have been.

It was already apparent the first reactions that institutional investors and securities houses were not sold on the idea. Many analysts, assuming that the total price of the three parts would not be that different from the price of a share of the common stock, tried to figure out is how the USU pie would be sliced.

Among their questions were, how much more valuable is the bond portion compared to the preferred stock? and Will the parts really be worth more than the whole? Financial theory says that in an efficient market, they cannot be. The answer could come only when the pieces started trading—and when they did so the results were not encouraging to the promoters.

Shearson continued to insist that the unbundling concept was sound. It would appeal to both the public and to the issuing corporations for the following reasons: unbundled shares reflect varying investor goals more accurately, and unbundling shares reduce corporate taxes. (The company substitutes interest payments that are tax-deductible for dividends, a different way of sweeping debt for equity.)

But investment managers who were asked to exchange their common stock for USUs balked. Many thought that the product was too confusing, that it would take away their voting power, and that the total of the three pieces might, in fact, sell for less than the original security, depending on how liquid the market was.

Three months after being announced, and under attack by investment managers, the USU became an embarrassment. Shearson Lehman Hutton management eventually had to bring in Goldman, Sachs to help pitch the idea to institutions. The product has been a more difficult sell than its originators ever thought it would be.

The Mexican securitization promoted by the U.S. government (and arranged with the help of Morgan Guaranty Trust of New York) is another example of an idea that, while it sounded good on paper, did not make market sense. The key to the Mexican debt/bond plan, proposed in the 1987/1988 time frame, was the collateral, consisting of U.S. Treasury bonds, that Mexico would be offering to back its new bonds.

The game plan was that interest rate would be 1 5/8 percent over Libor, maturity would be 20 years, and the collateral for principal would be as stated in the preceding paragraph. While the Federal Reserve was to hold this collateral, interest payments would not have been collateralized or guaranteed. Up to $10 billion of new Mexican bonds were to be issued according to this plan.

Creditor Banks were asked to participate with $53 billion of non-trade-related public sector debt eligible to be swapped.

Mexico was to dip into its reserves to buy non-marketable twenty-year zero-coupon U.S. Treasury bonds with a face value of $10 billion; and because zero bonds are sold at deep discounts, Mexico could pay just $2 billion but receive $10 billion when the bonds matured in twenty years.

After completing the purchase of the Treasury bonds, Mexico was to conduct an auction in which existing debt would be swapped for the new bonds, with discounts set by using the Dutch-auction technique. This meant Mexico should accept all offered discounts, from the biggest to the smallest, that could enable it to place $10 billion in bonds.

At the time of this offer, financial analysts expected the weighted-average discount to be about 30 to 35 percent. Hence, about $14 to $15 billion of debt might have been swapped, with Mexico extinguishing around $4 billion to $5 billion in outstanding debt total. Unfortunately, creditor banks, who would have to bid for the bonds by offering to cash in their loans at a discount, lacked enthusiasim for the scheme.

Chase Manhattan, for one, let it be known that it intended to delay its decision on whether to participate in Mexico's bonds-for-loans scheme until closer to the February 19, 1988 deadline. "It is very constructive development which provides an exit for banks who want to reduce their international lending. But it is, therefore, of little or no interest to a major international player like Chase," said chairperson Willard Butcher. Other large U.S. banks, such as Citicorp, said they would not participate because the scheme required them to write down their loans.

Securities analysts in New York were also critical. One said, "The U.S. Treasury made exception of taxation due to President Reagan's Tax Law for foreign governments. Zero-coupons by individuals now pay taxes on non-earned income. Mexico has been given a blank card to let participating banks off the tax hook."

At least one analyst suggested that the Mexican scheme might be the monetary equivalent of the nuclear-arms treaty between the United States and Russia, that is, a first step toward defusing an international time bomb: Mexico would reduce its total debt and its annual interest payments; the U.S. Treasury would market some new debt of its own at going interest rates; and banks could clear up at least a portion of their messy Mexican loan portfolios, writing off part of the debt but earning a better rate of interest on the remainder.

This seemed reasonable, as some banks had at the time sold Mexican loans at distress levels of 50 cents on the dollar. But a fire sale is one thing, and a preannounced financial swap, another. The debt reduction scheme was not credible and the results have been just as inadequate.

Endnotes

1. *Management Today,* November 1986.

2. *What's Wrong with Wall Street* (Boston: Addison-Wesley, 1988).

3. *Business Week,* 30 May 1988.

4. See D. N. Chorafas, *Simulation, Optimization and Expert Systems: How Technology Is Revolutionizing the Way Securities Are Underwritten, Analyzed and Traded* (Chicago, IL: Probus Publishing Company, 1992). Chapter 12 discusses the use of a client profile analyzer for investment purposes. The same principles, with the use of a different expert system, are applicable to marketing.

5. *U.S. News & World Report,* 25 May, 1987.

6. See also D.N. Chorafas, *Fourth and Fifth Generation Languages, Vol. 1* (New York; McGraw-Hill, 1986).

Chapter 9

Mortgage-Backed Financing

Chapter 9

Mortgage-Backed Financing

1. Introduction

The granting of credit is one of the services, rendered by the seller to the buyer, whose cost is included in the sales price of a commodity. In fact, credit itself can be seen as a commodity that is bought and sold.

When a business borrows money, it ordinarily gives the lender a note, or written promise to pay, that specifies the terms of the obligation, (maturity, interest rate, and so on). This note may be interest-bearing or non-interest-bearing.

In the first case, it states that interest is to be paid at a given percentage. In the second case, no interest is charged until after the due date. Interest may be charged at the legal rate for any time that the note remains unpaid after it is due.

The borrower will also issue a mortgage or a pledge of certain property as security. If the amount owed is not paid by the debtor, the creditor has the right to bring court action that may result in the sale of the property to satisfy the claim.

But, as will be discussed in this chapter, mortgages can also be repackaged, securitized and resold in the market.

2. Financial Instruments for Handling Debt

Mortgages were originally a transfer of property from a debtor to a creditor or the creditor's representative. If the debt was paid, the transfer would be nullified. Today, however, the mortgage is a guaranty rather than an arbitrary transfer of title.

Financial instruments for handling debt, while polyvalent, are generally based on notes and acceptances. As with a promissory note, a time draft is a debtor's written agreement to pay a certain sum of money at a fixed or determinable future date. Therefore, most accountants record acceptances receivable in the notes receivable account, and acceptances payable in the notes payable account.

If a company finds it undesirable or impossible to obtain the funds from one lender, an issue of bonds may be offered to investors. Bonds may be secured by mortgages on fixed assets or may be based on the general credit standing of the company. In any case, they represent a debt to be paid at some determined future date and are, therefore, included under fixed liabilities.

Whether in connection to companies or to individuals, bonds may be secured by first, second, or even third mortgages on the same property.[1] If the obligations are not met, and foreclosure ensues, the proceeds of the mortgaged property must go to the satisfaction of the first mortgage bondholders, any residue to the satisfaction of the second mortgage bondholders, and so on.

Hence, second mortgage bonds are a less desirable investment than first mortgage bonds, because they are secured by a secondary lien on the pledged assets. First mortgage bonds are called *prior lien,* or underlying bonds; second mortgage bonds are called *junior* bonds.

Bonds may be classified in three groups on the basis of registry. If they are registered as to both principal and interest, the name of the owner of the bond is recorded on the books of the issuing company or its fiscal agent; the interest is paid by checks drawn to the order of the bond holders. This method safeguards the owner against loss or theft, but it has two disadvantages: first, interest is paid by check; second, a sale and transfer can be made only by assignment and registry, not by delivery.

If bonds are registered as to principal only (with coupons attached for the interest), the owner is safeguarded against loss or theft of principal. At the same time, the debtor company is relieved of the burden of issuing numerous interest checks.

Unregistered bonds are transferable by delivery, without need for the owner's endorsement. Hence, the danger from loss or theft is much greater than for a bond that is registered as to principal. The interest is collected by clipping the interest coupons and presenting them to a bank for collection.

As financial instruments, bonds may be held by many people. This presents opportunities as well as problems. These people or companies are not known at the time of arranging for the issue. They (the bond holders) will tend to transfer a bond by selling it from one holder to another.

For these reasons, the borrower selects a trustee, usually a bank or trust company. The financial institution acts as a representative of the bond holders, and a mortgage, or deed of trust, is executed. This deed conveys a conditional title to the property. This is called underwriting.

In this procedure, long-term mortgage notes are considered to be the same as secured bonds, and vice versa. Thus, mortgage-backed financing (MBF) is essentially a conversion from one type of debt to another.

In order to identify a projected deal's strengths and weaknesses, both the construction of original debt and its repackaging require financial research.

Provided the investigation has positive results, one of two types of contracts is signed between the issuer and the underwriter(s): the first is a firm commitment made by the underwriter(s) to purchase the entire issue outright for resale to investors; typically, such a contract contains a market-out clause, which permits the banker to cancel the contract if certain specified events take place. Under the terms of the second contract, the underwriters agree without financial obligation to use their best possible efforts to sell the issue.

This type of contract is generally used for very strong or very weak issues, the reason being that in investment banking a relatively large sum of money is required to complete the average unit transaction. At the same time, the securities house operates on a relatively narrow margin of gross profit; and since security prices are highly sensitive to market whims, the risk in carrying inventories of unsold securities is quite large.

This is the environment in which mortgage-backed financing and other asset-backed financing solutions, such as corporate loans (corporates), operates. Securitized financial instruments share two fundamental aspects: the search for the right pricing, and the need to assume risk.

As an example of a useful model for the design and administration of securities, Figure 9.1 shows a bullet-bond solution to an integrative financial environment. The theme is primary asset pricing for noncallable bonds.

Callable bonds as well as options and futures are taken as derivatives of this approach, subject to boundary conditions, with term structure and risk management being the key factors. These notions are behind most asset-backed financing

Figure 9.1 An Integrative Financial Environment for Bullet Bonds

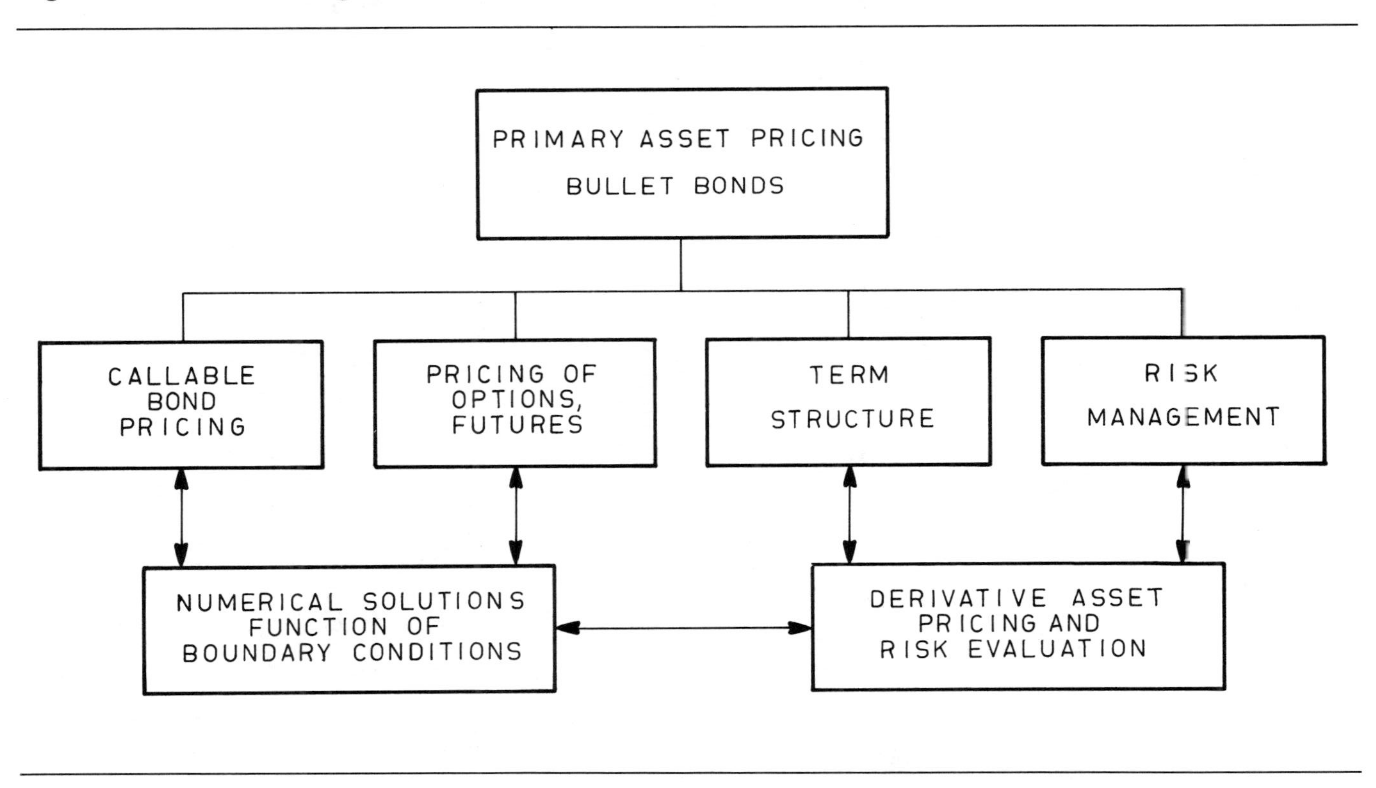

operations; the optimization of an offering requires substantial research, and here lies the great interest in simulation and experimentation.

3. The Process of Underwriting and the Role of Interactive Computational Finance

In offering securities to investors, an originating investment bank must do considerable homework; it is also likely to ask other securities houses to join in an underwriting or purchase syndicate, of which the first bank will be manager.

The terms of a syndicated loan are defined by agreement among the parties entering into the joint venture; these parties constitute the underwriting syndicate. Current practice typically limits the liability of each bank to the amount of its participation; but even so, the successful outcome will be largely based on the type and the depth of the qualitative and quantitative studies that have been made prior to taking on the commitment.

The more competitive the market is, the faster and more detailed these studies must be. Interactive computational finance (including the use of supercomputers and artificial intelligence) is a necessity; analytical studies of the magnitude and frequency that is required cannot be made by paper and pencil or through classical data processing.

Also, prototyping may need to be used in order to identify, select, and manage suitable projects. A serious approach will be based upon a project-management methodology as well as on practical experience in running such projects. The methodology should center around the concept of iterative refinement and focus on modular design principles.

An investment bank, and in particular the manager of a syndicated loan, has broad powers. These include undertaking the commitments and costs involved in underwriting, from feasibility studies to execution, borrowing to carry the inventory of securities in process of sale, and stabilizing the market price of the new issue by purchases and sales in order to facilitate distribution at the offering price.

Thorough experimentation is thus necessary, because while stabilizing the market for a new issue is permitted by the Securities and Exchanges Commission (SEC), the desirability of the practice has been widely debated. Because of the magnitude of the support required, low technolgy can lead to notable failures. It is always wise to study and experiment with all possibilities, with a focus on what can go wrong.

This process becomes crucial when engaging in operations such as stand-by underwriting, which occurs most commonly when a corporation that is recapitalizing or reorganizing offers new securities in exchange for its outstanding issues. Because of the longer time involved, the risk to the investment banker is greater than in ordinary underwriting.

Interactive computational finance is just as important in the domain of bond sales. The investment banker attempts to achieve a wide, rapid, and profitable placement of the securities. Organized and managed by the head of the underwriting syndicate, the selling group is the principal vehicle for the actual distribution of new issues to investors.

The participants in the selling group (which comprises some or all of the underwriters and additional dealers) may receive the right to take a firm subscription on the offering date for a fixed amount; subscriptions may also be made subject to allotment. As well, other dealers may make purchases of the issue at a small concession from the public offering price; this type of profit-sharing also needs to be studied.

Timing is of essence. The offering of a new security to investors is generally made on the day after the registration statement becomes effective. A good deal of computation, which must be done in real time, involves terms, risks, maturities, prices and costs.

As the volume of financial transactions has increased in the past decade and as the world's big banks and securities houses are now linked through electronic wholesale payment systems, panics can spread at alarming speed; thus, the timing or response is essential.

Today's liquidity and credit dependencies stagger the imagination. Daily financial transactions in New York alone are presently the equivalent of nearly one-fourth of the U.S. gross national product (GNP).

Furthermore, this financial system weathered several crises in the 1980s, including rampant Third-World debt, stock-market crashes, thrift bail-outs and leveraged buy-outs. That it has survived with only minor casualties is due probably as much to good luck as good management. But to repeat, luck is what happens when preparation meets opportunity.

Financial markets, that is the virtual economy, have become the shock absorbers for the real economy. Separately and together, the world's regulators, as well as private bankers, need to work to ensure that the financial system does not fail that test. This is why interactive computational finance is so important.

4. Tooling-Up for the Institutional Buyers

For the issuing corporation, the cost of obtaining funds includes the bankers' spread and discount, as well as the expenses paid by the issuer itself. The bankers' spread covers charges for underwriting and distribution. Other expenses are registration fees and taxes; legal, accounting, and engineering costs; and, if required, listing on an exchange and the associated logistics.

Who constitutes the market to which such offerings are directed? In recent years large and well-established issuers have frequently placed bonds and preferred stock with one or more institutional buyers, such as insurance companies, mutual funds, and pension funds. Also private placements are often made through a single investment banker, whose restricted service does not include underwriting and retail selling—but who faces significant requirements for computational wizardy, because institutional investors are sophisticated and demanding.

This is another reason why simulation, algorithmic solutions, and heuristic approaches are in increasing demand, even more so as the investment banker takes on the role of financial adviser to institutional investors and corporations. Both securities houses and institutional investors actively seek the advice of investment bankers who have mastered high technology. For example, the banker may give advice to corporations planning to market issues by competitive bidding, as well as to those contemplating a private placement.

An investment banker may also become an ongoing consultant to security-buying customers, furnishing information on securities in which they are interested, and helping them select securities that meet their particular requirements. Also, in order to protect clients' portfolios, the investment banker must experiment with the wisdom of switching in or out of an existing security and into a new or different issue. This requires profile definition, opportunity scouting, factual definition of constraints, and consistency. These activities pose significant computational challenges. Figure 9.2 shows an aggregate of functions and constraints made up of expert systems and simulators dedicated to the management of investments.

Because of the tools it makes available, interactive computational finance allows for optimal packaging of mortgage-backed securities as collateralized obligations. Similar packaging can be done with asset-backed debt instruments (see Chapter 8).

As the field of asset-backed financing expands, computation power will become essential. Even now, many firms have

Figure 9.2 **Consistency Maintenance Requires an Aggregate of Constraints and Knowledge Engineering Supports**

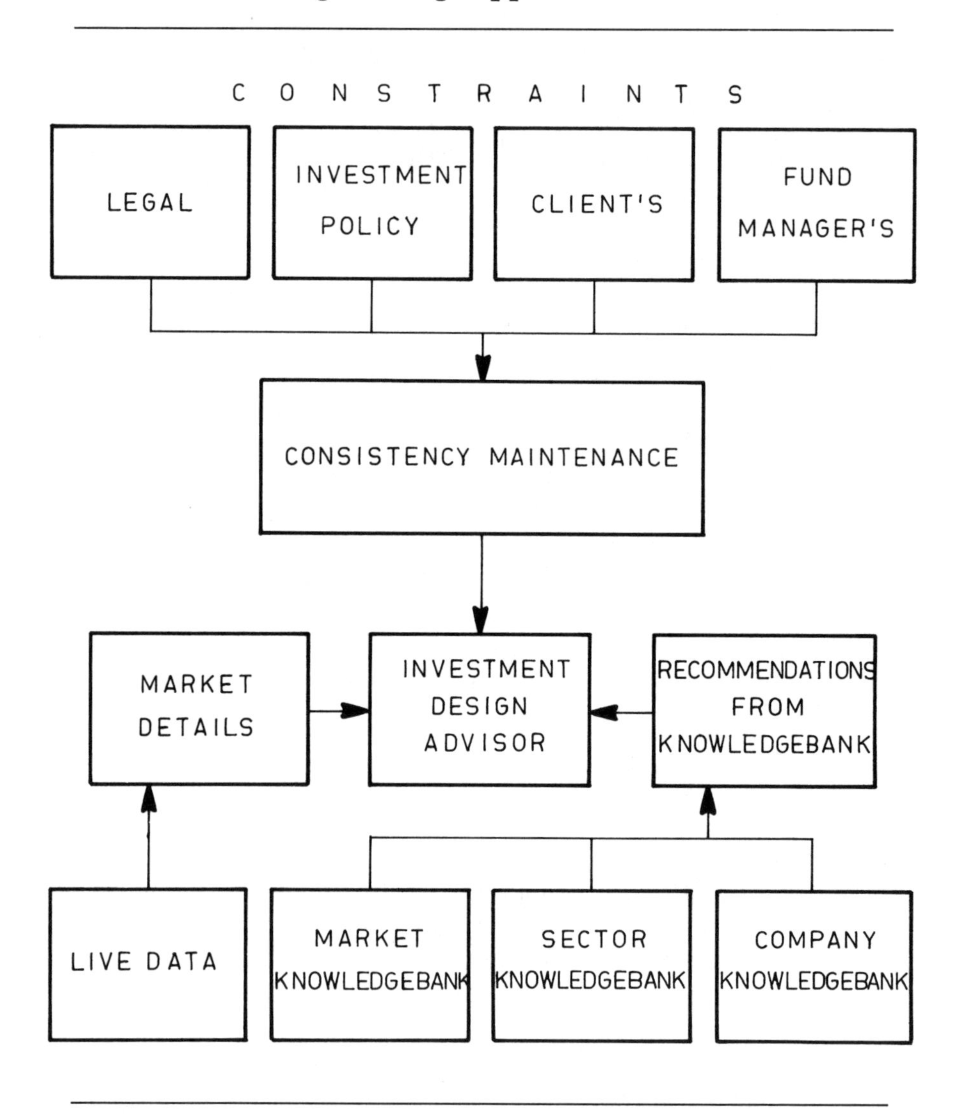

made their R and D departments more competitive by hiring "rocket scientists," that is, engineers, mathematicians, and physicists who have been working with the aerospace and nuclear industries and have moved into finance to help with their know how. Computer manufacturers are also hiring people with these skills; the tolerances involved in making a read:write head work on high density magnetic disks resembles the challenge of a Boeing 747 flying at an altitude of 10 meters from the Earth.

5. Understanding the Essence of Mortgage-Backed Financing

In order to understand the analytics of MBF that are handled by rocket scientists on supercomputers, it is necessary to understand the fundamentals of the trade.

Today on Wall Street, investment banks trade mortgage-backed securities that come mostly from mortgage loans by savings and loan associations and other financial institutions. As discussed in Chapter 8, these loans are administered through the U.S. government-status organizations known as Ginnie Mae, Fannie Mae, and Freddie Mac.

These three agencies have slightly differing status. Ginnie Mae's obligations are assimilated with those of U.S. Treasuries. Fannie Mae and Freddie Mac have a line of credit with the U.S. government, though there are no explicit guarantee.

These three agents have among them about 250,000 pools; these pools are essentially pass-throughs that involve all the principal and all but a small amount of interest. (See Chapter 8.)

Mortgage-backed securities are usually traded by pool number. Each pool contains $1 million or more in funds, and its creation necessitates transactions concerning which must observe a number of rules.

Within each pool, anywhere from fifty to five hundred home owners' mortgage loans may be packaged and sold. These home owners provide a reliable repayment base; nevertheless, they may have prepayment and other problems; hence, there is a need for the complex calculations that can be done by expert systems with AI.[2]

Typically, such calculations involve the use of analytical tools and require access to large databases. (The MBF operations of Ginnie Mae date back to 1980, and those of the other two agencies, to 1983; thus, today, the historical database consists of some 28 million prepayments.) That is why supercomputers, state-of-the-art database management, and the efficient implementation of AI are all required. MBF can be handled effectively if its analytics are mastered. Partial solutions are inefficient because they only address part of the problem and lead to suboptimizations. They may also involve quite substantial risks.

6. The Basics of System Integration

The more sophisticated financial instruments become, the more polyvalent they need to be. This requires having access to different databases (in contrast to past data processing practices, in which each application was developed in its own domain and for its own merits).

Today, the strategic use of information technology calls for integration; Morgan Stanley is one firm that has made efficient use of the process. Using a combination of IBM and Hitachi main-frame equipment, Adabas DBMS, and the fourth-generation language Natural, this bank was able to build a sophisticated back-office position management system that uses mainly nontechnical staff.

In the Morgan Stanley approach, high-level software facilitate rapid programming and enhance software maintainability as well as integrative solutions involving several distinct applications. This enables management to systematically examine any product and market changes that are currently taking place.

Nevertheless, system integration is not being used; yet this is an issue for the majority of financial institutions, perhaps because they are having trouble coping with the explosion of in-house information technology. Yet, with it a master plan and attention to detail, system integration can become, for the firm that uses it, not a product, but a solution.

For example, mortgage-backed financing can be run on supercomputers through a model that accesses on-line, rich databases (both private and public) and integrates programs that have been written in the past to answer discrete island requirements.

This model can be developed with the help of algorithms capable of analyzing the prepayment process affecting mortgages. It can also be used for scenario writing for securitization and for tailoring the financial product to client needs. End users should determine their own needs, whether they are using deterministic and stochastic models or heuristic scenarios. However, end users cannot, and should not, attempt to provide the infrastructure for system integration. This is the function of the system specialist.

Integrative solutions should make transparent to the end user the bridges necessary for linking to each other the formerly discrete islands of applications. For example, in one implementation the MBF code inputs a number of records, each representing a mortgage pool. It then computes key factors by accessing other programs that were written to compute monthly balance, principal interest, bond value, and cash flow (all of which relate to the pool structure). Subsequently, depending on the run identification, different prepayment and reinvestment factors are used in the calculations.

Some of the advantages that integrated systems can provide include a fast development timetable (on the order of three to four months per application), rapid job turnaround which allows for real-time handling of complex financial algorithms, and real-time response to market requirements. Solutions can serve both the modeling needs of end users and their communications requirements. This is why integrative approaches must be promoted over the stand-alone solutions that were the norm in the past.

7. Betting on Supercomputers for More Efficient Results

The packaging of mortgage-backed securities requires intense number-crunching; thus, it is a popular application for supercomputers on Wall Street. This enhances new product development, as securities firms not only buy up mortgages from lending institutions, but also package them and sell them to investors in the form of fixed-income instruments.

The first problem is for traders to estimate the value of mortgages. When consumers pay off their loans, the interest and principal is passed on to the securities firms. If consumers pay off their mortgages early, they pay less interest and the firms make less money; in addition, investors, such as pension funds, have their cash-flow calculations upset.

The prepayment of mortgages is, in itself, a complex function—it is affected by interest rates and other factors. Hence, securities firms try to simulate the process with computer models that assess the value and likely duration of the mortgages.

Once a lifecycle emulation of MBF has been done, the problem become one of finding an optimum way of packaging the mortgages and of deciding how much interest the fixed-income securities will pay. Rocket scientists pick up the debt and try to repackage it in a way that will satisfy customer requirements. The associated algorithmic and heuristic requirements now tax current workstations and main frames beyond their capacity, resulting in increased response time and higher costs than necessary. This is where supercomputers come in to play.

The cost/effectiveness of supercomputers is far greater than that of main frames. The following statistics provide a comparison, in terms of cost per floating operations per second, (FLOPS) between Intel's iPSC-2, and (a hypercube architecture with parallel processing characteristics) VAX and IBM mainframes.

At peak megaFLOPS, the ratio in cost/effectiveness is 1:47.7 to the advantage of the parallel computer when compared with the IBM 3090-600 E/VF (with vector processor); and 1:15.9 to its advantage when compared with the DEC Vax 9000/440. (Note also that the Vax 9000/440 is more cost/effective than the 3090/600 E/VF by a factor of 1:3.) Obviously, no firm wants to pay 47.7 times more for computing power; but it has to be substantiated by a well-tuned project that produces end-user oriented results.

Aside from cost differentials, one of the hypercube's major advantages is that because of its parallel architecture, it has a greatly reduced response time. This can be demonstrated through test cases (see Figure 9.3).

Note that at combined execution times of 150 to 2,000 pools, response has dropped by an order of magnitude, from more than 500 seconds with one processor, to 50 seconds if 16 processors are used in parallel. Also note that the 16-processor configuration of iPSC-2, on which this test is based, is only a fraction of the available power; this hypercube supports up to 128 parallel processors.

Nevertheless, power alone does not address the complexities of MBF; Also required are

1. immediate and direct end-user involvement in the application;

Figure 9.3 **A Mortgage-Backed Financing (MBF) Experiment on Hypercube Computer Architecture**

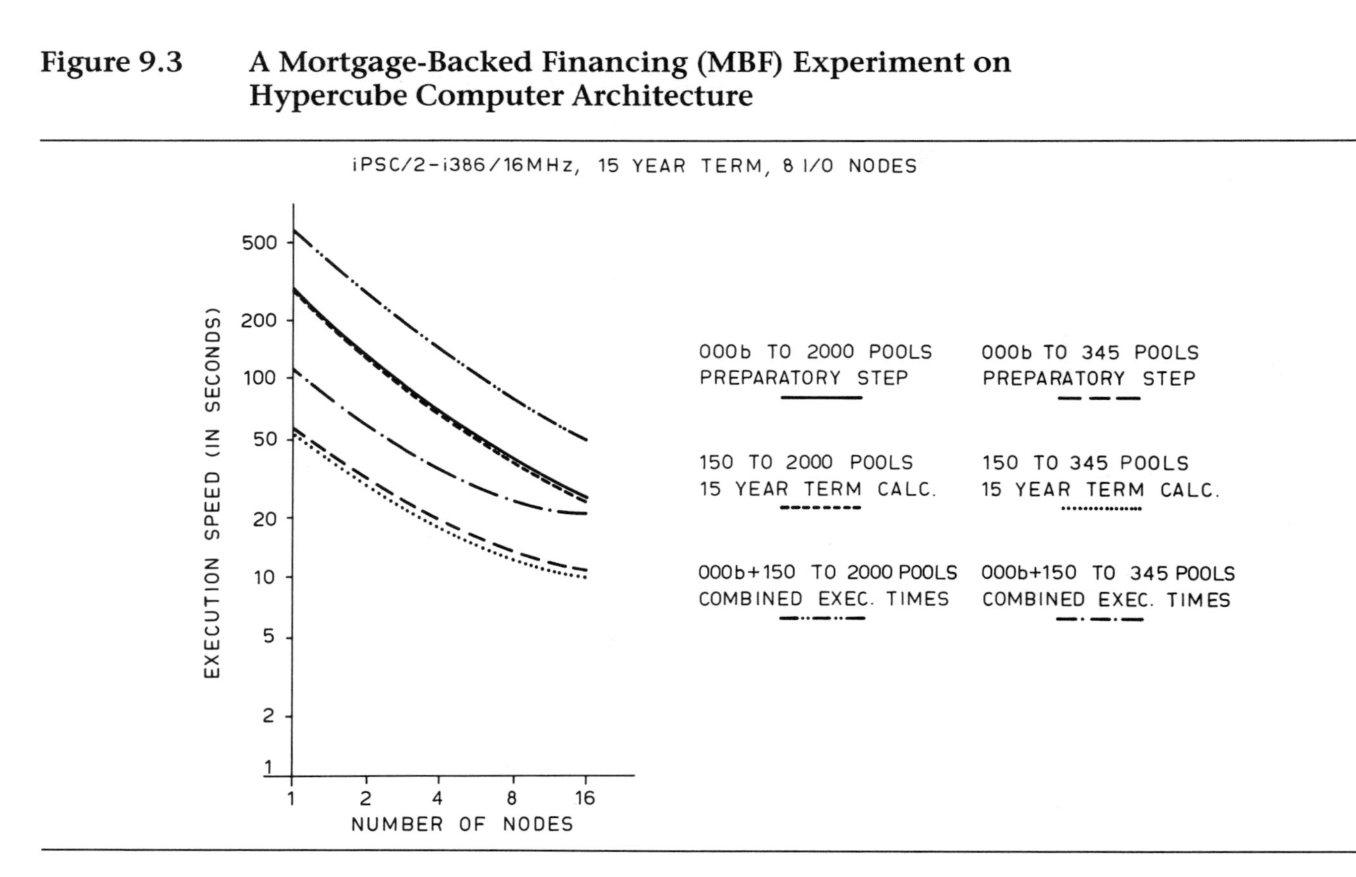

2. intensive end-user training to make such involvement feasible;
3. a mastery of database management, particularly regarding distributed database engines;
4. effective solutions to communications challenges, from links to integrative perspectives.

Also, once the supercomputer has been used as a number-crunching server, its applications should be steadily extended.

These applications should be clearly defined, and available alternatives examined. Questions asked should be focused and geared to adding value.

Take the example of a prepayment model, which is a set of data elaborated through mathematical statistics. A logarithmic decay exists in the mortgages backing up a new securities instrument; this decay is observable in the data.

Random walks (Monte Carlo method) can help in determining what will be the future basis of the security being offered. They can help also in weighing the economic incentives against the disincentives.

Multiple regression analysis and binomial lattices are helpful in investigating crucial factors. As will be discussed in subsequent sections, these approaches can be partly complementary and partly alternative, with each security analyst and rocket scientist having a preferred theory. There is nothing wrong with a plural approach, as long as the alternative modules are properly coordinated.

8. An Implementation of Second-Generation Expert Systems

Mortgage prepayment and delinquency prediction are domains in which second-generation expert systems, such as fuzzy sets and neural networks, can greatly aid implementation. Figure 9.4 shows the results of an experiment by Nestor Systems on mortgage-delinquency prediction. The host computer was a workstation (Apollo); the neural network was composed of 3,00 neurons, and speed of processing was about 1 second per pattern. The data set featured 4,000 files, of which 3,200 were the training set and 800 the test set. Nestor advises that the test set accuracy was 80 percent in conservative mode (with 5 percent through-put), and 57 percent in liberal mode (with 74 percent through-put).

The implementation of neural networks is not yet that popular among financial analysts on Wall Street, nor is it a mature tool, although it is developing. To date, Monte Carlo and binomial distributions are much more widely used; nevertheless, these methods are sometimes questioned as well.

For example, binomial approaches, according to some securities analysts, force operators to use a model which is path independent and, therefore, not robust; others prefer the binomial solution precisely for this reason.

Thus, as long as the modules being developed form part of a comprehensive system and are under control, there is no problem in having more than one. In fact, a firm should also have available an expert system that tracks the results of various approaches and determines which compares most favorably with real life.

Whichever analytical approach is followed, however, the goal is ultimately the same—to understand explanatory variables, their components, and their aftermaths. This is why phenomena such as coupon effect, burn-out rate, and so on are being intensively studied today.

Using new math and high-speed computing, securities analysts can look at a coupon and the dependability of a mortgage. Some mortgages will be prepaid early; this destabilizes the mortgage because there is no longer a source of ready

Figure 9.4 A Mortgage-Delinquency Predictor Using Neural Networking

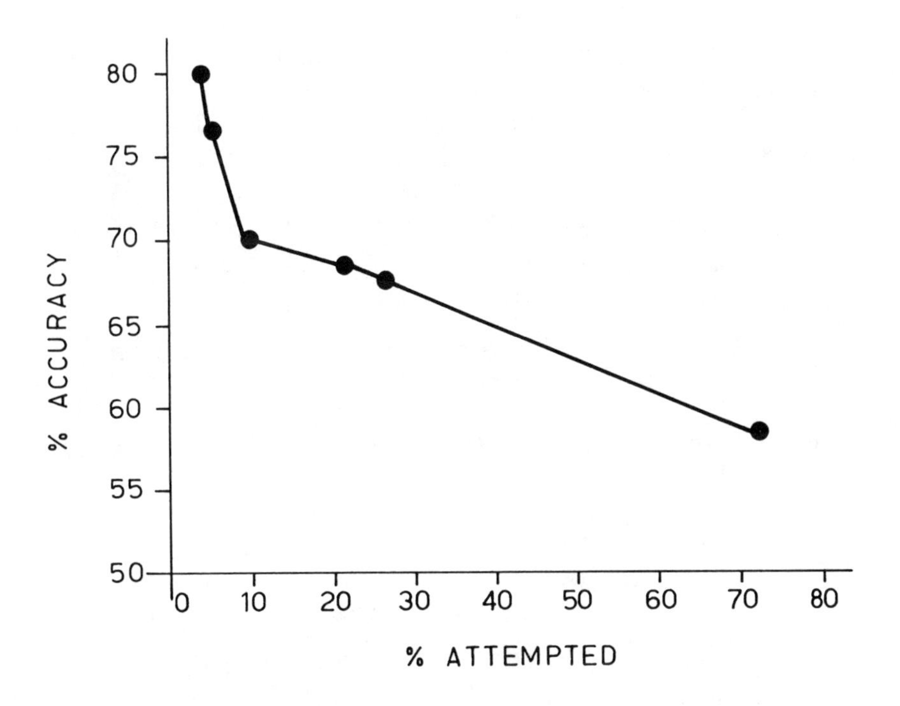

cash available to meet payment obligations over the originally projected lifecycle. This is the burn-out effect.

To study burn-out and other functions, advanced analytical models test a number of hypotheses under current and projected conditions. For instance, if the interest rate drops, the borrower has more of an incentive to prepay; this incentive increases as the rate drops further.

Some pertinent questions are: How aggressive are lenders going to be in offering incentives to clients so they do not move out of the mortgage? How much interest will there be in remortgaging?

Some of the most critical factors involved in algorithmic work currently being done include

1. delta function, which identifies the difference between current coupon and what the borrower pays;
2. lag or surge, a moving average that indicates how long have the rates been down;
3. seasonality, which is influenced by several variables, including the pool;
4. decay (i.e. burn-out);
5. housing activity (i.e., the numbers of new home permits and secondary home sales as well as inflation and unemployment);
6. the age of the pool. Thirty years is final in MBF, but two to five years are necessary to become seasoned; between eight and twelve years a mortgage becomes highly seasoned, hence, less sensitive to interest rates and more to demographics.

Six factors seem to be the ideal number to plot in a radar chart, as evidenced by Sanyo Securities' chart, which is currently used by every major securities house in Japan.[3] (This radar chart was shown in Figure 7.4.)

Because they give digested information without expressing compulsory opinions, these models help the traders and salespeople of brokerage houses to make decisions. However, as with all mathematical models using real-life data, they involve uncertainty and imprecision; these, however, are characteristic of any business and of any decision. If users appreciate this fact, they may find experimentation to be quite profitable.

9. Projects to Exploit New Business Opportunities

As discussed in preceding chapters, expert systems can be instrumental both in developing client profiles and in evaluating investment criteria. Among their applications are the calculation of the most likely pass-through rate ($ price), experimentation on repayment speed (with zero speed meaning that no mortgages are paid off early), comparison of returns from MBF against treasuries, asset/liability management (for example, pension funds take lower spread and less prepayment risk), and evaluation of the emotional criteria present in almost every transaction.

Mode- and computer-based experimentation helps bankers to recognize signs of trouble in new financial instruments. Experimentation can also be done with the aim of enhancing the appeal of existing products and developing new ones.

Some other ways in which the use of analytics can play a key role are as follows:

1. Analytics can be used to enhance total return on major accounts.

This application particularly appeals to money managers of discretionary accounts, pension funds, insurance companies, and banks with a trust department. It tends to look at a security over its holding period (one year is the bench mark versus Treasuries, although it can be ten years when long-term dominates) and examine return and repayment.

Many securities analysts feel that they can make significant contributions to their bank's profitability by examining client profiles and strategies through the supercomputer, then optimizing. Such an approach capitalizes on the fact that every year a money manager is judged against other money managers in-house, as well as against outside competition.

2. Analytics help to pinpoint Option-Adjusted Spread.

A senior executive of a Wall Street firm says, "Customers who do a $200 million to $300 million trade don't buy from us if we do not have OAS. The supercomputer may be the perfect tool because it is fast enough and we can do with it added value such as differentiation through financial service which consider life-cycle, burn-out and taxation."

Regulators have a similar viewpoint. The U.S. Office of Thrift Supervision declared that all thrifts should use the OAS algorithm because it will effect capital reserve requirements and help them to determine the amounts of money that can be invested.

Nevertheless, one should not underestimate the mathematical skill and financial know how necessary to calculate Option-Adjusted Spread. It needs to be computed against an index set of rates (e.g., Treasuries) which can then be used in a cash-flow scenario.

Thus, the securities analysts must compute spread over implied short-term forward rates of Treasuries that will equate discounted cash flows with market price; they must simulate bond behavior over a given time frame and compare it to alternatives. Only then can decisions be made on risks taken and profits to be expected.

3. Analytics help to calculate Hybrid Bond Obligations (HBO)

Straightforward bond analysis is no longer applicable if a firm wishes to competitively price its securities. The competitive edge has to be sharpened through experimentation; this is particularly important in developing HBO patterns.

Differences must also be accounted for; for example, European call options can be exercised only once, while U.S. call options can be exercised any time after a certain date to the end of the life of the bond.

4. Analytics can be applied to buy-and-hold

This function centers on asset/liability management and is oriented to pension funds, insurance companies (for annuities), guaranteed-income trusts, and banks with certificates of deposit (CD) portfolio.

Like the preceding application, buy-and-hold can greatly benefit through artificial intelligence. Another challenge for quantitative and qualitative approaches is to evaluate the option spread for corporate bonds, a task that may include scrutinizing a whole portfolio.

As soon as the models are developed and tested, they should be utilized in a consistent fashion. In the case of a Wall Street bank, one of the expert systems in operation is being used three hundred times a week by the salespeople in almost every case for client accounts. "Corporate bond is Dr. Jekyll and Mr. Hyde," said a senior securities analyst, "because of the embedded options and other variations. We must find out what a bond is really worth and value it precisely."

5. Analytics Prepayment Algorithms

As practiced by Wall Street firms, prepayment algorithms follow one of three methods—Multiple regression analysis, binomial lattice, and Monte Carlo. All three are well known mathematical routines and are available in existing libraries. The most challenging part of the routine is doing the organizational work that both precedes and supplements the analytics of the model, as well as the organizational work involving the methods used for treatment.

For instance, in the case of binomial lattices, statistical tables are based on a normal distribution. To skew this distribution, analysts use weightings that can best be done through possibility theory rather than probability theory.

10. Models, Components, and their Linkages

When experimental approaches are followed in dealing with management problems, each problem should be thought of as a system of interrelated components. Components are interrelated when the output of one is the input of another, when all (or at least the majority) of them need to work for the system to function, and when such functioning is conditioned by the way these components are designed and, hence, operate.

The components of a system are never random; they exist to perform a function that is related to the performance of the system itself. In the case of an overall economic model for securitized commodities, for example, the factors integrated into it must account for markets to be addressed, prepayment characteristics, population mobility, demographics, interest rates, volatility, state laws, age of mortgage, transferable loans, and present value of cash flow. These basic variables change with time and have to be recalculated.

To contend with increasing computational requirements, Morgan Stanley is said to have installed a Cray supercomputer for interactive computational finance; Goldman Sachs is using a time-shared Cray computer; Bear Stearns and Yamaichi Securities have purchased Floating Point supercomputers.

All of the major investment banks have a number of projects that need supercomputer-based solutions. These projects fall into areas such as risk management, bond portfolio immunization, worst-case analysis, stochastic programming, and so on. At the same time, supercomputers are being used to enhance the construction and analysis of microeconomic and macroeconomic models.

Heuristics and algorithms are becoming increasingly complex; already many securities houses are applying sensitivity analysis that involves spread, duration, mean value, and dispersion of net present value. They are also doing cross-evaluations of an immunized portfolio, as well as cash-flow matching under generated interest-rate scenarios.

Assisted by rocket scientists,[4] securities specialists are applying necessary mathematical financial methodology, such as the esoteric algorithms that enrich a prepayment model. Specialists are also finding solutions for accessing heterogeneous securities databases (private and public) that must be reached on-line during the workday.

Firms, today, prefer to develop sophisticated software internally, rather than subcontracting to outside firms and losing control. Thus, confidentiality is another major point. Also proper attention has to be paid to R and D activities for the development of new financial products.

Almost all the investment banks on Wall Street feel the requirement for a steady stream of new services. Some existing financial products (e.g., collateral-based obligations) are not profitable anymore.

"As more people come up with securitized products—mortgages, junk bonds, corporates, and so on—we have to evaluate them," says one investment banker. "And this is a field where excellence in performance is needed now, not in two years." Finally, the growth of the client base must be considered. As more investment accounts are handled, it becomes mandatory not only to do portfolio management by means of computers but also to automate the whole procedure through AI.

Endnotes

1. Unsecured bonds are sometimes called *debentures*. Since they are not secured by a pledge of any specific property, their value depends upon the general credit of the borrower.

2. See also D.N. Chorafas and H. Steinmann, *Expert Systems in Banking* (London: Macmillan, 1990).

3 See also D.N. Chorafas and H. Steinmann, *Implementing Networks in Banking and Other Financial Institutions* (London: Macmillan, 1988).

4 The way "rocket scientists" work and what they produce is treated in D.N. Chorafas, *Simulation, Optimization and Expert Systems: How Technology Is Revolutionizing the Way Securities are Underwritten, Analysed and Traded* (Chicago, IL: Probus Publishing Company, 1992).

Chapter 10

Mergers and Acquisitions

Chapter 10

Mergers and Acquisitions

1. Introduction

Many solvent companies with strong market bases were acquired during the corporate takeover frenzy of the 1980s; and nowhere was the mergers and acquisitions (M and A) fever stronger than in the U.S. Now, with the integration of the Common Market, the fever has spread to Europe; it is also starting among Japanese companies who are interested in foreign acquisitions.

At the end of January 1990, Yamaichi Securities reported that during 1989 Japanese companies took over a record 404 foreign firms, the majority of them in the U.S. Some of these acquisitions, like the takeover of Columbia Pictures by Sony, have made bigger news than others. Among financial institutions, Nippon Life bought a 13-percent share in Shearson Lehman; the Sumitomo Bank purchased a 12.5-percent share in Goldman Sachs; Lloyds got a major stake in the U.S. investment manager Weiss, Peck and Greer; British and Commonwealth bought Mercantile House Holdings; and Hong

Kong-based Jardine Matheson bought a 20-percent stake in Bear Stearns.

In Europe, Aachener and Muenchener, a German insurance firm, acquired Bank fuer Gemeinwirtschaft; Deutsche Bank acquired Banca d'America d'Italia; Primerica got control of Smith Barney, and Xerox purchased Furman Selz. Shearson Lehman bought E.F. Hutton in a bid to challenge Merrill Lynch for first position in the brokerage business, but ended in second spot.

Finance is not the only domain in which acquisitions are strong. According to Morgan Stanley, in one year alone (1987), overseas acquirers spent a record $40.6 billion for U.S. real estate and industrial corporations; nearly $17 billion of that was invested in smokestack America. Many of these acquisitions capitalized on existing tax and accounting rules.

The U.S. has proven to be a tax shelter for Japanese and European companies. For example, the blended federal and local tax rate for a Tokyo-based firm is 56 percent; in the U.S., the blended rate runs around 39 percent. Again, British companies can quickly charge off goodwill (the excess of purchase price over book values) against equity. For a U.S. company, goodwill can be a drag on earnings for up to forty years.

Meanwhile, Americans are suffering from a growing fear of and resentment toward foreign investment. This is most evident in Hawaii and on the west coast, where the impact of new Japanese wealth on the economy has been the greatest, but examples are turning up throughout the country. There seems to be a vague but widespread sentiment in favor of limits on foreign ownership of U.S. real estate and businesses.

Not all Americans share this reaction. As the *Washington Post* remarks:

> America has been extraordinarily reckless to run up the debts of the last seven years. Having run them up, it is going to have to deal intelligently with the consequences.

> U.S. prosperity depends on persuading the new owners of those dollars to keep them in the United States. One effective way to do it is to assure them that they can invest on the same terms, under the same laws, as Americans.[1]

2. A Decade of Big M and A Deals

Merger activity benefits a company only when that company has a well-defined strategic goal. As the focus has shifted to complex international deals, successful mergers and acquisitions, have generally involved companies who observe the fundamentals of sound financial business, valid pricing, careful planning, and decisive postmerger integration.

By and large, sound M and A rules were not observed in the 1980s. Therefore, it comes as no surprise that the decade of the big deals is now being criticized by many, including those who took part in the M and A activity. As of December 1989, Campeau Corporation's banks reported that the firm might be in technical default on $2.34 billion of debt (Campeau's retailing operations filed for bankruptcy in January 1990), while other leveraged buy-outs that lavishly used junk bonds in wheeling and dealing were also in big trouble. Drexel's demise was largely caused by the collapse of its $1 billion junk-bond portfolio.

Among the better-known big M and A deals of the 1980s is Kraft's merger with Dart to the tune of $2.5 billion and Sun Company's buying of Texas Pacific Oil ($2 billion), both in 1980. Also, DuPont purchased Continental Oil Company (Conoco) for $6.8 billion; Elf Aquitaine bought Texasgulf (for $2.7 billion), Sohio/Kennecott ($1.8 billion), and Fluor/St. Joe Minerals ($2.3 billion), all in 1981.

In the following year, 1982, Marathon Oil was purchased by U.S. Steel (now USX) for $6.2 billion; Connecticut General merged with INA to form CIGNA ($4.3 billion); and Baldwin merged with United/MGIC ($1.2 billion). In 1983 came Santa

Fe Industries' merger with Southern Pacific ($2.3 billion) and Allied's buy-out of Bendix for $1.8 billion.

In 1984, Chevron acquired Gulf Oil for $13.3 billion; and Texaco bought Getty Oil for $10.1 billion and Beatrice/EsMark for $2.7 billion. Three big deals took place in 1985, with Royal Dutch/Shell acquiring the remaining 30.5 percent of Shell Oil for $5.7 billion, Philip Morris taking control of General Foods ($5.6 billion), and Triangle Industries acquiring National Can and American Can for $1 billion (the latter in the 1985–86 time frame).

There was not to be another single takeover of more than $10 billion till 1988; but, some big deals occurred in 1986, Kohlberg Kravis Roberts acquired Beatrice in an LBO for $6.3 billion; General Electric bought RCA for $6.1 billion, as well as Wells Fargo/Crocker National Bank ($1.1 billion); May Department Stores/Associated Dry Goods ($2/4 billion); News Corp/Metromedia ($2 billion); and Honeywell acquired Sperry Aerospace for $1 billion.

In 1987, British Petroleum purchased the remaining 45 percent of Sohio for $7.6 billion; a group led by Merrill Lynch acquired Borg Warner LMO for $4.4 billion, Gran Metropolitan/Heublin ($1.1 billion), and Blue Arrow/Manpower ($1.3 billion). The Campeau/Allied Stores and Federated Department Stores deal spread over three years, 1986, 1987, 1988, and involved $10.1 billion.

Then, in 1988, Philip Morris bought Kraft for $12.6 billion and in 1989 came the biggest LBO of them all: Kohlberg Kravis Roberts acquired RJR Nabisco in a neck-to-neck race against a management buy-out supported by Shearson and Salomon Brothers for $24.7 billion; while Bristol-Myers merged with Squibb in a $12.5 billion affair.

In the span of one decade, the 1980s, $1.3 trillion was spent on assets that changed hands mostly through leveraged deals. This is an amount at par with the annual economic output for West Germany, or equal to more than one quarter the gross national product of the United States.

Not all these mergers and acquisitions worked out. One that did was the General Electric/RCA merger; one that didn't, the Campeau/Federated Department Stores merger. Though there are no fast and hard rules, the chief executives of the corporations that fared the best planned their takeovers meticulously and focused on an efficient integration of the acquired assets.

Are M and A good or bad for the economy? Many people disagree on their effects. Some argue that as a result of mergers and acquisitions, the U.S. companies are leaner and meaner than they were at the start of the 1980s; others say mergers are a two-edged sword, because as companies take on more leverage to feed the increasing expectations of their new owners, the economy is put at risk.

Long-term statistics seem to show (though not conclusively) that bad M and A deals may outweigh good ones. The sheer weight of too much leverage is having a visible negative impact on long-term investment and competitiveness.

As far as the fate of the companies themselves, it is still too early to tell how the chips will fall; nevertheless, at least two indicators suggest that there may be no easy ride in the 1990s. One of these is the crisis that started in the junk bond market, and in which $200 billion[2] is now at stake. (As of February 1990), the default rate had reached an estimated 10 percent.)

Another, more subtle indicator is the currently hot profession of turnaround consulting, which involves rescuing troubled companies, particularly those that have been overleveraged.

The moment it becomes a massive business, turnaround consulting is going to be of dubious value. There is, however, no denying that lack of focus, not to mention strategy, is found in the background of many M and A failures. Another critical issue is price; companies that overpayed made a bad deal. Merger experts note that the better the acquiring management understands the business of the acquired company, the less likely it is to overpay.

At the same time, it is true that a seemingly good price can become a bad one quickly if the M and A deal is rushed and salient problems are overlooked. Making an acquisition demands attention to detail and a proper evaluation of the integration of the new business. Success does not come automatically.

If there is a lesson to be learned from the events of the 1980s, it is that charging headlong into unfamiliar territory is the best way to invite failure. Nevertheless, when greed is involved at the beginning of a major acquisition, there is generally no analysis of synergy along product or market lines; there is only leveraged money to be invested somewhere for quick profits—or ready cash to be hidden.

In 1974, when the oil industry was responding to critics' charges of overly high profits by saying that it had to reinvest in the search for new oil, Mobil Corporation put up $1.8 billion to buy Montgomery Ward and Container Corporation of America. Neither acquisition worked well, and in 1988, with energy prices low, Mobil geared up to sell a revitalized Montgomery Ward for at least $1.5 billion.

But this extracurricular deal proved to be in no way profitable to Mobil. Montgomery Ward limped along in the early 1980s, surviving only because the new parent pumped in $609 million. Then, in 1985, Mobil took a $508 million write-down to restructure Ward, driving its own corporate profits lower by 18 percent. And with intervening inflation, the proceeds from Montgomery Ward's sale were not what they would have been in 1974.

Exxon fared little better in the 1970s when it jumped on to an acquisitions merry-go-round with the aim of diversifying into electronics and business equipment. The office automation companies that it bought ran out of talent and out of the market, as their original promoters resented Exxon's stringent management control.

This is precisely what happened with Zylog, one of the best chip companies of its time, after it fell into Exxon's net; and with Rolm, after it slid into IBM's. Many entrepreneurial start-up firms have been victims of subsequent acquisitions by large corporations; size squeezes talent out.

Mergers and acquisitions do not necessarily fare well even when there is a seeming product line compatibility. In September 1983, Manufacturers Hanover Trust (MHTC), the fourth-largest U.S. bank, bought CIT Financial Corporation from RCA for $1.51 billion. Up to this time, no bank holding company had spent as much on one acquisition. There were two reasons for this purchase. One was that MHTC, being mainly a wholesaler, wanted to expand its product line. (CIT addresses itself to the small consumer.) The other was that, as an MHTC executive put it at the time, "CIT covers the U.S. and practically doubles our number of branches."[3]

With the agreement to buy CIT, MHTC added more than $7 billion to its $63.3 billion in total assets and saw its nonbank subsidiaries account for 20 percent of total earnings.

In topology, as well, having CIT's business increased Manufacturers Hanover's reach. The acquired company raised most of its funds on the west coast, in the Southwest and in Georgia, while Manufacturers Hanover's financial base has traditionally been in New York. MHTC thus had good reasons to make its purchase, and CIT was profitable from the start. Nevertheless, five years later Manufacturers Hanover sold CIT. What happened?

MHTC sold CIT because it was strapped for cash. The grounds for disinvestment were different than the reasons for purchase, but the arguments that were advanced in favor of acquisition were no longer heard, which implies that management had not necessarily abided by its own plan.

A valid merger (of the mid 1980s) was Wells Fargo's merger with Crocker National, which paired the British owner's desire to disinvest with Wells Fargo's need to consolidate market share. This deal became a success because Wells Fargo's management moved fast to integrate the two banks; thus, while revenue growth at Wells Fargo trailed other Western banks prior to the merger, it picked up afterwards.

3. The Business of Mergers and Acquisitions

If fees are wed as a frame of reference, mergers and acquisitions are a lucrative business for an investment bank. Sometimes a similar statement can be made about an acquiring company, but in many cases, M and A involves commitments that, when the chips are down, have more negative than positive aftermaths.

Among the better deals, RJR Nabisco (prior to being itself subject to an LBO) sold Grand Met at a bargain price to Heublein, one of its not-so-profitable operations. The acquirer turned Grand Met into the world's largest purveyor of wine and spirits; as a result, Heublein's profits grew twice as fast as before.

Quaker Oats also found the business of acquisition to be a lucrative one; after the firm acquired Stokely-Van Camp, it sold off everything except the firm's canned pork and beans and Gatorade sports drink, then focused on these two operations. After some ingenious marketing on Quaker's part, Gatorade registered in 1989 an annual operating profit of about $125 million, a fifth of Quaker's total.

In more wheeling-and-dealing fashion, Triangle Industries, a maker of wire and pinball games, bought American Can and National Can for $1 billion. It then achieved economies of scale and sold out to Pechiney, a French chemicals company, for $3.7 billion.

This deal, which spanned the 1985-to-1989 time frame, is reminiscent of another that took place in the early 1950s. Kaiser-Frazer, an automaker with huge operating losses, obtained a loan from the Bank of America and bought Willys, a very profitable jeep manufacturer. Subsequently, the two companies merged and Kaiser recovered from the U.S. government the taxes that were paid by Willys; it then used this money to pay off the bank loan while the assets of Willys remained the property of Kaiser.

Unfortunately, many acquisitions will not fill the roster of financial success stories. Britain's Blue Arrow (whose annual revenues were $500 million) bought Manpower, a company over twice its size. Management clashes and faltering earnings dashed hopes of a global organization in employment services. As a result, in early 1990 the company's stock traded at half the price of the shares floated to finance the deal.

Even an acquisition that seems to perfectly complement an existing product line may turn sour. Rumor on Wall Street has it that Honeywell never really studied the books of the aerospace unit of Sperry before buying it. Overruns on defense contracts and other woes cost $185 million in 1988 alone, and the company has had to restructure in order to placate angry shareholders.

In similar fashion, top management at LTV failed to achieve the efficiencies it needed after the acquisition of Republic Steel. As a result, when steel prices fell, LTV's annual interest bill of $300 million became unmanageable, and LTV went into Chapter 11 bankruptcy.

Again, Pan American acquired National Airlines on the assumption that National's domestic flights would feed passengers into Pan Am's international routes. However, Pan Am seems to have been ill-equipped to run a short-hop domestic schedule; this situation was compounded by a recession and damaging feuds between the airlines' unions. The result was that Pan Am's business steadily deteriorated.

Strapped for cash, Pan Am sold its lucrative Pacific route to United Airlines. Up to a point, this was a profitable deal for United; since the merger, the Pacific traffic of United Airlines has grown by 22 percent (although domestic traffic has been shrinking). Such growth has meant good profits; Pacific route margins are double those of United's flights in America.

But in 1989, United Airlines itself became the target of an LBO. Wall Street initially thought that UA would sail through its buy-out, which was being paid for mostly by $7.2 billion in loans; but, there was nothing in United's past history of acquisitions (Hertz, Western Hotels) to justify such optimism.

As securities analysts examined the proposed deal more closely, they began to see that the new owners might easily find themselves struggling to prevent United's slide into second-class status. As a result, the banks backed out and this LBO never materialized; however, when it fell through (in October 1989) it created a 200-point drop in the Dow-Jones index.

In mid-1989 USX Corporation (formerly United States Steel) came under pressure to restructure and possibly split the steel-and-energy company into its major components to avoid hostile takeover bids. Management, however, disavowed any intention to sell its steel division, even as it moved increasingly into the energy line, which by 1988 amounted to 58.6 percent of business as opposed to 0 percent 10 years earlier (see Figure 10.1).

Securities analysts suggest that if the steel unit of USX is sold, the separate steel and energy operations could be run quite profitably, despite some problems on the steel side; they also suggest that a spin-off of the steel unit is inevitable. This is a far cry from 1982, when the chairperson of U.S. Steel was asked why he bought Marathon Oil instead of building a new steel plant, and he responded, "If we were borrowing for a steel plant, we would not be able to pay (the money) back."[4]

Figure 10.1 The Business of USX Corporation in the Late 1970s and Ten Years Later

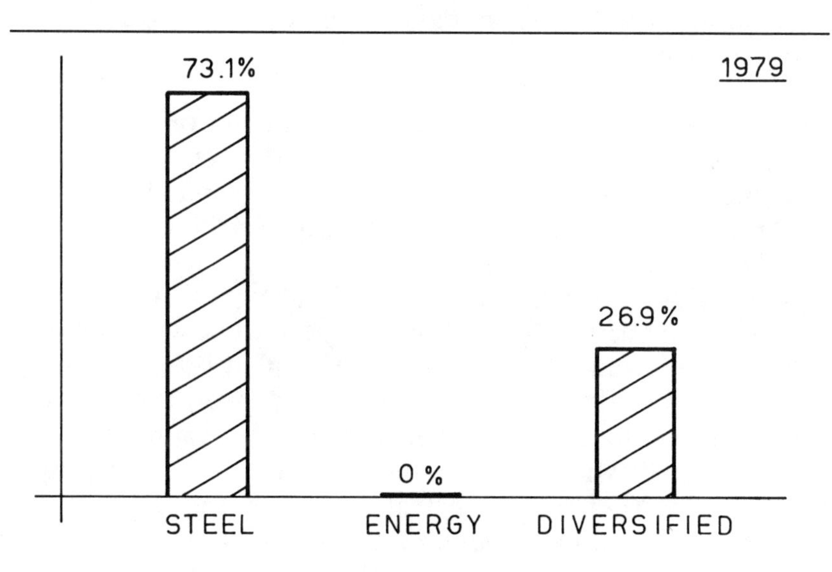

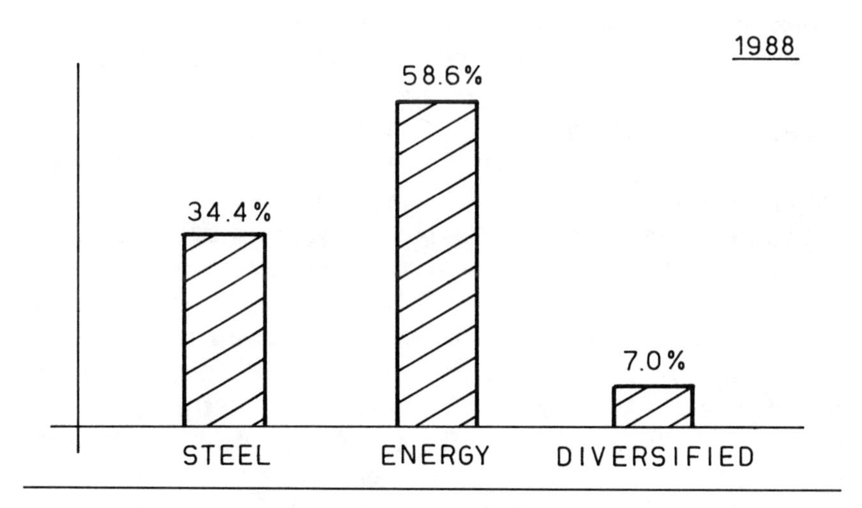

Acquisitions can also run into trouble when they are made cross-border. Avis Europe provides an object lesson in how transnational problems can have significant effects on a deal's ultimate cost.

For about three years, until mid-1989, Avis Europe was an independent company that had been spun off from its parent when the American rental-car concern underwent a leveraged buy-out. Then, a consortium of Avis (US), General Motors and Lease International (a Belgian company) decided to acquire Avis Europe in a $1.6-billion transaction.

By the end of 1989, Avis owned about 9 percent, GM, 26 percent, and Lease International, 65 percent of Avis Europe. But in order to acquire this company, and at the same time allow for a healthy increase in working capital, the consortium decided to arrange a permanent loan of about $2.5 billion; this is where the trouble started. The consortium's headquarters (hence the logical source of the debt) is in London; however, British interest rates are around 15 percent, 5 percentage points higher than those in France and 6 percentage points higher than those in West Germany, where much of the income to service the debt will be generated.

The consortium also thought that it would minimize its exposure to currency fluctuations if the debt was more equally distributed across the Continent and serviced with local currencies. Unfortunately, each of the twelve countries Avis Europe operates in has a different set of laws governing how much debt can be assumed by a local subsidiary and how much interest they will allow to be deducted from corporate taxes.

As 1992, the year of the projected European integration, approaches, many of these legal and accounting nightmares might fade but it is far from certain that everything will be normalized. Recent discussions about a common currency may eventually lead to a simpler deal-making environment; nevertheless, this is not yet done, and the acquisition of a company that operates in even two or three Common Market countries may result in many problems.

Interestingly enough, to facilitate the Avis transaction, Lazard Freres designed a computer model that could figure out the optimal placement of the debt to minimize taxes, could experiment with and maximize the effect of lower interest rates, and could avoid running afoul of corporate laws on currency and dividend outflows.

The solution that has been provided by this simulator, after nearly ten weeks of analysis, seems to have been the equivalent of ten leveraged buyouts. This is a pertinent example of how much high technology banks need to contend with market complexities and requirements.

4. Bridge Loans: A Challenging Environment for the Intermediary

Business Week commented that few dared challenge Lewis T. Preston's wisdom when in the early 1980s, the former chairman of J.P. Morgan began steering the bank into investment banking.[5] Success has proved to be elusive, however.

J.P. Morgan has spent millions in its efforts to transform itself into a merchant bank. By recruiting in-house, it built up its own inventory of deal specialists, but not without incurring significant costs. Staff salaries and bonuses totaled $1.1 billion in 1988 alone, almost double what they were in 1985; nevertheless, corresponding profits did not result, and today the mergers-and-acquisitions business in the U.S. is no longer what it once was.

Internal staff costs are only one side of the story. In a complex LBO an investment house may also seek outside advice or retain other investment banks to keep them from acting as competitors. Authors Bryan Burrough and John Helyar estimate that Kohlberg Kravis Roberts incurred nearly $400 million in costs (including the money they paid to lawyers and to retain firms such as Morgan Stanley and Wasserstein Perella) in their bid for RJR Nabisco.[6]

There are also risks involved in acting as an intermediary; in November 1989, a Delaware chancery court questioned Wasserstein Perella's advice that Interco reject a $74-a-share, or $2.7 billion, bid from the Rales brothers. The investment bank had recommended a recapitalization, which kept the existing management in power but proved disappointing to investors.

And did Wasserstein Perella assess values and risks correctly in the purchase of Northwest Airlines' parent company? Along with Bankers Trust, this investment house represented the buyer, a group led by California financier Alfred Checchi.

When the takeover battle began, Northwest's stock was trading in the high 50s. The opening bid was an offer of $90 a share by Marvin Davis; Wasserstein Perella advised its client to offer $121 per share all cash, and the deal was done. As a result, Checchi paid 35 percent over the original hostile bid and more than twice the value the stock market had placed on the company.[7]

While it earns a big fee from advising on M and A, an investment bank may also have to sustain hefty losses if the acquisition turns sour. One problem is the bridge loans made to tide clients over while they try to sell bonds or get more permanent financing for deals.

In order to facilitate the client's deal, the bank puts up its own capital as a way of closing the gap between the offer being made and the time it actually has to be funded.

The hope is that by the time of funding, the investment bank will have placed much of, if not all of, the debt with bond buyers. The proceeds of the sale of bonds are expected to pay the bridging loan; if the investment bank leaves some of its capital in the deal, the proceeds will pay part of it.

But it does not always work that way, as the example of First Boston shows. As of early 1990, the bank stood with some

$1.1 billion in bridging loans that resulted in what management called "an undisclosed earnings adjustment."

The Campeau acquisitions where First Boston calculates its exposure in the Chapter 11 filings at $293 million are not the only problem. The investment house also has bridge loans to Ohio Mattress—a deal that went under because of the collapse of the junk-bond market. Another sore point is its bridge loan to Medical International.

At one time, the bridge loan seemed like a great way to make money. Now it looks more like a financial form of Russian roulette, and a number of investment bankers blame Michael R. Milken for its invention. This is not because Drexel Burnham Lambert pioneered them but because, Drexel competitors argue, they themselves need a way to assure clients that they could complete offers as Drexel was able to do with junk bonds.

A bridging loan can mean profits to a bank, but also inordinate risk. In their unsuccessful bid for RJR Nabisco, Shearson Lehman Hutton and its partners were ready to risk $5 billion of their own money in a short-term bridging loan. If the loan was later refinanced by selling off an equivalent quantity of junk bonds to insurance companies, thrifts, mutual funds, pension funds and others, Shearson could expect more than $250 million in fees; but if the market turned away and the bridge loan was not refinanced, Shearson would have had to carry the debt in a way similar to the way First Boston has had to carry Campeau's.

Shaky bridge loans have brought Wall Street firms near the crisis point. Low liquidity, rising interest rates, worries over inflation—which played a role in the late January 1990 bond collapse—initially hit the weakest strata of the market in which junk bonds and bridge loans lie.

A good deal of the problem comes from the fact that most of the aggressive acquisitions-oriented companies are overleveraged. The Campeau Corp. owes millions of dollars not only to First Boston, but also to Paine Webber and Dillon Read, to a total of $400 million. These bridge loans, securities analysts say, helped Campeau spend too much in buying Federated Department Stores. And as Shearson Lehman Hutton prepares to sell stock to raise capital, Wall Street is worried about Shearson's $500 million bridge loan to Prime Computer.

Of course, bridge loans are not the only way to lose money. Consumer, real estate, and business loans can also turn bad when they escape management control and supervision. One recent case in real estate is that of the Bank of New England (BNE). In January 1990 it disclosed that fourth-quarter 1989 losses could reach $1.2 billion, offsetting a $74-million profit just a year earlier.

At BNE, nonperforming loans, mostly sour real estate credits, are estimated at $2.3 billion; but the bank seems to be suffering largely from self-inflicted wounds. Lending standards were lax in many cases, according to *Business Week*.[8] This was not the bank's only problem, either. Sloppy recordkeeping obscured the growing lending problems; lines of authority and responsibility were blurred; and management overexpanded without the appropriate infrastructure to go with it.

The whole business started with important mergers and acquisitions activity. Between 1987 and 1989, BNE set out to acquire community banks that were pushing for double-digit loan growth. Over these three years it acquired fourteen banks and thrifts, and these purchases did not come at bargain prices.

One of BNE's bigger deals was Conifer Group, a holding company with six community banks. GNE offered $656 million for Conifer, a full $100 million more than the next-highest bid from Fleet/Norstar Financial Group of Providence. Done in a rush, the acquisitions proved difficult to digest. As a result, too many people became involved in loan approvals, while few took overall responsibility for making sure borrowers were qualified.

In a way reminiscent of other acquisition deals that have gone sour, each acquired bank apparently kept its own lending standards and computer systems, making it difficult to follow deposits, loans, and other business in an integrative sense. That made it tough for headquarters to monitor business and created a bookkeeping nightmare.

Thus, uncontrolled growth, as well as mergers and acquisitions which cannot be digested, is hazardous to any company's health. If this is compounded by vulnerability stemming from leverage, a company could end up with bad debts and a tarnished reputation.

5. The Restructuring of Investment Banking

At the end of 1987, Shearson Lehman Brothers acquired E.F. Hutton in a cash-and-stock transaction valued at about $1 billion, or about $600 million less than what Shearson had offered for the ailing concern in 1986. At that time, Hutton, seeking $55 a share, had rejected the $50-a-share offer as inadequate; following the October 1987 stockmarket collapse, however, it settled for less than 60 percent of what it had been originally bid.

Was Shearson Lehman's move wise? At first sight, it paid what looked like a bargain price. "There would be enormous economies of scale gained in merging Hutton in Shearson," said Jeffrey B. Lane, then president of Shearson,[9] after observing Hutton's large retail system. But the bargain-price argument ignores the fact that after the October 1987 crash, the New York stock market was no longer the same place. The ranks of private investors had thinned out, and Hutton's problems had mounted over the couple previous years. Its untarnished image was blackened by a guilty plea in 1985 to 2,000 felony counts stemming from a check-kiting scheme.

It also suffered from high overhead costs, costly trading setbacks, and a persistent inability to build an investment banking business to complement its retail brokerage operation.

Hutton's earnings had slumped, and so did the growth of its capital, but Shearson/American Express was still living on the laurels of the Lehman merger, and the gathering storm did not attract serious management attention in time to stop overexposure.

Prior to the Hutton acquisition, securities analysts on Wall Street had focused on the news that private investment houses like Kuhn Loeb and Lehman Brothers decided to sell out—in effect, trading independence for money. It was an omen of sorts, with Lehman's sell-out further reducing the already small number of old-line private investment houses. Table 10.1 shows how investment banks and brokerage houses stood in 1984 right after the Shearson/Lehman merger.

There is another side to the argument that a merger is lucrative. First, in their rush into the investment and M and A market, many large acquiring companies (such as large retailers) have been learning that it is difficult to manage businesses in which they have little expertise. Sometimes they cannot even exploit the strengths of the unit that they buy.

Sears, Roebuck encountered trouble selling its customers the financial products of Dean Witter Reynolds, which it acquired in 1981. A mailing to some 19 million Sears cardholders in January 1982 generated only 1,000 new Individual Retirement Accounts for the brokerage. "It was not a very successful program," Dean Witter's chairman, Robert M. Gardiner, observed.[10] (Yet Sears was extremely successful in a domain which it knew well—that of the Discover credit card.)

A merger in the financial business yields the best results when the acquired company is well-run already or when the new parent has the in-house talent to turn it around. More-

Table 10.1 Wall Street's Largest Companies Ranked by Total Capital as of Early 1984

	Total Capital in Millions of Dollars Rounded to the Nearest $10 million
Merrill Lynch*	$2,030
Shearson Lehman (1)	1,700
Salomon Brothers (2)	1,270
Dean Witter (3)	970
E.F. Hutton*	750
Goldman Sachs**	720
Prudential-Bache (4)	500
Paine Webber*	450
Bear Stearns**	420
Drexel Burnham Lambert**	410
First Boston*	410
Donaldson, Lufkin & Jenrette*	340

(1) Subsidiary of American Express
(2) Subsidiary of Phibro-Solomon
(3) Subsidiary of Sears
(4) Subsidiary of Prudential Insurance
* Public company
** Private company

over, merging alien corporate cultures requires a strong leader who can push the companies together and pool their strengths.

Besides, regulatory authorities and the government have a word or two to say regarding such mergers. In the stages of building Shearson Loeb Rhodes into a large brokerage house, then chief executive Sanford I. Weill got a routine call from the Justice Department inquiring into possible antitrust violations in his latest merger. "Can I tape this call?" asked Weill. "Of course, but why?" was the response. "Because I want my mother to hear that I'm doing something big enough for the U.S. government to be interested in," replied Weill.[11]

Another fact often forgotten in the restructuring of investment banking is that while venerable firms like Loeb Rhodes had prospered, racking up record profits and turning partners into multimillionaires, as the financial-services industry underwent a massive change, the grand old houses that once dominated investment banking were pushed into a secondary role. In fact, the demand for more capital and the fragility of financial partnerships sent some of these firms into the arms of a rich corporation or encouraged them to go public.

Other ways, too, were tried. Credit Suisse got its stake in First Boston through an unusual joint venture agreement in 1978. Ten years later First Boston and Credit Suisse came toward the merger of the London-based Credit Suisse First Boston (CSFB) with the U.S. firm. "The substance of these discussions is fusion rather than fission," said a person privy to them. "Divorce is too costly for both sides and the status quo is seen as unworkable long-term."

Nevertheless, there still remained some doubt about a number of legal and financial problems in the aftermath of this move. "If we do a deal, it will be the most complicated merger First Boston has done for anybody," said a senior official at the firm, as Credit Suisse increased its 24-percent hold on First Boston.[12]

Generally, investment bank acquisitions work if they

1. reduce costs per unit of output,

2. help control risks,
3. improve overall management, and
4. result in new products with market appeal.

Rarely have all four factors come together, and certainly not in the Shearson environment and in many others. But investment bank restructuring does leave an impact on the financial industry as a whole. In the early to mid-1980s, some experts speculated that in the future Wall Street would be divided between two types of firms—huge financial conglomerates that offer a full range of financial services (the so-called financial supermarkets) and small firms (called boutiques) that specialize in a narrow range of activities.

Between these two poles were private investment banks, which were under constant pressure to decide which road to take. Growing big required enormous sums of capital, the kind that becomes available only by joining a larger organization or by going public. But securities analysts suggested that these firms could stay small and by staying within their own niche of services, profit handsomely. Lazard Freres followed this strategy and now prospers.

Throughout the 1980s, the financial industry evolved toward firms that would provide both investment banking and distribution capability under one roof. This meant having both capital resources and investment banking expertise.

Those that did not offer these two types of service are now in a hurry been to get them. For example, Wasserstein Perella, as opposed such full-service firms such as Morgan Stanley or Salomon Brothers, has been centered on M and A dealmaking, with little backup in trading and no distribution network for securities.

Acknowledging this imbalance, the firm hired junk-bond salespeople from Salomon Brothers and opened offices in Los

Angeles, Houston, London and Tokyo. In order to help pay them, it sold 20 percent of its equity to Nomura Securities.

It is also important to retain the best of the staff after a merger. "The income generators are going to be treated with respect at Bache," wrote the newly appointed CEO George L. Ball in a corporate-wide memo after the Prudential purchase. "Preach the message," he exhorted managers. "Next practice it. Third, warn once, and the next time—nicely but firmly—replace recalcitrant workers. We have no safe harbors for the inept...."

Wisely, in the Bache case, there was no intervention in the newly acquired broker by the seasoned insurance executives of Prudential. This was probably done in the belief that insurance and brokerage have different cultures; that is, brokerage houses attract fast-moving risk-takers, while insurance draws managers who like security.

The acquiring company may also have some egos to accommodate. Organized either as a partnership or as a private corporation, private investment firms generally follow some type of partnership structure. Many creative, entrepreneurial people are attracted to the freedom in partnerships.

There may also be some wounds to heal when a merger takes place. The sale of Lehman Brothers appears to have resulted from internal strife that had become so bad that it crippled the effectiveness of the firm. A team that once banded together can easily split into warring factions as the pressures and pace of business increased.

One looks at which investment houses are gone and which survived, more often than not the deciding factor has been not capital considerations, but the human element. Hence, people must be well-treated after a merger. If firms do a good job of managing their human capital, they will survive. Those that do not, will disappear altogether, or into the fold of larger, more successful financial corporations.

6. Bank Takeovers

The $1.3 billion (about $2.1 billion) surprise bid by Lloyds Bank for Standard Chartered, the international group, was the largest in the history of British banking. It was also the first major hostile bid bankers had ever seen. The merger would have turned Lloyds from the smallest into the biggest of the British Big Four, with combined assets of around £105 billion ($170 billion), and operations in an international domain sweeping from the Orient to the Americas, and from Europe to Africa and Australia. The bid failed as Standard Chartered's three white knights, Sir Y.K. Pao from Hong Kong, Tan Sri Khoo from Malaysia, and Robert Holmes a Court from Australia, came to the rescue, buying up 19 percent of Standard Chartered shares just three days before the Lloyds offer closed.

"The acquisition of Standard Chartered would have made us the leading trade finance bank in the world," said Lloyds Bank's chief executive, Brian Pitman. "That was really why we were interested in it."[13] It was part of a strategy to survive in the savagely competitive world of banking and financial services, Lloyds' solution has been to concentrate on sizeable markets in which it can achieve leadership; these markets were in international trade finance.

Mergers with other banks are not necessarily a solution to a bank's problems, either. In the early 1980s, Mellon Bank's acquisition of Girard Bank brought more problems than Mellon's management bargained for.

Since it was founded in the nineteenth century, the Mellon bank has been entrenched in Pittsburgh's economic heart. But market changes sent its major smokestack customers into the doldrums, and the developing needs of its traditional customers forced it to devise new strategies.

With the advent of deregulation, Mellon decided to buy the venerable but troubled Gerard bank in Philadelphia. Because of Gerard's outstanding problems, the move sent Mellon's profitability tumbling. Its balance sheet, once one of the strongest of any U.S. bank's, fell below average. Moody's then reduced Mellon's credit rating; its rate of loan losses more than doubled, and the value of its stocks lagged behind its Pennsylvania rivals.

This put Mellon at disadvantage as a new round of acquisitions began and the major American banks struggled to expand in a highly competitive financial environment.

In 1986, securities analysts said that Mellon Bank was losing market share, particularly after some of Girard's small and medium-sized corporate customers took their accounts elsewhere. At the same time, management correctly perceived that Mellon had to be equipped to compete against the New York money center banks in providing sophisticated investment-banking services to big companies (Mellon Bank's traditional customer base).

At the same time, Mellon was by no means a troubled bank. It is the 11th-largest U.S. banking company with nearly $40 billion in assets. It dominates financial services in the Pittsburgh area, and its balance sheet is basically strong.

Mellon's acquisitions strategy started in 1983 and was based on two pillars; one was new market orientation. Though it did not plan to abandon institutional clients, management wanted to broaden the bank's base of consumer deposits, which are government-insured and pose no liquidity threat.

As a result, Mellon decided to grow geographically, particularly in the lucrative mid-Atlantic area, believing that it would be easier and less expensive to do so through mergers.

Girard, with its strong retail position in Philadelphia, offered that opportunity, and so too did the other Pennsylvania banks (CCB Bancorporation, Citizens National Bank, Commonwealth National Bank, and First National Bank of Mapleton) that Mellon acquired just after the Girard merger. Acquired between September 1983 and November 1986, these smaller banks added $2.8 billion in assets and $2 billion in deposits.

The longer-term goal was to become one of the five most profitable big banks in the U.S. In contrast to the widespread retrenchment among financial institutions trying to enhance profitability, at Mellon top management launched a hard-driving growth strategy—but with the acquisitions in hand Mellon was discovering that growth can be costly.

Numerous departures of executives from Girard Bank in Philadelphia blunted Mellon's thrust into the eastern end of its home state. In Pittsburgh, Mellon's backyard, unemployed steelworkers staged demonstrations and poured skunk oil in the doorways of Mellon branches as retribution, they claimed, for the bank's abandonment of Steel City.[14]

Weighting on Mellon's balance sheets have been expenses related to consolidated acquisitions and the boosting of loan-loss reserves. Once Philadelphia's third-largest bank, the Girard Bank (now Mellon East) suffered from merger pains a year and a half after being acquired. Financial analysts also suggested that Girard Bank was a hornets' nest of delinquent loans. "Girard was in much worse shape than Mellon thought," said one banker. "They miscalculated."

Mellon's profitability dropped sharply after the Girard acquisition. The Mellon Bank's primary capital, a gauge of a bank's basic financial strength, has long been one of the strongest among big American banks. But other financial institutions increased their primary capital at a faster pace than Mellon did in its postmerger years.

Mellon is not the only example of bank mergers that did not work out as planned. In the 1970s Chase Manhattan suffered losses from its involvement with Drysdale Government Securities. According to some estimates made at the time, losses stood at $285 to $310 million—and resulted in large part from the liquidation of the U.S. Government securities positions that was necessary when Drysdale failed to pay the interest it owed on these funds.

By borrowing securities and lending on them again, Drysdale had built up a loan portfolio estimated at more than $4 billion. Subsequently, Wall Street was shaken when it emerged that Drysdale defaulted on a substantial interest payment due on this portfolio. Chase, arguing that it had acted as an agent rather than a principal in the transactions, initially refused to accept liability for Drysdale's debts; however, it later changed its mind and took on the liabilities, while reserving the option to take whatever steps it could to recover any part of its losses.

Mergers are a means for consolidation in banking, and while the examples just mentioned have negative overtones, the bottom line is that consolidation within the banking industry seems inevitable. Given the changing financial conditions, bank mergers are expected to gain substantial momentum in the 1990s.

A consensus prediction sees the number of banks in the U.S. declining by approximately one third; it is also estimated that more than one-half of all banks will be involved in consolidation, either as acquirers or targets.

As might be expected, this attrition will greatly affect small banks, while the number of medium-size banks also is expected to contract. Consequently, total bank assets will become more heavily concentrated in large banks.

Sometimes mergers and acquisitions happen by necessity. When in August 1990 the National Bank of Washington became insolvent, federal authorities welcomed a bid by Washington's Riggs National Bank to take it over.

In 1991, the same thing happened with GNE.[15] Since New England's third-largest bank has been in the hands of federal regulators, Bank of America, Banc One, and several foreign financial institutions have all expressed interest in its acquisition.

Opinion on Wall Street has it that the most attractive acquisition candidates are banks with a strong retail base, statewide or regional market coverage, and marked potential for earnings growth. An additional attractive characteristic is a sound middle-market commercial loan portfolio. These business traits suggest that medium-size regional banks will be the most appealing to suitors.

The basic hypothesis behind these estimates is that size will permit powerful financial service empires to provide the cheapest and most varied services to consumers. Consolidation and growing competition will ensure that the walls between banking, insurance, and brokerage crumble. Competition will become international as regulatory barriers are dismantled and market-driven economies look for greater operational efficiency. But as these examples have shown, mergers and operational efficiency are not necessarily one and the same thing.

7. Partnerships and Acquisitions Made to Improve the Product Line

In 1978, LTV, the owner of Jones and Laughlin Steel, bought Lykes Corp., the parent of bankruptcy-bound Youngstown Sheet & Tube. The deal was greeted with derision. "That is not a merger," said a securities analyst at that time. "It is a suicide pact." But then LTV chairman Paul Thayer seemed to have seen some things others had missed.

Youngstown's modern and underused Indiana Harbor plant, in East Chicago, took some of the burden off J and L's Cleveland plant, which at the time was straining to meet demand. A year after the merger, LTV's steel operations earned $171 million; they even made money during some of the industry's roughest times, though LTV itself had major financial troubles. Then came the downturn, and after another ill-judged acquisition (Republic Steel), LTV filed under Chapter 11.

Stroh Brewing Company had new markets in mind when it bought control of the ailing F and M Schaefer Corp. Burdened by a mountain of debt, Schaefer operated in the red two out of the five years prior to the acquisition; but it owned a large, efficient brewery in Pennsylvania's Lehigh Valley that was running substantially below capacity. Detroit-based Stroh was to expand to the Northeast, so it could put to use this idle capacity; thus, the acquisition seems to have made sense.

Buying performing assets outside one's industry or area of expertise requires a special breed of businessperson—one with insight, inclination, and a lot of faith. Royal Little, Textron's founder and one of the leading conglomerate builders, once suggested, "I never thought Textron was competent to take over any company and straighten things out. It's fantastic the number of things you can do that don't work."

In May 1982, after the death of C. Laning Hayes Jr., a longtime family adviser, Gordon Getty suddenly found himself sole trustee of the Sarah C. Getty Trust (named for his grandmother). The fund controlled 40 percent of the oil company with the same name. When he began looking at the firm closely, Gordon Getty seems to have concluded that its performance was poor and its stock undervalued.

Getty Oil market price at the start of 1983 was just $48.50 a share. In the first nine months of 1983 profits fell 51 percent, to $225 million. Getty questioned the company's diversification ventures, including those into insurance and cable television. The firm had, in 1979, acquired an interest in the money-losing Entertainment and Sports Programming Network (ESPN) and, in 1980, had purchased the Kansas-based ERC insurance group.

As a result of these findings, Getty Oil joined the list of companies for sale. Texaco, the third-largest oil company in the U.S., snatched fourteenth-ranked Getty from its nearly consumed deal with a much smaller suitor, Pennzoil. Only three days earlier, before Texaco jumped into the bidding, Pennzoil Chairman Hugh Liedtke and Gordon Getty had sealed a $5.2 billion deal to buy Getty Oil's stock jointly for $112.50 a share and make the company a private firm, but then came Texaco's offer of $125 a share.

Pennzoil sued in court and won the case; Texaco nearly went bankrupt in paying damages, and another merger joined the long sick list. Even partnerships that should have been working well are far from successful—yet strategies and alliances that are formed today may well help determine who will be left to fill market niches tomorrow.

AT&T joined forces with Philips of Holland and with Olivetti of Italy in order to break into European markets; then it opted out of Olivetti, swapping its investment for equity in Olivetti's holding, and cooled down its proposed partnership with Philips. Not all expansion plans are followed through.

In order to get the market share and economies of scale that it thought were necessary to maintain technological competence, Philips took management control of West Germany's Grundig. The move was a strategic one against such rivals in consumer electronics as Sony and the Victor Company of Japan. Rolls-Royce and General Electric joined forces to develop a new engine because neither could risk the R and D costs alone.

Both parties can contribute to a partnership, and some of these partnerships can be quite successful. In 1879, Thomas A. Edison teamed up with Corning Glass Works to make his experimental incandescent light bulb. Railroads formed partnerships in the late 1880s for what were at the time large-scale projects in transportation. Whether in the nineteenth century or today, partnerships as well as mergers and acquisitions are driven by the imperative to ensure that at least some activities add value.

To reach a value-added goal and gain efficiency, companies decentralize functions, contract out for some services, turn to specialist suppliers, and reduce the need for themselves to manage activities largely unrelated to their core business. But they also sometimes acquire dead weight through unnecessary acquisitions and convert equity into debt faster than they can feed such debt.

Companies also make projections, not all of which prove to be valid. Any product, even the best, follows a more or less bell-shaped curve in terms of market appeal. In the mid-1980s, one computer manufacturer plotted a graph depicting product curves (see Figure 10.2).

As this graph shows, the decay of some services has taken place as projected. At the same time, the market for both data communications and personal computers (PC) has grown fast; nevertheless, there is no reason to believe that the PC market will be as exponential as projected. There is plenty of wishful thinking in this graph.

From partnerships in product development and marketing to mergers and acquisitions, the goal should be to do more with less by reducing the staff, making fixed costs lower, and clarifying various departments' roles in the business. But when management is lax, as it is in many cases, things do not turn out this way.

There are many examples of corporate collaboration, but all too often experiences fall short of expectations. Joint projects are sometimes too late (as with British Telecom's collaborative telecommunications effort System X) or are abandoned (as was the German and Austrian BMW-Steyr-Daimler-Puch diesel engine project). Many run over budget, particularly defense deals, such as the British, German, and Italian development of the Tornado fighter aircraft.

The Visicorp-Software Arts battle shows the dangers inherent in having one company create a program and having the other sell it. Personality conflicts may contribute to the

Figure 10.2 Product Appeal Tends to Follow a Bell Curve. Exponential Growth Is Just the Beginning of Such Cycles.

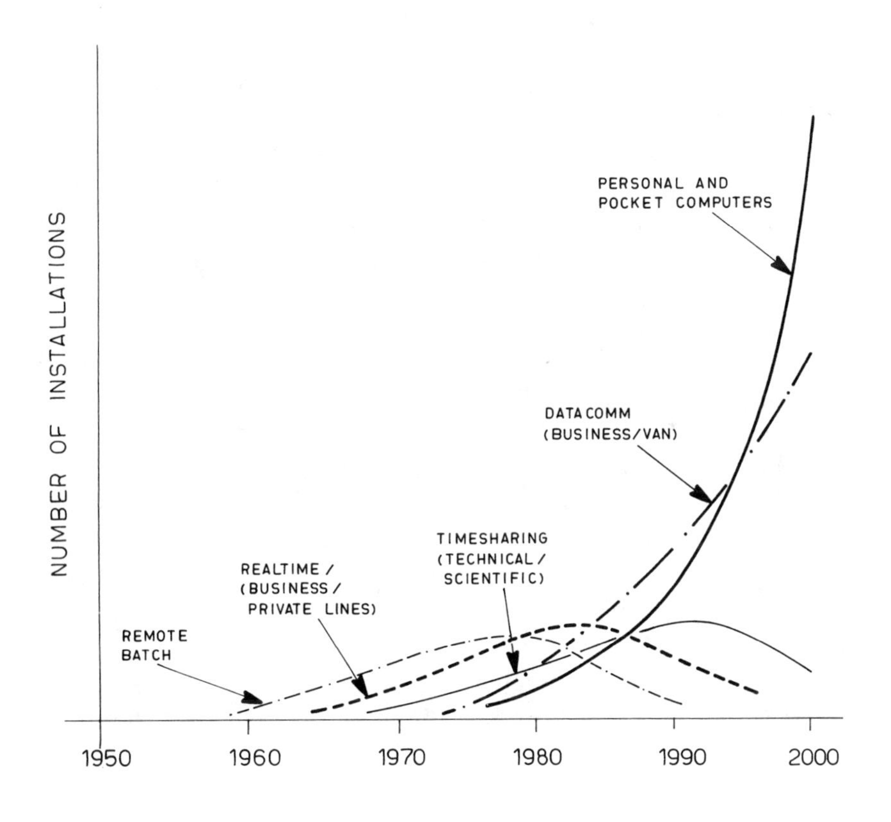

inability of two or more companies to do business together, or the chemistry may simply be wrong.

The Visicalc story begins in 1978, with Daniel Bricklin sitting in classes at the Harvard Business School, watching professors manipulate figures, and having to recalculate many numbers if just one figure changed. He came up with a brilliant idea; he would build an electronic blackboard that could do all the recalculations automatically.

Introduced in October 1979, Visicalc was the world's first spreadsheet program (spreadsheet being a reference to the ledger worksheets used by accountants). Through its appeal to professionals, it changed the nature of the personal computer industry. A subindustry grew up around it as smaller software companies and users of the product devised ways to make Visicalc more helpful; and since Visicalc initially ran only on the Apple-II computer, Apple's sales surged to the lead in the personal computer industry.

The firm's fortunes began to change, however, when Microsoft introduced Multiplan and other players also entered the game. When a Visicorp employee, Mitchell Kapor, formed Lotus Development Corp. and produced the much superior 1–2–3 spreadsheet, sales of Visicalc began to dwindle.

"I think what happened is that success overcame them," said a software industry executive around the time when the relationship between Visicorp and Software Arts began to deteriorate. "They got bogged down in who would take the credit and the money. What is kind of ironic is that by arguing over the golden goose, in essence they ended by killing it."

Endnotes

1. *The Washington Post,* 2 June, 1988.

2. Eventually, however, MHTC resold CIT well before merging with Chemical Banking.

3. Nearly equal to the outstanding loans of Mexico and Brazil, and somewhat more than 50 percent of Third-World debt.

4. *The Dines Letter,* 18 June, 1982.

5. *Business Week,* 29 January, 1990.

6. Bryan Burrough and John Helyar, *Barbarians at the Gate* (New York, NY: Harper and Row, 1990).

7. *Forbes,* 7 August, 1989.

8. *Business Week,* 5 February, 1990.

9. *Business Week,* 7 December, 1988.

10. *Business Week,* 20 December, 1982.

11. *Business Week,* 20 December, 1982.

12. *The Wall Street Journal,* 22 June, 1988.

13. *Management Today,* November 1986.

14. *Business Week,* 24 December, 1984.

15. The Bank of New England was seized January 6, 1991, in a rescue that is likely to cost the federal insurance fund up to $2.3 billion, making it one of the costliest bailouts ever.

Chapter 11

Leveraged Buyouts, Liquidity and Junk Bonds

Chapter 11

Leveraged Buyouts, Liquidity and Junk Bonds

1. Introduction

Mega-deals have created a wave of anxiety in the investment community. Investors are concerned that these debt-financed, multibillion dollar takeovers will put upward pressure on interest rates. Economists worry that the leveraging of corporate America could either worsen any downturn or trigger a recession.

Alan Greenspan, the Chairman of the Federal Reserve Board, says, "The Federal Reserve has been monitoring the LBO and corporate leveraging trends for some time now; both I and my predecessor as Chairman have noted our concerns about the risks that these developments might carry for lenders and the economy more broadly."

One issue that brought the leveraged buy-out (LBO) into prominence is that interest expenses are tax deductible, while dividends are not. Hence, by raising the after-tax cost of equity capital, the current tax system favors debt capital (which is an imbalance that legislators should correct).

In an LBO, an investor uses borrowed funds to buy all of the shares in a publicly owned company. The result is a large amount of debt, which is secured against the assets and the cash flow of the leveraged company. But leveraging carries a high interest cost, and there is no guarantee that cash flow will be able to meet the financial obligations.

One form of LBO currently receiving a lot of attention is the management buy-out (MBO). An MBO is structured the same as an LBO, except that all or part of the management group of a company provides a small equity investment portion in the takeover deal.

Another popular form is the management buy-in (MBI), which emerged during 1988 as a venture capital product. In this case, outside management, together with the MBI's financial backers, obtains boardroom control, significant shareholdings, and usually voting control. The MBI enhances the growth of the target company by providing fresh management and finance; to the quoted group, the opportunity of adding these ingredients to a neglected subsidiary can be attractive if it shows a better return than an outright sale.

MBOs, on the other hand, offer the advantage of retaining continuity of management. For example, in order to avoid a hostile takeover, Safeway, a supermarket chain, agreed in 1986 to be acquired by Kohlberg Kravis Roberts (KKR) in a $5.7 billion buy-out. The deal left the existing management in charge, and offered top managers the right to buy up to 10 percent of the new company.

Immediately after the buy-out, the privatized Safeway had to face a debt of $5.7 billion, which through asset sales, it whittled down to just over $3 billion; nevertheless, total jobs have fallen from 185,000 to 106,000, with the number of stores reduced from 2,330 to 1,160.

An employee stock-ownership plan (ESOP) can be seen as a nonaggressive type of management buy-out. No ESOP gets much attention on its own, but all together they represent a significant shift in leverage in the business world, inasmuch as they are transferring billions of dollars' worth of equity and crucial margins of power to the companies' employees.

Table 11.1 shows the ESOP stake in the some well known deals. Some people hail ESOPs as a new era, while others criticize them as a tactical move by managers, who choose to toss company assets to their employees rather than succumb to a hostile raider, while exploiting tax loopholes in the process. Aside from these criticisms, ESOPs may also present a risk to worker-owners. When Drexel Burnham Lambert went under (in February 1990) the firm's employees, who owned 54 percent of the stock, saw their holdings evaporate.

Table 11.1 ESOP Stake in the Better-Known Deals

Company	*Millions of Dollars*
Avis	$1,750
Healthtrust	1,700
Procter & Gamble	1,000
Epic Healthcare	856
J.C. Penney	700
Anheuser-Busch	500
Texaco	500
U.S. West	500
Polaroid	300

2. The Pros and Cons of LBOs

Leveraged buy-outs have led to the shrinkage of corporate America, a development that has had a profound impact on the financial markets. Most merger negotiations are a form of psychological warfare. Various issues, such as which party is in control, which management has more negotiating power, which changes should be made, and which divisions or subsidiaries should be sold, often depend on the mood of the negotiations, the personalities of the players, the type of financing, even the surroundings.

Immediately after an LBO has taken place, the new owners are left with almost the same entity as before, but assets are sold to reduce debt. Still, this leaves the company highly geared (the British term for "leveraged"), with a huge ratio of borrowing to shareholders' funds because of the large amounts of debt incurred to finance the takeover deal. The funding for leveraged buy-outs is structured in three layers, called equity, mezzanine debt, and senior debt. Only about 10 percent of funding comes from the buyer itself, or equity.

Mezzanine debt, which constitutes about 30 percent of funding, traditionally comes from a handful of major insurance companies, whose commitments might take months to obtain; however, junk bonds will now likely constitute this funding. Senior debt, constituting the rest of the total, is provided by banks.

This structure assures tremendous leverage by inflating balance sheets with high levels of debt, thereby swamping equity, or more precisely, using the assets of the company in order to buy it out.

Leveraged and other buy-outs have reduced the supply of corporate equity by an estimated 25 percent. Equity has become less valuable than debt; equity's traditional function as a claim on a company's future earnings is being replaced by the concept of a potential value in a company's breakup.

Proponents of LBOs say that this is for the best, as debt induces a company to become lean. In many LBOs, the fight for survival has given management the leverage necessary to win concessions from workers. But while increased efficiency is a characteristic of some LBO deals, the overburdening servicing of debt often makes the bottom line worse.

Dr. Merton Miller, 1990 Nobel prize winner in economics, defended LBOs, suggesting that much of the criticism of modern financial practices was based on misunderstandings; he predicted that of the practice would eventually gain acceptance.

Dr. Miller said, "Developments in a lot of the financial markets are much misunderstood. New markets and new developments are always unsettling." He added that leveraged buy-outs have helped to restructure bloated American companies.

There are two sides to the coin. With good reason, opponents of LBOs believe that in the end they will destroy one of industry's great strengths—the capital base. At a time when the U.S. faces stiff competition in world markets, one of its key advantages is being taken away. Instead of creating jobs and new products, management is focusing its attention on paying back debt. The fact is, through the decade of the 1980s there has been a fundamental shift toward new types of investing, including Leveraging and Securitization.

New investment vehicles, such as mortgage-backed financing, usually make it necessary to develop control metrics, such as option against spread (OAS). Similar metrics should be designed to gauge the possible aftermaths of an LBO.

LBOs and securitization are related. Through LBOs, bankers have been converting equity into debt, and debt into a financial instrument that not only has tax advantages, but also provides the bank a fee for matching buyer and seller. Former dividing lines have disappeared; a junk bond, for example, is an equity in the form of a debt with a high dividend but also unsecured repayment of capital.[1]

Even if the high default rate on junk bonds causes them to lose favor, put on the back burner, financial firms will likely continue to develop products to capitalize on new trends. This is particularly true of equity conversion into debt, which boosts takeover capital by 10-to-1 ratio (customary in leveraging).

3. The Fallen Angels Fly Again

When Drexel started trading high-yield, low-grade bonds during the late 1960s, the only junks around were the so-called fallen angels. These were former investment-grade issues that were downgraded when the companies fell into difficulty. Drexel was more or less alone in this market till 1977, when Lehman Brothers and Goldman Sachs underwrote the first bond considered to be "junk," an LTV issue that has since defaulted—after having traded at 35 percent of face value.

A number of factors, including mezzanine debt, junk bond issues and not-so-secured debt by commercial banks, helped to make 1990 a year that corporate America would like to forget. In all, $510 billion in corporate-debt issues were downgraded by Standard & Poor versus $174 billion in 1989. Some $14 billion in issues went into default in 1990, more than five times the level of previous years. Standard & Poor lowered ratings for 411 financial institutions in 1990 and raised a mere 44. (The figures for 1989 were 149 downgrades against 70 upgrades.) Furthermore, the slump in the credit standing of financial institutions badly hurt the credit of state and city governments, many of whose housing issues are backed by banks and insurance companies.

Nevertheless, while junk bonds may be "funny money" they are not necessarily easy money. The key to a successful LBO is using computational finance to create a set of projections; these are cash flow, profits, and sales (in that order). Because they identify the amount of debt a company can safely repay, projections are basic to formulating a bid. The right price means everything to an LBO. The higher the acquisition price is, the higher the debt; and too much debt can crush even the healthiest corporation.

LBO specialists understand very well the risks that leveraged deals entail. If the investment house they hire cannot swiftly market the junk bonds for refinancing, thus retiring the bridge loan, the loan's interest rate grows. If for any reason the broker cannot sell the bonds at all, the acquirer is liable for the entire amount. And since the money is not available, the acquirer is forced to bet the entire deal on whether the investment house that is hired to do the job can unload the bonds.

This effect of leveraging is not usually mentioned, yet it is the reason why as much debt and as little cash as possible is used to purchase a company. The purchaser may be an arbitrageur, the management of the firm itself, or any other entity. No matter who this party may be, its underwriter must have money to see through the deal in case something goes wrong.

Burrough and Helyar make this point in a discussion KKR's business methods:

> They began raising the new fund in June 1987....When the fund closed just four months later, Kravis and Roberts sat atop a $5.6 billion war chest, more than two times the size of its nearest competitor's. Of the estimated $20 billion in equity poised for LBO investments worldwide, the two grandsons of a Russian immigrant controlled one dollar of every four.[2]

Who are the investors that contribute these large sums of money to an LBO? The public perception is that they are wealthy individuals. In fact, wealthy individuals account for a mere 5 percent of the lot. The top two capital providers are mutual funds and insurance companies, to the tune of 30 percent each. These are followed by pension funds, foreign investors, and savings and loans (see Figure 11.1)

And there are other aftermaths of the debt-for-equities swap. David D. Hale, of Kemper Financial Services, estimates that in 1989 some 30 percent of all corporate cash flow was devoted to interest payments—up from 22 percent in 1982. The drain from debt servicing means that companies must scale back on investments for productivity. Profits are getting squeezed by the debt load as well as by rising compensation, which may have something to do with the shortfall in federal taxes.

For this reason, LBOs are taking their toll even among leading firms. Of forty-one corporations that recently dropped out of the top one thousand list of corporate America, five left via LBOs, five were acquired by other companies (three of which are foreign), and thirty-one now possess a market value that is insufficient for their inclusion in the list.

Nevertheless, the 1988 market value of these forty-one firms was over $89 billion, which surpassed that same year's market capitalization of the top 1,000 firms in many countries, including Italy and Switzerland.

How long will LBOs last? Edward Dunne of UBS Securities says, "I see LBOs continuing as long as large amounts can be raised, because many lenders don't understand the risk they are taking. The myth that there will always be liquidity in the junk bond market ends by destroying liquidity in the market as a whole." And it sometimes destroys the companies themselves.

Figure 11.1 Origin of the Contributors to the U.S. Junk Bond Funds

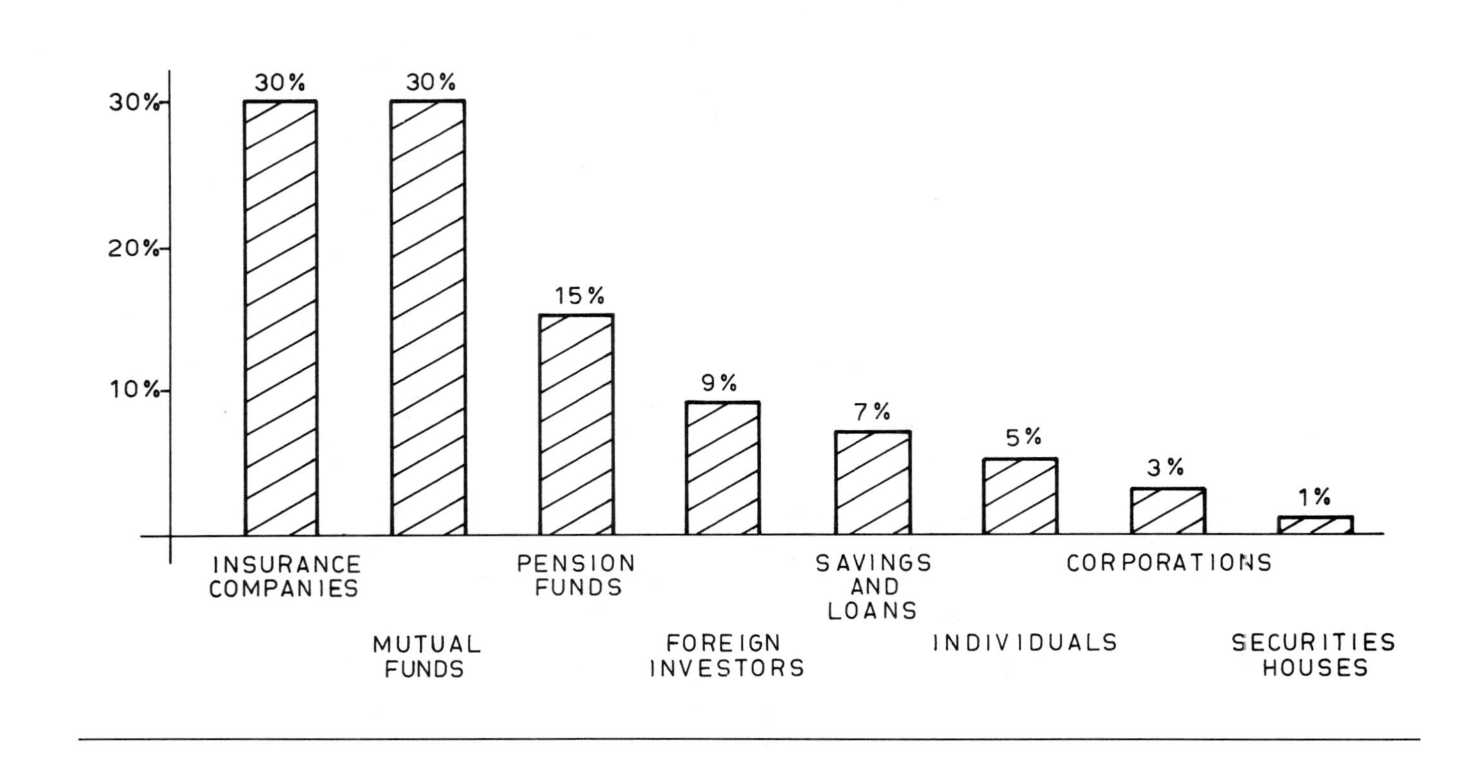

4. The Necessity of Careful Planning

No doubt some LBOs have been highly beneficial to entrepreneurs who knew how to manage them. In 1982, William Simon purchased Gibson Greetings, a Cincinnati company, from RCA for $80 million—and took it public for $290 million 18 months later. In 1986, he bought from Beatrice its Avis Car Leasing, which he then sold at a $485-million profit just 14 months later.

Many deal makers, hungry for huge fees and anxious to get a buy-out at any cost, boost LBO prices; nevertheless, operators who do their homework properly stand the best chance of making profits. They ensure that the new owner(s) of their target will be able to service the massive debt and, above all, know how to target on the acquisition price.

No fast and hard rules foretell the likelihood of a profitable LBO, but cognizant securities analysts believe that, among other factors, the target company should have market dominance in its field, be subject as little as possible to business or commodity cycles, have a strong and predictable cash flow, and have undervalued assets (so that they can acquire it at a discount). The chances for profits increase if the management team is committed and competent—or if the new owner(s) have the management skill to turn the company around.

The payment of debt will be much easier if the LBO target has minimal requirements for future capital expenditures, with little if any need for expansion to remain competitive. The purchase price must be a true bargain if the new owners are to make a healthy profit. Also, there must be a lucrative disposition of assets, or a favorable market climate to refloat the company.

Until management is able to restabilize the company and come out of heavy debt, some people may make money but many more may be hurt. This is just as true for those who extended credit to a company prior to the LBO. Holders of

RJR Nabisco's bonds, for instance, watched the value of their securities fall by about $1 billion in the autumn of 1988, when rival groups began to bid for the firm.

Bond prices plummeted because the prospect of the company being saddled with huge debts post-LBO hurt its creditworthiness. By contrast, those who owned the company's equity saw its value rise from $13 billion before the bids began to about $25 billion at the end.

Some people gain and some people lose because the corporation is a collection of long-term contracts between shareholders and lenders, many of which are implicitly there but not legally stated as such. A supplier may invest in a new plant if it believes that the client company will survive and be a source of business; and bankers will extend credit if in their judgment the company that takes out a loan can pay the interest and repay the principal.

While these are common notions, and basically valid, there are other factors that must be considered:

1. The world is beginning to feel the effects of currency and debt swings.
2. Debt is easier to trade on a global scale than equity; hence in the 1990s, debt will have the upper hand.
3. Debt is promoted by the tax laws, while profits derived from equity are penalized.
4. Debt owned to foreign investors is growing at a tremendous rate. In America 30 to 40 percent of new issues are purchased by the Japanese. (The interdependency of financial markets is such that when the Japanese did not buy for three weeks, American bond interest rates went up one hundred base points.)

5. Investors who do not hedge find themselves overexposed, and hedging is increasingly done in the futures market.

On a worldwide basis, futures markets do not have the same resiliency as in the past. The root of the problem is that nobody can control the futures or the debt market; and the rules of global money management are still unfamiliar to many investors. With LBO or any other type of debt, investors should expect liquidity.

Also, money will be made or lost in relation to the cost of liquidity (see Section 5). If the cost of liquidity increases, then the cost of capital (and inflation) will also increase, making it much more difficult to pay the interest, repay the principal, or restructure the loan.

The mood of the market changes constantly, and one of the risks in LBOs is the possibility that there may be fewer new ones in the future. A slowdown in deal-making deprives investment banks and other institutions of the profits that come from being active in LBO deals. As a result, they lose the fees made from originating, distributing, and even making a market in them. Those financial institutions that are overexposed will go under, as happened with Drexel Burnham Lambert in mid-February 1990. The danger is all too real that Wall Street's merger machine has run out of steam after having loaded corporate America with all the debt it dares (or cares) to take on.

Apart from opportunistic raiders who repackage assets for quick resale, those merchant banks who take positions in an LBO will also be hurt. Origination fees and distribution gains have been a sort of lifesaver, as have the equity kickers that banks have been accumulating in LBO deals. Loss of this income may not be crippling to the earnings of some financial institutions, but it will definitely further reduce liquidity; and this may put in motion a snowball effect.

5. Can Business Be as Usual?

Opinions vary about what is and what is not an LBO. Jackie Mason says:

> This business, on a legitimate basis, is a fraud. You need money to be in this business. But not a lot. You need more money to open a shoe-shine shop than you do to buy a $2-billion company; let's be honest about it. But to buy a shoe-shine store, if it costs $3,000, you need $3,000. If you don't got it in cash, you need to bring it by Thursday. But if it's an LBO, not only do you not have to bring it, you don't have to see it, you don't know where you are going to get it, nobody knows where they got it from.[3]

Edward Yardeni, the chief economist of Prudential-Bache, takes a diametrically opposite viewpoint:

> Just how leveraged is corporate America? The pessimists observe that interest costs exceed 20 percent of corporate cash flow. They are also disturbed that the portion of earnings that US corporations need to finance their debt is up to 50 percent, on average. But it doesn't make any sense to compare interest expense to income after expenses. The ratio of short-term liabilities to internal cash flows is no higher today than it was in the 1950s.

Behind the LBO wave, Yardeni and other New Wave economists see a trend: Investors are swapping equity for debt. (See Figure 11.1) Pension funds alone account for 15 percent of junk-bond funding in the U.S. In fact, *The New York Times* reported that several large pension funds were to provide the $2-billion down payment on the $20.3-billion buy-out offer for RJR Nabisco (negotiations for which were still in progress). The funds might have been planning to reinvest some of the cash from the sale of their RJR stock in RJR's junk bonds;

however, they have no business in betting pensioners' money in low-grade debt.

Thus, statements such as the following, made by George M. Salem, seem inappropriate: "While LBO loans may present risk, the risk is not anywhere near that presented by LDC (less-developed countries) loans, nor does the scale of LBO lending approach that of LDC lending."

What Salem and others are trying to say is that money locked into different LBO deals may not be as exposed as if it were loaned to the Third World. And they further add that the top ten American banks hold "just" $18.1 billion in LBO debt compared with $60 billion of Third World debt, the latter averaging 150 percent of their equity. But this is not the point.

In the early 1970s, banks suffered severe losses on money they had poured into the Real Estate Investment Trusts (REITs), and it was said that such risks do not exist in Third-World debt because sovereign governments pay what they owe.

In other words, financial history is repeating itself. In the 1980s, LBOs are being justified in the same way that sovereign lending was in the 1970s.

The one striking parallel between the two is the heady optimism felt by many that the recipients of lavish funding will be able to repay. One should therefore keep in mind the first law of finance: "Making a loan is not the same thing as collecting."[4]

It may be true that total LBO loans on the books of the big U.S. banks have risen little in 1989 and that foreign banks purchased a great deal of dubious paper; nevertheless, U.S. regionals have taken some 20 percent of the load—the rest went to U.S. insurance companies, pension funds, mutual funds, thrifts, and so on. What all this means is that the LBO paper remains in the system and one day it may blow up.

This could happen with the onset of a liquidity crisis such as the one that erupted in January and February of 1990. Liquidity risk is growing, whether we want to admit it or not.

As with Third-World debt, it is not individual LBOs, but the cumulative size of them that is disturbing. In the 1980s, LBOs involved 2,800 companies; as a comparison, there were 1,713 companies listed on the New York Stock Exchange.

Furthermore, according to some calculations, for every $1,000 increase in shareholder wealth in LBOs, various companies' top managers enjoyed an increase of $60 to $70 in personal wealth. This fact undercuts the arguments that as managers become part-owners through LBOs, they have greater incentive to improve performance; or that the discipline of meeting debt repayments forces managers to cut costs.

Also, LBOs often involve selling companies off in pieces. Critics consider this practice to be a perilous financial game played to enrich a few savvy manipulators, and one that is leveraging up companies in a way that will eventually end in a debt explosion.

The fixed income markets around the world cannot afford for too much longer the fast and steadily growing debt positions of the 1980s. As less-secure debt grows, the number of intermediaries drops. This is how the bond market crashed in January 1990 in New York (with some help from the Federal Reserve, which let interest rates go up to prop up the dollar and prevent massive foreign sales of U.S. securities). The same thing can happen in bond trading in other financial markets around the globe if financial institutions continue to show a lack of leadership in providing the financial accountability necessary in the 1990s and beyond.

6. Junk Bonds and the Liquidity Trap

In the junk-bond and LBO markets, high returns are said to offset the high risks. Junk bonds are seen not as debt but as an improved form of equity; yet there is a big difference between this "new equity" and the real thing. Nevertheless, capital and credit poured into the LBO market in the 1980s for six reasons.

First, because of the spectacular returns earned in the preceding years, investment banks had at their disposal equity capital amounting to a double-digit of billions of dollars (some $25 billion by 1988). Second, low-grade bonds that were always around but had never really become star performers were renamed and repackaged into a high-yield, widely traded financial instrument. The name junk bonds became popular, with little thought given to the fact that these are less than investment-grade securities, whose only advantage is that they yield some five percentage points above Treasuries. It is worth remembering that, in the long run, steep rates mean big risks.

Third, the 1987 stock-market crash scared many individual investors out of stocks and into junk bonds, which took things from bad to worse. Fourth, given that their traditional business of lending to large corporations had eroded, commercial banks too pushed aggressively into the LBO arena, in which both fees and interest spreads were high.

By the mid-1980s many boards and chief executive officers, who in the past had had little regard for low-rated bonds, began to be impressed by the profits made by Drexel Burnham Lambert. As shown in Figure 11.2, in 1984, Drexel Burnham Lambert made a market of low-grade bonds that was twice as big as that of all other American financial institutions taken together; by 1986, the Drexel share of junk bond market had fallen to about 41 percent, but the yearly business had reached $17 billion for this institution alone, and $41 billion in the whole U.S.

Figure 11.2 Percent of Junk-Bond Offerings with Drexel as Lead Underwriter

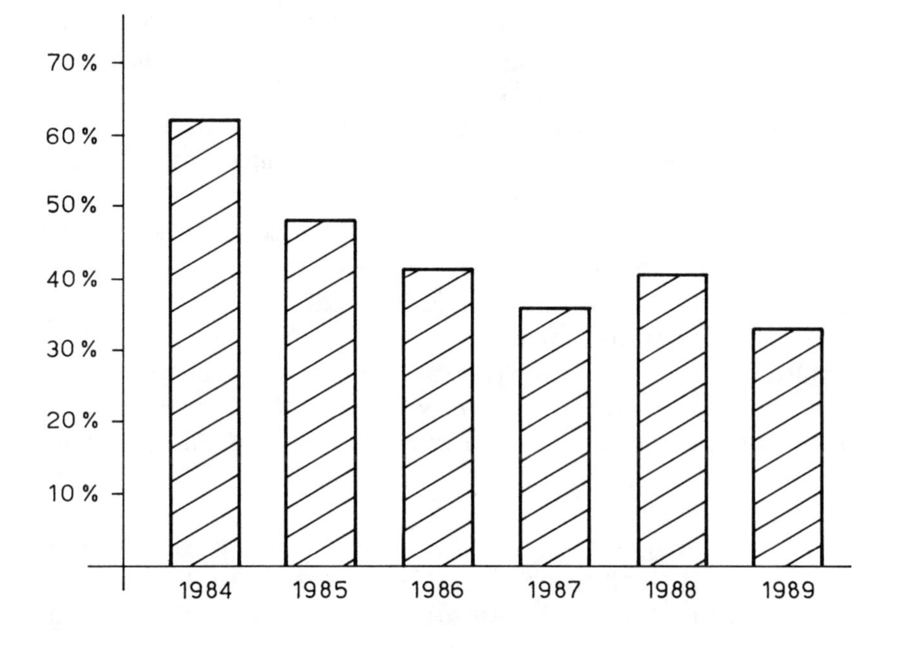

Year after year of junk-bond sales accumulated, until, according to some estimates, by the end of 1988 the total LBO exposure of 28 major American banks was $47 billion, which was equal to 5.6 percent of total loans and, as stated, about 60 percent of the banks' equity.

A fifth factor in the junk-bond explosion is that foreign financial institutions, particularly Japanese banks, were lending heavily to LBOs. They provided, for example, major funding for the RJR Nabisco deal.

A sixth is that as junk bonds used in LBOs started getting into trouble and began to be questioned as takeover tools, investment banks began a new business—trading the bonds of troubled companies. "We think that this will be the great opportunity of the 1990s," said one securities analyst.

Many financial analysts do not see the growing LBO risk because they fail to realize that for every security there is an option, and this is liquidity. Liquidity is becoming more valuable and less available today, and this fact alone may nullify many calculations made on Wall Street.

Yet the optimists will not give up. According to some financial analysts, shrewd repackaging (involving interest payments and capital repayment up front) can ensure that junk bonds receive an AA or even AAA rating. Also, metrics such as option against spread can be used to help the buyer assess the product.

Wisdom suggests the need to reevaluate our position. Dennis Healey is the author of the first law of holes, which says, "When you are in a whole, stop digging." Bear in mind that what was thought to be a great market liquidity led to frenetic bidding between companies for the same asset (e.g., Macy's and Campeau Corp. for Federated Department Stores, and Shearson and Salomon against KKR in the RJR Nabisco case). This produced high-priced deals, compounded by corporate boards' reacting to charges that they might be selling their company too cheap.

Also, many companies go private or take on heavy debt loads as a defense to hostile bids. Examples are Harcourt Brace's LBO to avoid Robert Maxwell, Holiday Inn's effort to escape Donald Trump, and Union Carbide's recapitalization to stop advances by Sam Heymann.

Too much liquidity not only leads to more expensive deals in more cyclical industries, but it also produces more risky results for the wrong reason.

One potentially incorrect reason for doing deals is that of reacting to pressure (often felt by LBO funds) to aggressively promote business. This is aggravated by the fact that investment and merchant bankers can raise large amounts of capital from pension funds, foreign investors, and U.S. citizens by touting their track records and asserting that there are still plenty of lucrative investment opportunities available.

Even an M and A business that ultimately goes sour will generate a big bonus for the investment bank that arranges it. Few calculate the risks that may be involved. First Boston earned $100 million from its role advising Campeau Corporation on its takeover of Allied Stores. However, to earn that fee it had to risk $865 million of its own capital as a bridge loan to Campeau in order to seal the deal.

How can LBOs manage to deliver the promised spectacular returns after paying big premiums for what are in many cases average or even mediocre companies? The answer, say takeover specialists, lies in the

1. much greater efficiency of private, debt-strapped companies that are run to maximize cash flow rather than reported earnings (which, as discussed, is a half truth);
2. fact that the tax advantages of debt versus equity in current law make it possible to capitalize (which is one of the problems with the current tax law);

3. payment of debt incurred in LBOs by selling assets and subsidiaries (which involves a good deal of wishful thinking).

According to some arguments, interest on the junk bond is serviced not out of cash flow from operations, but from arbitraging the difference between the stock-market value and private market value of the company's assets. This argument, however, does not take into account the fact that market prices vary according to the economic law of offer and demand.

In the late 1970s, when the efficiency and cost-effectiveness of optical fiber communications were proven, enthusiasts predicted that AT&T would install optical fiber all over the United States, down to local loops; afterward, said the enthusiasts, AT&T would pull out the twisted pair wire and sell the copper, thus making enough money to pay for all the optical fiber (i.e., expenses for material and installation) while still showing a healthy profit.

Unfortunately, this never happened; aside from technical difficulties and delays, there was no market for aging copper that had been installed overhead or underground for over one hundred years. If anything, copper prices crashed. Furthermore, while the laying of fiber optics is progressing, it is a long way from replacing all of the twisted pairs and coaxial cables used in telecommunications.

Just the same, when Mike Milken was studying at the University of Pennsylvania's Wharton School of Economics, he discovered while doing a project that low-grade bonds had a default rate of only 1 percent. This discovery led to Milken's proposing junk-bond packaging after he joined Drexel Burnham Lambert. His bank even offered to buy back the 1-percent default,[5] by capitalizing on the wide margins of junk bonds.

In practice, the 1-percent default rate proved to be a miscalculation. As many players entered the LBO market, surplus junk bonds began to accumulate. The resulting dynamics in trading substantially increased the amount of risk assumed by every player, and what was once a 1-percent default rate became 3 percent and kept growing. As of early 1990, the junk bond default rate stands at an ominous 10 percent.[6]

As a result, junk-bond defaults are already slashing investment returns more drastically than is widely perceived. Also, one of the flaws in this methodology of calculating failures is that a bond is much less likely to default in its early years.

When the junk bond market was growing exponentially, most of the outstanding issues were one to four years old (when default rates were lower). The picture changes radically when one asks a different question. What proportion of the junk bonds issued in a given year have defaulted after, say, six years?

The answer seems to be, close to 16 percent, even though the companies in debt did not have to repay principal, but only pay interest. It is also well to keep in mind that companies have experienced benign economic conditions during the 1980s.

7. Arbitrage and the Many Aspects of Leveraging

As discussed, during the 1980s, a fairly profitable, albeit financially risky, leveraged buy-out model was developed in the United States. These transactions slowly became one of the hottest investment activities in the financial markets; while condemned by some securities analysts, they were highly regarded by many others.

The appeal of the LBO is its high debt and low equity ratio; because of these, the acquisition price is effectively paid by the company itself. Since substantial debt is added to a company's balance sheet, current cash returns to investors are often forsaken for an elusive, later-on capital-gain appreciation. Sometimes, however, owners infuse new life into an acquired LBO company. When this happens, they have the best of all possible worlds, that is, good current cash flow and greatly appreciating assets.

But this is not the way to bet. The best bet is that there are risks involved in this game. While many leveraged buy-outs have been taken public or resold, most merchant banks, arbitrageurs, and other investors had to wait prior to partaking of the spoils. Others ended by managing the acquired assets (and did so quite well, as shown by the example of Carl Icahn's takeover of TWA and other companies).

Thus, the arbitrageur's task does not necessarily end with a leveraged buy-out. A significant amount of entrepreneurial energy may need to go into management if profits are to be made. Also, financial-engineering wizardry is needed to take companies private. If all these missions are accomplished, fortunes can be made, in finance or in other fields.

Where does the game start? Following the dictum of the English recipe for cooking rabbits, which says, "First catch the rabbit," the arbitrageur must find a company that is ripe for an LBO; this takes financial analysis and quite a bit of consulting. The next step is to find money to purchase the company; this generally means convincing a bank to grant a loan or act as an intermediary.

Throughout most of the 1980s, the Mecca of junk bonds was Drexel Burnham Lambert's office in Beverly Hills, California. During that period, chances were that when an arbitrageur or corporate official needed money to acquire a company, that person traveled to Drexel. Once there, after being screened by some of the junk-bond specialists, the pilgrim would be granted an audience with Michael R. Milken, Drexel's senior vice-president and wizard of the junk bond market.[7]

Investment banks such as Drexel Burnham Lambert (now bankrupt) act as underwriters by buying a block of junk bonds from an issuer and selling the bonds on debt markets. Over the years, some banks expanded their knowledge of junk bonds into sophisticated corporate takeover strategies and made investment banking a gold mine in highly visible, very lucrative corporate takeover games. Drexel Burnham junk-bond customers have included Rupert Murdoch, the chairperson of News Corporation International; T. Boone Pickens, of Mesa Limited Partnership; Oscar S. Wyatt Jr., of Coastal Corporation; Sanford C. Sigoloff, of Wickes Companies; William F. Farley, of Farley Industries; Ronald O. Perelman, of Revlon Group, and many others.

The Wickes Companies were once a bankrupt concern; Sigoloff has been using Drexel-raised funds for his empire-building efforts. Carl C. Icahn, Samuel Belzberg, Irwin L. Jacobs, and Ivan F. Boesky (a man who controlled a limited partnership under his own name) were other Drexel clients. The Drexel-Boesky relationship made big news when it came into the spotlight and eventually led to the downfall of both Boesky and Drexel.

Thanks to the junk bond business, Drexel Burnham Lambert grew from an obscure firm to a high-profile business with revenue of $4 billion a year, largely derived from a large number of public offerings in junk bonds. Its pretax profits hit about $550 million in 1986, making the firm a leader among its peers.

Figure 11.3 shows the growth of the junk bond market in the 1984-to-1989 time frame. While 1986 was the peak year, junk bonds still accounted for about $30 billion in 1989—and Drexel Burnham Lambert had a commanding share in that market, practically till the company crashed.

Yet, the demise of Drexel's parent company finally came (in mid-February 1990) because of a cash shortage, allegedly caused by the collapse of its $1 billion devaluing junk-bond

Figure 11.3 Annual Public Offerings of Junk Bonds in Billions of Dollars

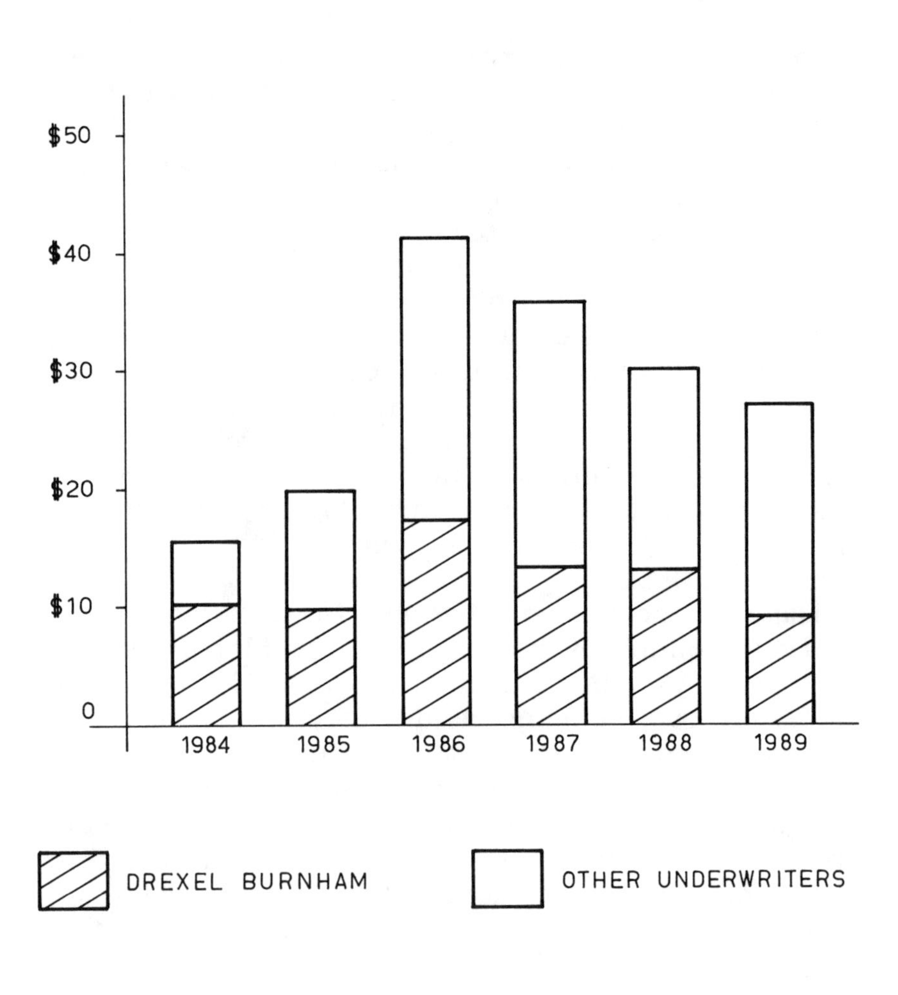

portfolio. As the firm's credit rating began to slide, its banks cut off credit. Said *Time* magazine: "The parent company, starved for cash, began to siphon money from the investment firm's coffers, until government regulators halted that maneuver."[8]

Numbers alone do not convey Drexel's power in its heyday. Financing arranged by Drexel Burnham Lambert has given some of America's most formidable raiders the go-ahead. Prior to October 1987, high-yield junk-bond securities accounted for an estimated 20 percent of all publicly held corporate debt in the U.S. Morgan Stanley and Merrill Lynch tied for second place in junks, with each underwriting only a fifth of Drexel's volume.

Because of its unmatched ability to place these bonds with a network of buyers, Drexel could raise billions of dollars on short notice. Of deals underwritten or co-managed by this investment bank, the following have been recognized as outstanding: BCI Holdings (Beatrice Cos) for $2.5 billion; SCI Holdings (Storer Communications), $2.2 billion; Metromedia Broadcasting, $1.9 billion; Turner Broadcasting, $1.4 billion; Safeway Stores Holding, $1 billion; Coastal, $0.9 billion; Rapid American, $0.7 billion; and Pacific Lumber, also about $0.7 billion.

At first, junk-bond dealers that prospered were those that knew who the buyers were and what they liked, and could also (it is alleged) twist the arm of recalcitrant buyers if necessary. These dealers also had a knack for singling out up-and-coming companies from the apparent losers that the rating agencies had lumped together.

But Drexel Burnham Lambert took junk-bond underwriting a step farther. If the issuing companies got in trouble, it would intercede quickly to keep default rates low. As long as its finances were strong because of booming business, it also stood ready to buy bonds back if no one else would. That is how Milken's Beverly Hills-based junk-bond operation built up a powerful network of bond buyers.

When Drexel began underwriting leveraged buy-outs and hostile takeovers during the early 1980s, the network absorbed the added volume. Since only Drexel could arrange financing for the trickiest deals, clients did not rebel even when this investment bank represented parties on both sides of a transaction. Further, nobody minded that Drexel demanded equity stakes in the deals it financed.

These practices were not necessarily illegal, but they were unconventional when introduced. In all fairness, it must be said that despite their reputation, junk bonds have not always been used to finance takeovers.

According to Federal Reserve Board estimates, direct-acquisition financing has probably been about 20 percent of all junk-bond issues, or around 40 percent if corporate restructuring is included. Another major bundle of low-grade bonds has been employed to finance ordinary capital spending by companies who could not qualify for a bank loan.

A substantial portion of these junk bonds under other circumstances might have been bank loans. They gave thousands of unrated companies direct access to capital markets, enabling them to bypass the banking system and other intermediaries such as insurance companies. It is also worth noting that only about 700 U.S. companies are rated by the major agencies.

8. Workouts for Highly Leveraged Transactions

Because of a possible drying up of lenders and investors, loan-loss risks in highly leveraged transactions are now greater than they were in the past. The second law of finance, that "Any debtor's likelihood of default is highly dependent on the willingness of creditors to lend more money," while once forgotten, seems to have been rediscovered.

The temporary memory lapses had a profitable aspect. For nearly a decade, highly leveraged transactions provided handsome revenues to investment banks in the form of wide loan spreads, fees for managing bank lending syndicates, gains on sales of loans, and subordinated and equity participation in the deals.

But an economic slowdown can change all that, and liquidity reverses the gains that are made; however, investment houses can find new and lucrative business in debt restructuring.

In this business, creditors are asked to accept stock, lower coupon rates, debt stretch-outs, and any other solution that will keep failing companies alive and out of bankruptcy court. Such deals need ingenuity to develop and good management to keep them alive; this is where turnaround consulting enters the picture.

These exercises, known in Wall-Street jargon as workouts, are very similar to Third-World debt restructuring. They often involve selling off pieces of a business to raise cash and usually end with old loans being replaced by new, lower-cost ones if at all possible.

But such workouts will be little more than cosmetic unless and until the effort behind them focuses on reestablishing public confidence. "Restoration of public confidence is a condition prerequisite to success and future prosperity of institutions," said A.P. Giannini, the founder of Bank of America.

In studying the markets, one may be surprised at the ease with which a panic can get hold of a market or even of a whole nation. Once this panic settles in, it can wipe out the gains of a day, a month, a lifetime. In *Breaking the Bank—The Decline of BankAmerica,* author Gary Hector suggests that at the turn of the century markets in the United States were particularly vulnerable to panics because of the nation's system of issuing currency.

> The United States did not have a single, unified currency. Coins...circulated along with currency issued by both the federal government and the national banks....any bank with a national charter could issue its own paper currency. But the paper was only as good as the bank that issued it. When a bank got into trouble, merchants discounted its currency....Anyone stuck with paper from that bank lost out, and if the bank failed the paper would be worthless.[9]

A parallel may be drawn with Drexel Burnham Lambert and its junk bonds. Few appreciate the wisdom of A.P. Giannini, who advised his friends and employees not to gamble on leveraged deals. "Pay off your debts and sit tight," he said. "If you own your stock you have nothing to fear no matter how deep a crisis may be."

Successful restructuring requires having both public confidence and the ability to sit tight, as well as sound financing; but not everything is as straightforward as it might seem. For example, off assets might cover interest payments or the repayment of part of the capital—if there are any valuable assets left to be sold; in many cases, what is still around is not salable. If it was, it would already have been disposed of.

Before it went private in April 1986 through a $6.2-billion LBO carried out by Kohlberg Kravis Roberts, Beatrice Foods sold everything from brassieres to car rentals and chow mein. The new management put in by KKR has sold off about $7 billion of assets, including Avis car rental, International Playtex, Max Factor, and Samsonite.

These sales cut total debt to about $3 billion. At the same time, all that remained under the Beatrice shell was domestic food operations, which proved hard to sell. Total employment has fallen from 100,000 to 20,000, but the reduction means little in terms of productivity, as it mainly reflects on the sales of operating divisions.

Thus, it is not always easy to restructure old loans with what remains after reckless sales of assets. Nevertheless, restructuring makes up more than one-third of American banks' long-term corporate lending. This amounted to a staggering $105 billion in 1989 alone, and reintroduced debt into a system that was eager to securitize prior debt and sell it out.

What will the future bring? As the LBOs of the 1980s followed the wave of the conglomerates built in the 1960s and 1970s, the specialty of the 1990s may appropriately be the turnarounds. In the opinion of investment analysts on Wall Street, workouts are what lies ahead. "Many of the leveraged buyouts done in 1987 and 1988 were bad ideas," says Robert J. Edgreen, president of KD Equities, an LBO firm. "It's a matter of time until they will need rescuing."[10]

For companies in distress, some securities experts consider these workouts to be an alternative to filing for Chapter 11 protection against creditors. This has been a strategy followed by LTV, Allegheny International, and others. But by now the bad debt loans have become big, and there are many creditors with money at stake but no cash, which makes it hard for management to negotiate restructuring plans for turnaround.

This is not to say that in the past Chapter 11 has always been a good solution. First Republic Bank of Dallas went into Chapter 11 after suffering major losses. Its legal costs, after protracted battling, are running at $500,000 monthly. Still, turnaround also has its problems; typically, management needs the co-operation of 80 to 90 percent of its creditors to make a workout financially viable.

Investment banks look at this subject, LBOs and workouts, as business opportunities.

In either case, there are huge fees to be earned. In the LBO for RJR Nabisco, one investment bank earned a rumored $150 million as its fee for selling junk bonds to raise the debt financing due to the large proportion of debt in the deal.

Today workouts are starting cautiously, but this also characterized the beginning of LBOs. Huge leveraged transactions began in the 1970s as modest deals; it was only a small company or a division of a larger company that went private in a leveraged buy-out. At the time, such deals were limited to businesses that had established, mundane, proprietary product lines with a dominance or significant share in a fragmented industrial market; the firms also needed to show continuity of experienced management and demonstrate consistent profitability even during recessions.

Had turnarounds been necessary at that time, they would not have been that difficult, because emphasis was usually placed on companies with a good cash flow, a low need for capital investment, minimal requirements for R and D, a debt level not greater than 20 percent, and assets carried on the books well below fair market value. Turnarounds were facilitated also because during the high inflation of the 1970s real-interest rates were low, which reduced the burden of interest expense, and high inflation had depressed stock prices, which enabled deal makers to buy assets cheaply in the stock market.

It should be noted that one of the basic reasons for the success of LBOs in the 1980s (and a reason often overlooked by the architects of LBOs) is that the economy was "cooperating." From 1982 through 1986, real GNP expanded while interest rates declined; and though interest rates rose in 1987 and 1988, economic growth accelerated and profit margins expanded impressively.

The year 1989 thus shaped up as a year of slower (though still acceptable) growth and shrinking profit margins but leveling interest rates. Meanwhile, slack labor markets and weak unions had made it easy from 1983 on to cut labor costs; in such an environment, chances could be taken, with positive results, on risky transactions.

Also, prior to the 1986 tax reform, International Revenue Service (IRS) rules regarding depreciation were liberal. Financiers could write up assets of an acquired company from book value to current market value and depreciate them from this higher base, thus enlarging the cash flow available for servicing debt.

These conditions were ideal for workouts. By contrast, under the now prevailing financial climate, debt financing strains companies and investors, which is one reason why throughout the industry today, more emphasis is being placed on cash flow than on profits.

Some securities analysts think that it took the takeover and leveraged buy-out wave of the 1980s to teach the importance of cash flow. Also, it seems that investors will need to learn the third law of finance, which says that in order to get meaningful information out of financial statements, skill and patience are necessary in examining them.

Companies with rich cash flows (the so-called cash cows) can be expected to demonstrate the best financial staying power. Cash flow gives a more accurate picture of the state of a business than do earnings. It is a measure of how much spendable cash a company's operations generate. A sound financial analysis starts with net income, then adds bookkeeping charges, such as depreciation.

One difficulty of using cash flow is that many financial analysts have their own definitions of what it is and what it is not. Most definitions of cash flow begin with the same data, but they do not all use the same algorithms. Most differences between them lie in how each estimates free cash flow. This is a measure of how much cash flow remains after subtracting the amount that must be spent to keep the company running. This amount can be broken down into capital expenditures, the cost of doing business, and the cost of staying in business.

Free cash flow will increase whenever capital spending declines and depreciation increases—or when management exercises tough cost control. And while cash-flow investing has for some time been a contrarian move in pricing a company's stock, it is now an integral part of looking for LBO deals that will be able to face debt requirements as well as for workouts. Financial staying power has become key to not only success, but to survival.

Endnotes

1. Junk bonds are rated BB+ or lower by Standard & Poor, and Bal or below by Moody's. The rating agencies do not consider repayment, in Moody's words, "well assured."

2. *Barbarians at the Gate: The Fall of RJR Nabisco.*

3. Ibid.

4. Gary Hector, *Breaking the Bank—The Decline of BankAmerica* (Boston: Little Brown, 1988).

5. A figure derived by dividing the number of defaults in a given year by the value of all debt outstanding in that year—a false way of accounting.

6. *Time,* 26 February, 1990.

7. As of February 1990, Mike Milken was preparing his defense against 98 counts of insider trading and other alleged crimes.

8. *Time,* 26 February, 1990.

9. *Breaking the Bank—The Decline of BankAmerica.*

10. *Business Week,* 11 December, 1989.

Chapter 12

Strategies Followed by Financial Institutions

Chapter 12

Strategies Followed By Financial Institutions

1. Introduction

In order to prosper in the market a firm needs a master plan; yet as recently as 1990, about half the major U.S. banks had none. In Europe, the situation is even worse; the idea of strategic planning is only now being examined.

The five most important steps towards establishing a strategy include:

1. appraising prevailing conditions,
2. defining a set of options,
3. examining each of these options in detail,
4. making informed choices among alternatives, and
5. elaborating a master plan.

Key questions must be dealt with directly in order to help identify goals. Short of this, a firm will have a strategy by default. This is unacceptable because there is no room for error in the investment banking industry.

Because the securities business is now both global and highly competitive, certain strategic weapons have become fundamental requirements. A firm must have

1. a comprehensive strategy for the next ten years;
2. exact knowledge of the depth and range of its resources;
3. innovative financial products;
4. qualified professional staff;
5. high technology.

Goals must be defined by the top management of an investment bank or securities house, and should be directed toward ensuring profit, cash flow, and liquidity; strengthening the client base; developing specialized expertise; and maintaining capital adequacy, that is, financial staying power.

Financial products should be developed with customer needs in mind. Cross-selling of products and services improves profitability, and innovation enhances the bank's image.

A policy for managing change should promote the testing of new ideas and the development of new opportunities. This process should involve many people at all levels, and in particular, those at the top. "Anytime I do not understand the data, I look at the people who are involved," says a senior banker. "Particularly the people at the peak of the organizational pyramid."

2. The Reasons for Globality

The number one reason for globality in financial operations is expanding business opportunity and, therefore, greater potential for profitability. The second reason is the opportunity for gains through securities trading in foreign exchange. The third reason is diversification and spread of risk.

But global operations do not happen by accident; they call for a great amount of preparation and for a different culture. Multinational organizations are driving the banking industry into providing a greater quality of service, more polyvalent services, and opportunities for cross-market profits.

Global firms have a different orientation than national organizations, whose priorities are reconciliation (the squaring of accounts) and eliminating fraud.

All financial, manufacturing, and merchandising firms today aim to swamp costs and to assure compliance to rules and regulations. Financial institutions must abide not only by the rules of the different stock exchanges, but also those of reserve banks in their country of operations. In a global setting, this makes compliance much more complex, as the regulations in many countries contradict one another.

Nevertheless, all reserve-bank and stock-exchange regulations emphasize control of settlements and set some guidelines for market behavior. At the same time, the market landscape itself is changing with the emergence of twenty-four-hour banking and worldwide transaction business.

Such changes are forcing corporate treasurers and money managers to reassess existing banking relationships. Sophisticated customers want to trade any security or currency, on any exchange, any place in the world, at any time of the day.

A strategy that merely pays lip service to the requirements we have been examining, or ignores them altogether, is doomed to failure, because it cannot guarantee account control.

In investment banking the concept of account control extends well beyond the time-honored notion of a bank as financial intermediary, calling for a significant amount of databasing and distribution power. If a financial institution wishes to be successful and profitable, it has to have distribution power on a global scale.

As recent studies have indicated, distribution is regarded by 40 percent of the leading firms as being a key factor in success; one international securities house was quoted by a competitor as being able to determine in only four minutes how much of a proposed new issue it can distribute.

To achieve feats such as this, leading financial institutions have developed impressive technological support to enhance their distribution facilities. Because firms are battling to reach global status, or to maintain such status as they have acquired, this effort is vital.

Nobody disputes that knowledge and information are key commodities. Nevertheless, while computers and communications are an integral part of planning more efficient operations for a bank, there is no such thing as a strategy based solely on information systems; nor are there purely financial or marketing strategies. In banking, if strategy is not global, there is no strategy.

Strategic planning must be based on clear vision and unambiguous management choices. If management does not make timely decisions about goals, products, competitive position, and a concrete plan, a firm cannot move forward.

Therefore, the first task of bank management is to set the strategic perspectives. Strategic planning in a financial institution must rest on four pillars:

1. market evolution
2. human capital

3. innovative products
4. modern equipment

Financial and legal criteria tie these four pillars together. Aside from compliance with the rules of stock exchanges and reserve banks, various tax laws must be observed; in the international arena, these may be quite complex.

Modern equipment does not refer to mainframing junk software and obsolete communicating protocols but to any-to-any networks, intelligent databases and expert systems. The network of a global investment bank must work round the clock nonstop; it must also be secure and reliable.

Not all twenty-four-hour banking is twenty-four-hour trading, but in order to have a competitive edge in trading, a firm needs efficient after-hours networks. As of this writing, leading banks are actively installing them.

The international financial network of tomorrow will be quite different than that of today. Because many of the current solutions are of mid-1970s vintage, firms are revamping them to include global real-time approaches—a solution which I call real space.

Global intelligent networks are not for every investment bank. Many financial institutions would never conceive of doing worldwide banking; rather they choose to focus on domestic distribution or even local marketing. But those securities houses and investment banks that go global will require not only the highest grade of technology, but also superior employee talent.

While the reasons for globality may be sound, if the logistics and the infrastructure do not follow (or even lead), a bank is not going to have much success. Furthermore, computer literacy is a must; this means being able to effectively run all the functions of a modern system (see Figure 12.1). Operations include:

Figure 12.1 An Investment Banking System Enriched with Knowledge Engineering from Data Filtering to Database Mining and Portfolio Management

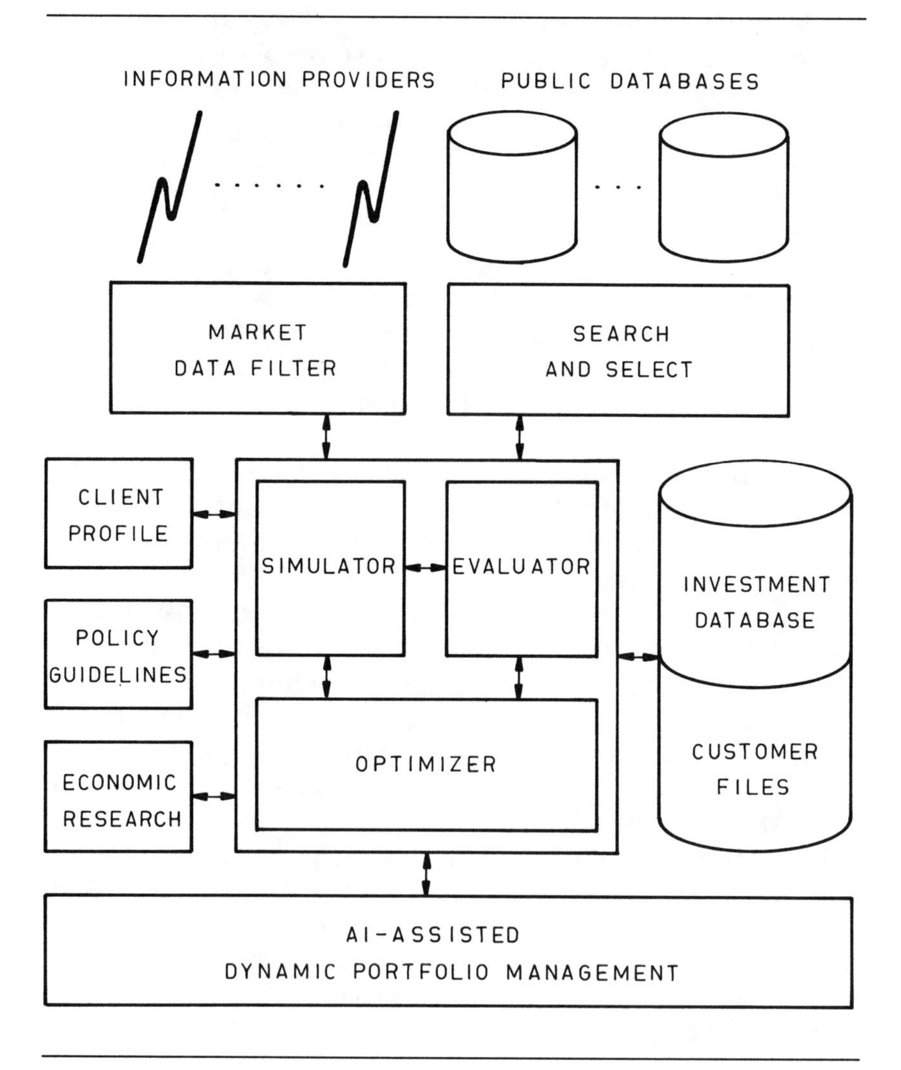

1. not only receiving a stream of information from providers, but also developing and applying market data filters;
2. not only accessing public databases, but also using expert systems to search for and select information;
3. doing value-differentiation by developing client profile analyzers and matching their results with policy guidelines;
4. experimenting with simulators, evaluators, and optimizers, as well as AI constructs (as, for instance, in dynamic portfolio management).

In this fast-developing economy, the costs of entry—and of holding one's own—are steadily rising; only with a global market can financial companies raise the money necessary to cover R and D costs, not to mention the implementation of advanced technology. Also, if a firm introduces a product to the market, it then has the option of spreading its breakthrough in a wider client base. That firm can also work on the basis of more accurate market forecasts because it sees further than its competition.

Since faster development times allow a greater number of innovative product experiences, user's skills develop more quickly. In addition, because they are obliged to collaborate closely in order to sustain fast timetables, bankers and securities experts develop more trust and loyalty across functions both vertically and horizontally in the organization. In contrast, if the development process is slow, frequent changes in the market impel researchers to constantly rework product design, which slows even further the process of product introduction and the development of effective market strategies.

It therefore comes as no surprise that in both the financial and the manufacturing industries, faster developers continually gain on slower ones. And as their experience improves, the gap with the laggers increases.

Topping the list of those elements common to successful financial institutions is appreciation of the fact that time is a vital resource. Naturally, cost and quality goals are important; but the clock is the ultimate arbiter of a financial product's success or failure in the global market.

3. Controlling the Quality of Banking Services

Expectations of improvement in banking services are driving the wave of interest in supporting intelligent networks, deductive databases, workstations, and artificial intelligence resources. Today, quality is the realm in which competitive advantages most visibly demonstrate themselves.

Hard to define, impossible to legislate, quality is an attitude of mind. It is also the manifestation of a new culture in the financial industry. Therefore, product quality should have a prominent place in a strategic plan. But is not it true that automation blurs the focus on quality?

Competition and the advancement of technology have driven banking management toward the industrialization of the services offered to the client base. As with products in the manufacturing industry, financial services are now a result of institutionalized research and development, and in order to swamp costs, assembly-line production methods are being used; they are also marketed and delivered on-line.

But far from swamping quality, computer and communications emphasize it—the whole process of automation is an emphasis on quality control.

During and after World War II, statistical quality control (QC) became a basic ingredient in manufacturing. The service industries are only now adopting QC methodology, revamping systems and procedures to adapt to its requirements.

Quality control should enter into all the services that a firm provides to its customers. In the long run, the way to stay competitive is to ensure the best possible service. (Albeit not necessarily the cheapest.)

Furthermore, quality means consistently maintaining the values embodied in the financial product. Unwanted variety may occur if there are no established and normalized methods for controlling outgoing product quality. Low quality occurs when services offered are not kept within tolerances established at a product's inception.

Both financial transactions and customer-oriented applications are fertile areas for the implementation of quality-control measures. But benefits have probably been best documented for applications visible to customers.

In weighing the advantages and disadvantages of different standards of quality, a firm may find its judgment influenced to a considerable degree by its closeness to the product. Fair judgment, however, demands not only objectivity and impartiality, but also a merit system. Merit rating is a useful tool for measuring the performance of bankers at the front desk and the back office; it is a means for assessing how well various employees' personalities suit the jobs they are doing; it is a way of sizing up, with the help of customer feedback, the quality of the financial product itself.

While across-the-board quality is a fine idea, there should be a certain statistical distribution that characterizes every process, whether natural or synthetic. But can it be identified? Pareto's Law states that 20 percent of something represents 80 percent of something else (See Fig. 12.2a).[1] That is,

1. 20 percent of products will have 80 percent of the defects;

2. 20 percent of the drivers create 80 percent of the accidents
3. 20 percent of workers are responsible for 80 percent of the absenteeism;
4. 20 percent of customers represent 80 percent of a firm's profits.[2]

A firm's quality products should thus be geared to the 20 percent of customers who account for the bulk of its business.

Mathematics can be instrumental in fine-tuning a QC system, particularly if that system is computer-based, thus benefiting from databases and networks. A theoretical background has developed to support the necessary applications; Dr. Markowitz and Dr. Sharpe, who shared the 1990 Nobel Prize in economics with Dr. Miller, have made major contributions in this domain.[3]

Harry Markowitz developed Modern Portfolio Theory (MPT); Sharpe's research has been instrumental in developing methods for pricing financial assets. He is also known for taking the stance that computerized trading helps to make markets more efficient, in opposition to other analysts' charges that the practice fueled the stock market collapse in October 1987.

Computerized trading based on selling shares into a falling market could be destabilizing, but more recent strategies, which emphasize contrarian strategies or buying stocks after a fall, tend to stabilize share prices. Successfully implementing such strategies, however, requires comprehensive analytical guidelines.

At one time, by handling some key financial evaluation points and half a dozen ratios that are simple to calculate, financial institutions attempted to give investors some idea of whether a particular company was a good or a bad investment. But as financial operations became more complex, it

Figure 12.2a Pareto's Law: 20% of "A" Represents 80% of "B"

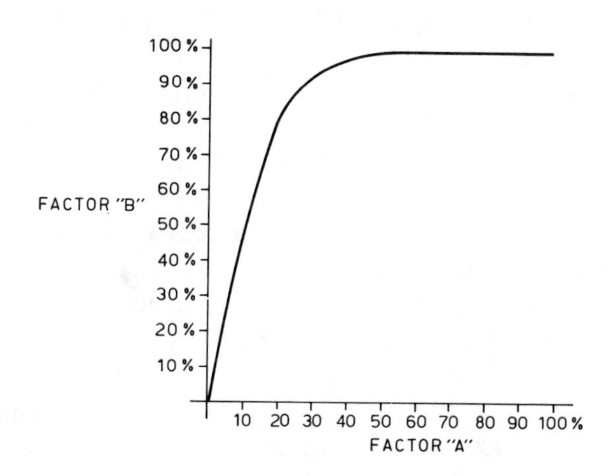

Figure 12.2b Poisson and Binonial Distribution

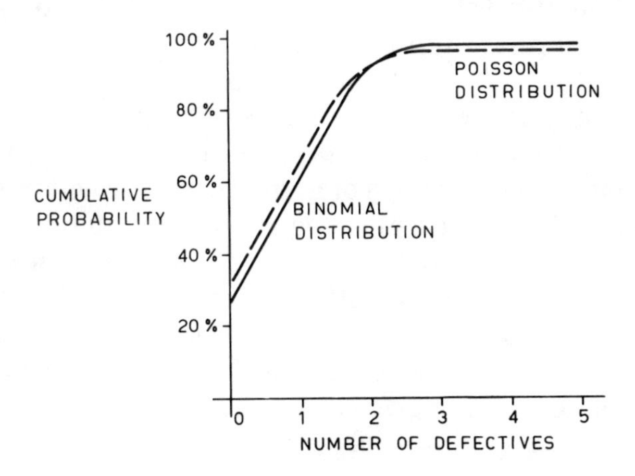

became clear that before analyzing figures, a financial analyst should ask whether a company has clearly defined its objectives and strategies. Vague statements alluding to "a rewarding place for employees" or "a commitment to excellence, quality and duty" were no longer sufficient.

So how can a trader determines whether a firm's directors know what they are doing and why? He or she can make an in-depth business audit of plans, means, products, and finances and then begin mathematical analysis. Conversely, a thorough quantitative study may reveal weak spots that require careful business analysis. In other words, a trader may mathematically scrutinize financial, product, manufacturing, inventory, and marketing data and then ask strategic questions.

Accuracy rather than precision is the crucial issue. In real life, rare is the case in which measurements, values or events will follow the normal (bell-shaped) statistical distribution. But in many cases the normal distribution is a good approximation; also, it is endowed with rich tables and graphs that permit a trader to do valid statistical tests at a predetermined degree of confidence.

In mathematical statistics, the Poisson distribution is based on findings similar to those of Pareto. Poisson was a Prussian cavalry officer who observed that 20 percent of the soldiers got 80 percent of the horses' kicks. Similar observations have been made of factory scheduling and production, as well as in what happens in a bank's branch offices. We will never find the errors taking place unless we are truly analytic.

Sampling inspection is the way to go, and the Poisson distribution is in contrast with the binomial in Figure 12.2b. This example shows that more than 3 percent of the samples will have 4 or more defective items. Such samples were taken from a production function connected to documentary credit for export trade—a financial product.

To understand the theoretical basis, take as an example a system subject to instantaneous changes caused by the occurrence of random events, such as telephone calls. All changes are assumed to be of the same kind; what is significant is their total number. Each change is represented by a point on the time axis; the collection of changes forms random distributions of points on a line.

The physical processes being studied are characterized by two properties: (1) they are homogeneous in time, and (2) their future changes are independent of what happened in the past.

In documentary credit, for example, the errors that take place the with *nth* customer, and are due to a human operator, are independent of those that have happened in the past. By the same token, the forces and influences that determine a given process remain unchanged; hence, the probability of any particular event is the same for all time intervals of length *t*, independent of where this interval is situated, as well as of the past history of the system.

In other cases encountered in business life it may be the other way around. In a telephone exchange, for example, incoming calls are more frequent during the busiest hour of the day than, say, between midnight and 1 A.M. The process is therefore not homogeneous in time and, for obvious reasons, telephone engineers are concerned with the busy hour of the day. However, within a given period the process can be considered homogeneous.

Experience also shows that during any specific hour the incoming traffic follows the Poisson distribution with surprising accuracy. Similar considerations apply to all sorts of accidents, loan defaults, and repayments of mortgages.

Progress and improvement in terms of quality can be determined, and their extent evaluated, only by comparing what was done before with what is done after a change for the better. Comparisons can be made by putting earlier and later records side-by-side and expressing them in the same terms and identical units. Herein arises the necessity for measuring quality and operational results.

Units and methods for accurate, impersonal measurement and comparison are the foundation for controls and statements of operation, analysis of quality performance, and quantitative determination of what must be done to bring improvements.

These forms of measurement also permit a comparison of quality performance in-house with that in other financial institutions, and with that in the financial industry as whole. Hence, they are basically important in any financial operation and are essential in all work in investment banking.

The four essential elements in any quality measurement, include

1. a definition of quality characteristics to be measured;
2. a selection of standards for each quality characteristic;
3. a determination of the unit (or units) in which measurement is to be made;
4. a creation of accurate means (methods and instruments) by which to compare the quality characteristic of produced results with the standards that were selected.

Because it is difficult to measure human performance by accurate means, the difficulty of satisfying these requirements in connection with financial operations is apparent. However, numerous methods have been developed covering a wide range of activity. Prominent among these are performance ratios, percentages, rates and ratings, experiential factors, methods of comparison, and mathematical statistics.

Ratios, percentages, and rates are simple mathematical quantities. Ratings are employed through rating scales or evaluation sheets. Experiential factors are values or quantities determined from experience. They aid in setting up attainable standards of performance.

In the implementation of mathematical statistics, emphasis must be placed on identifying opportunities for improvement of quality and establishing procedures to achieve increased quality with lower costs. The procedures sound simple, but it takes know-how and effort to design systems that are able to produce services (and their information) without defects.

With the proper methodology, and the use of mathematics, the job can be done. Figure 12.3a shows an operating characteristics curve that was developed during World War II at Columbia University for the Manhattan Project. The author has used it many times, once in conjunction with an expert system, to control loan risk.

The operating characteristics curve is a powerful means of underpinning management decisions of an accept/reject nature, including the calculation of risk. It can also be employed in securities, particularly in controlling liquidity risk.

The chart in Figure 12.3b was also developed during World War II and used to control the quality of production in manufacturing, in particular the observance of tolerances. Since the early 1940s it has been extensively used in factories, but it can also be used in investment banking to do quality control of outgoing financial products.

It may seem out of place to discuss mathematics in a chapter on strategic planning. On the contrary, the use of mathematics in finance should be part and parcel of any strategic plan. This is the mission that rocket scientists are entrusted with, and their business on Wall Street is now booming.

A good idea might be to use statistical analysis to create the background for the implementation of quality control. There are three sources of quality problems relative, for instance, to

Figure 12.3a The Operating Characteristics (OC) Curve

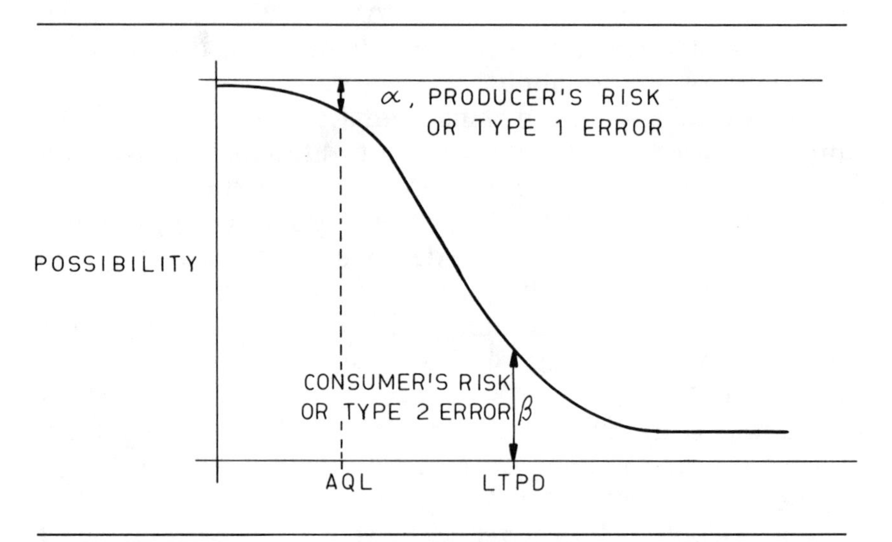

Figure 12.3b A Statistical Quality Control Chart

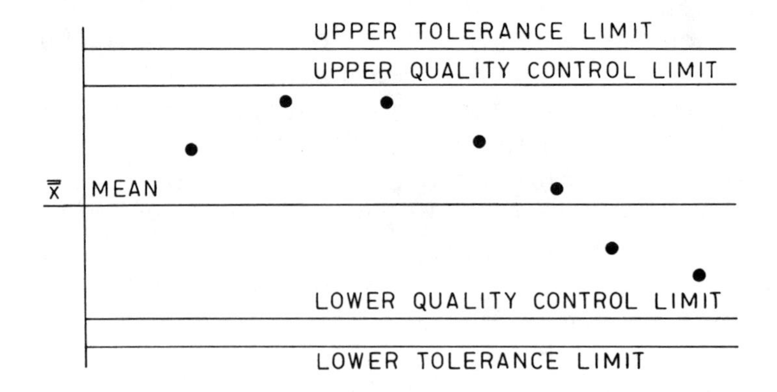

management information, accidents, unforeseen circumstances, and defects in the system of production and distribution. By curing the defects in the system, the firm has done the best that it can do to assure service quality.

Although statistical approaches were originally applied in the management of hard-good industries, such as electronics and automobiles, they can be very well used in the services industries and they have recently made inroads in banking. Information services could certainly benefit from quality control; let's keep in mind this reference when we establish our next strategic plan.

4. Swamping the Cost of Doing Business

According to statistics from the Association of British Clearing houses (APACS), 70 percent of a bank's real resources are tied up in transaction processing. Hence, only 30 percent is left for the banking business proper, such as, product development, sales, account management, customer hand-holding, dealing and trading and risk management.

A report by McKinsey and Salomon Brothers analyzed the breakdown of expenditures for *securities trading;* its results are startling. Back office and settlements represented 65 percent of costs and trade support, 25 percent, analysis product research, and market development the area with the highest potential returns to an investment banker accounted for only 10 percent.

These regrettable results bear witness to the fact that as long as profits have been fat, top management has showed little interest in cost control, and some departmental efforts were even misdirected. With information services, for instance, the approach which has classically been taken is basically numeric, data processing, as contrasted tot he true automation of payments documents, which requires imaging.

This is a *cultural failure* that has cost investment banks and securities houses dearly. Also, mere lip service has been paid to professional and managerial productivity. Until the mid-1980s, when expert systems came into use, data processing was focused on transaction handling—with negative results, as the APACS statistics show. Not surprisingly, a 1988 Peat Marwick study, made in the United States, Western Europe and Japan, concluded that 90 percent of financial institutions did not benefit from technology, in spite of the huge sums of money they invested in it.

In most financial institutions today, overhead is running too high because little attention, if any, is paid to the use of technology in supporting the most vital individuals in an investment bank's structure; that is, its senior managers and its top professionals. Those banks who do pay attention to priorities prosper (e.g., Morgan Stanley).

Part of a firm's strategy must be an integrative approach oriented to management productivity. Figure 12.4 shows figures based on personal research among financial institutions on three continents.

Managers and professionals represent about 60 percent of employment costs in the financial sectors; yet they benefit from only 7 to 20 percent of the investments made in technology. This is a skewed distribution, with 20 percent corresponding to the practices of the most progressive banks, while a large group neglects the productivity of managers and professionals. A rational, merit-based approach will allocate 70 percent of technology investments to the top echelons.

The reason for this discrepancy is one of culture. Data processing began in the mid-1950s; it was used in accounting and worked largely in the batch mode. With the advent of real time in the late 1960s, DP was expanded to transaction processing, but otherwise did not change or extend to senior layers of management to any appreciable extent.

Figure 12.4

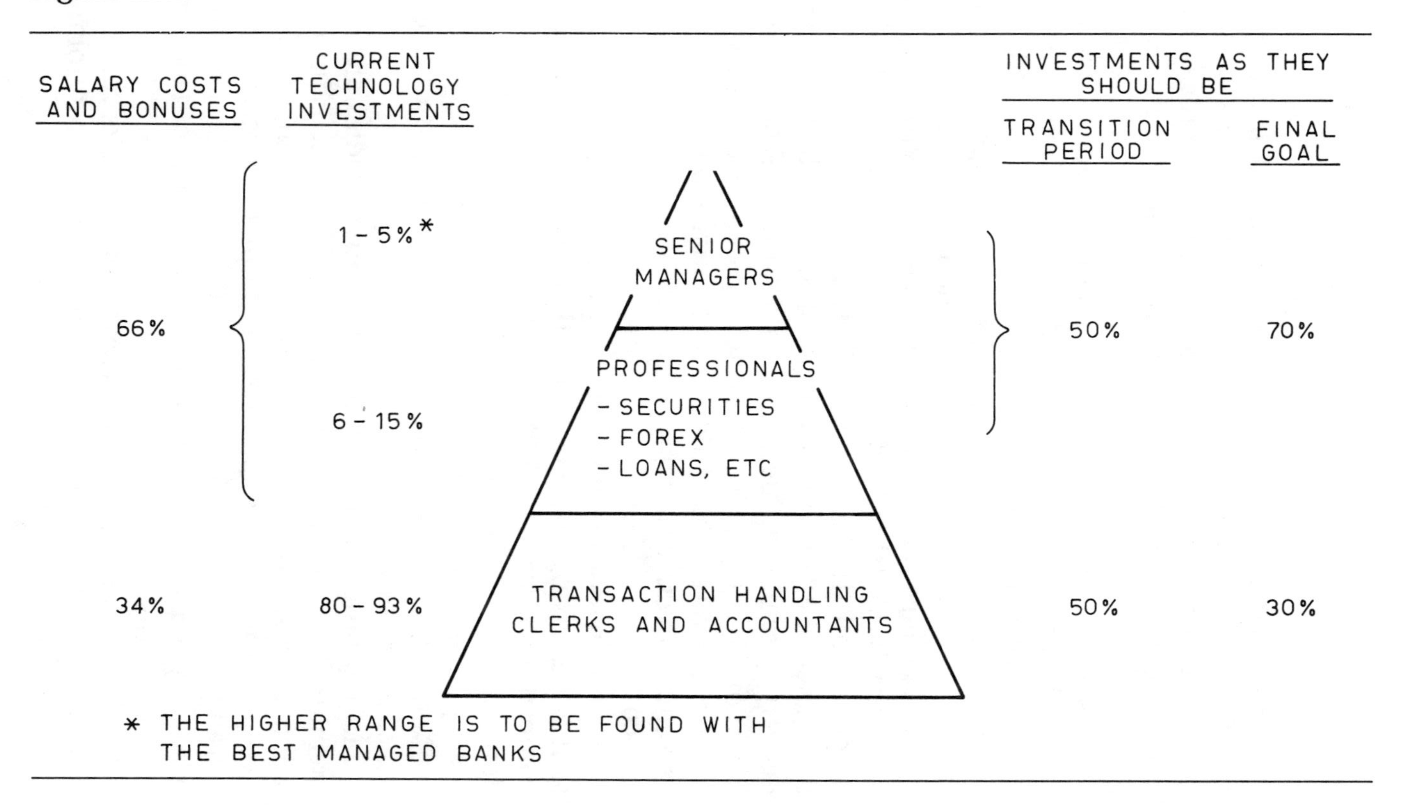
SALARY COSTS AND BONUSES
CURRENT TECHNOLOGY INVESTMENTS
INVESTMENTS AS THEY SHOULD BE
TRANSITION PERIOD
FINAL GOAL
1 - 5% *
SENIOR MANAGERS
66%
50%
70%
PROFESSIONALS
- SECURITIES
- FOREX
- LOANS, ETC
6 - 15%
34%
80 - 93%
TRANSACTION HANDLING CLERKS AND ACCOUNTANTS
50%
30%
* THE HIGHER RANGE IS TO BE FOUND WITH THE BEST MANAGED BANKS

As discussed, studies done among financial institutions show that salaries and social expenses represent between 65 and 75 percent of noninterest costs, with two-thirds of this amount going to managers and professionals. Yet, this is the group least well served by technology. Eighty percent to 90 percent of the important management functions have *not* been automated, and cannot be automated without artificial intelligence, say Japanese sources.

The suggested transition period shown in Figure 12.4 still weighs considerably on the transactional side, because the cultural change takes time to implement. Nevertheless, investment banks should thoroughly revamp their imaging practices and the technology of their delivery mechanism now. There is a growing, urgent need to study the cost of the delivery system. Securities houses and banks must be in search of an equilibrium between information processing and information delivery. The delivery of financial products must become simpler, more rapid, very accurate, fully on-line and low-cost.

The automation of the delivery system is strategic in nature, as it is provoking changes in the financial industry and its competition. Non-competitive services are obliged to abandon some sectors that are not profitable. Services which were once practical may cease to be so. Even Swift is no longer economical, now that thousands of messages must be produced and expedited.

Factual, progressive, and comprehensive studies are at a premium because investment banking as a whole is in transition. In order to stay ahead of the wave of changes that is sweeping the financial industry, appropriate strategic goals must be established followed by tactical moves. Cost control is synonymous with the thorough automation of labor-intense activities.

First, as seen from a tactical viewpoint, the chief function of cost accounting is to guide management in controlling costs associated with the daily operation of the business. Many financial executives with experience in this domain are convinced that the form of measurement called standard costs serves this purpose better than any other method.[4] In order to have reliable data, reliable standards are needed.

The diagram in Figure 12.5 shows the operating factors that affect profits, as well as their relationship with each other. The income side is simpler, consisting of business done with financial products and by-products, as well as fees.

The costs side is more involved, making it necessary to distinguish between interest and non-interest costs. It is also necessary to determine within each group the different levels of reference, making it possible to examine analytically all types of cost distribution and appropriation rules. Second, examined from a strategic viewpoint, the population to which high technology-intense solutions should be addressed are the bank's professional and senior managers. Albert Einstein once said that it was a pity people understood no more about the technology they use than cows do about the biology of the grass they eat. The comparison might be somewhat exaggerated; yet, it is true that as far as information technology is concerned, our society cares very little about what it is, what it means, and how it works.

Cost control in banking is intimately related to the practical application of technology. Therefore, it is best to examine the time frame of an investment bank's future requirements rather than "stumbling backwards" into the future.

For example, six years ago, a well-known French bank was advised not to rewrite its transaction-processing programs on main frame; nevertheless, the firm did it, with assurance from a software company that the project would cost only 8 million francs (about $1.4 million).

This project began in 1985. As of 1990, the transaction programs were still not ready, the software company had been fired and replaced with another just as incompetent, and the

Figure 12.5 Main Elements of Operating Profits and Going Costs

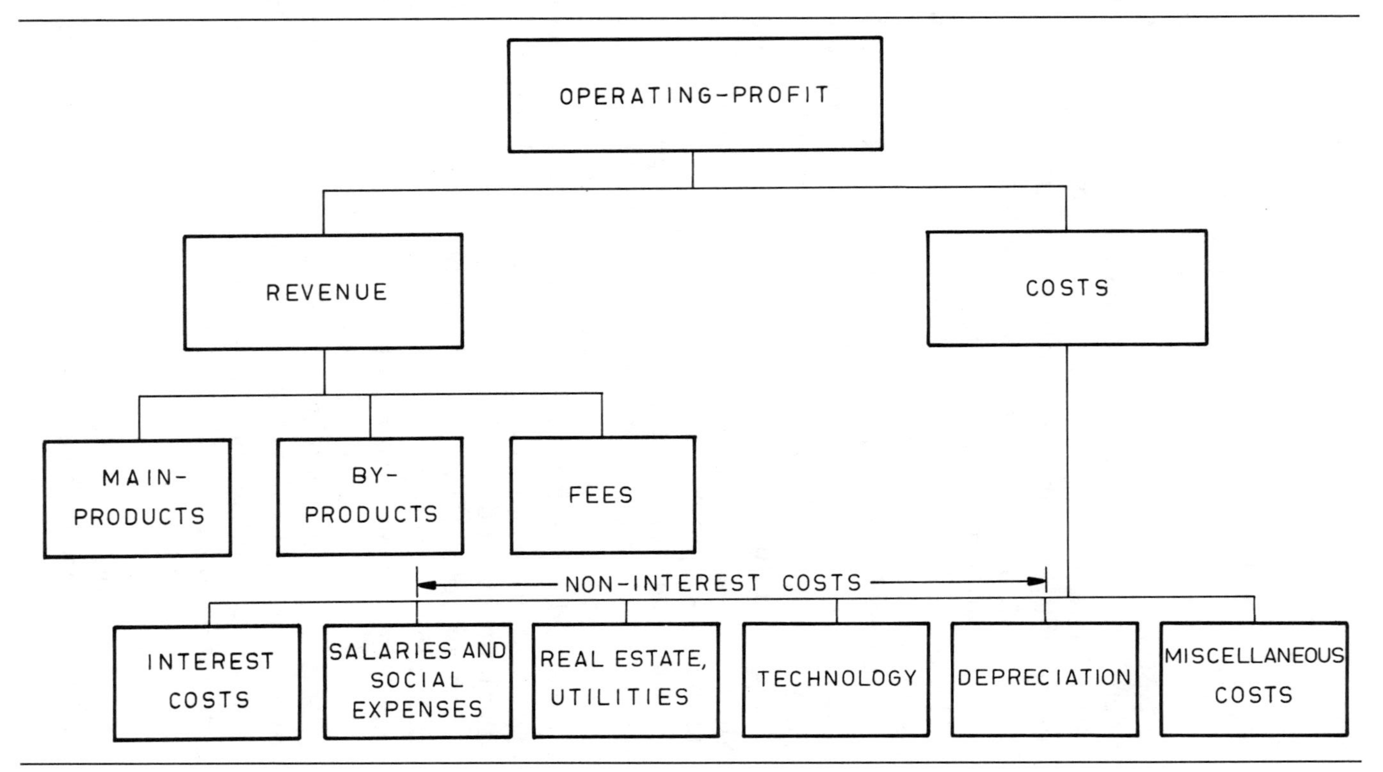

budget had ballooned to 75 million francs (about $13 million). It is the classic case of the unable asked by the unwilling to do something in controlling costs—and they did the opposite.

5. What Global Risk Management Must Consider

Risk is not a concept alien to banking, but with deregulation and globality it has both been magnified and became polyvalent. It is crucial, therefore, that global risk management become one of the fundamental strategies of an investment bank or securities house.[5]

A thorough evaluation of risk requires that a firm identifies

1. all exposure to customers, no matter in which channel, country or currency they deal,
2. all exposure to other financial institutions, specifying every commitment to every bank, in every currency and every country, and
3. the firm's own and other parties' daily overdrafts, as well as the liquidity and other risks that the firm is assuming.

The financial institution should establish limits for all products, all trades, and all officers. It should monitor these limits constantly, as if doing a perpetual inventory control. This includes watching follow-the-sun overdraft, evaluating hedges, staying informed on experimental results, and taking advantage of artificial intelligence constructs that can recommend specific action.

Follow-the-sun overdraft is a notion that, while not yet part of the banker's daily business, is crucial in twenty-four-hour banking. The underlying concept is that credits and overdrafts mean exposures, while a major banking failure can snowball, with the aftermath hitting the financial system.

Hedging requires having a global-market viewpoint and considering trends in currencies and in industry sectors. One of the most important of these is the revolving liquidity risk that exists in the different markets in which a firm operates.

In order to calculate the risk inherent in a banking operation, it is necessary to identify fundamental risk factors, determine linkages, establish metrics, take measurements, reach conclusions, elaborate dynamic correction capabilities, and take decisive action. Management must do more than give strategic directives—it must also control the execution of its orders regarding risk management.

Risk management cannot be based simply on common sense. It requires perspective and proper methodology. For example, it may be structured in terms of

1. global, worldwide markets,
2. the principal market in which a firm invests,
3. the principal currency in which investments will be made,
4. industry risk within the principal market,
5. the specific stock (or bond) in which investments are made,
6. expected dividends (or interest rate), and
7. carry or the cost of leverage to hold a position.

Strategic directives must be established with regard to managing risk globally. A firm must be able to integrate, by channel, client, industry, currency, and country (including interdisciplinary effects) the risks being taken in real space.

A real-space implementation will typically involve intelligent networks, supercomputers, rich databases, and AI. All four are important for intelligence gathering on companies and industries and the control of risk.

High technology can be used in evaluating risk for global operations providing dealer-support systems for securities and foreign exchange trading and in portfolio management and financial planning. It can also handle the continual process of assessing liquidity risks of various kinds, analyzing these risks, and integrating them into a global model.

A thorough risk management system must consider customers who want differentiated products and regulatory environments that bring change and complexity. It should also monitor the competition, as well as the products competitors may rush onto the market. Quite often, new products by competitors induce another firm to take inordinate risks because of a "me too" attitude.

An approach to continuous risk assessment must be all-inclusive; it can only be realized if

1. the applications horizon focuses on global risk,
2. the time horizon is appropriately chosen,
3. a clear methodology is elaborated, including weights for each transaction type, and
4. risk tolerances are established by transaction and integration (see Sec. 3).

Risk management requires that every trader be monitored every minute and his or her activities evaluated every day. This should be done constantly as the trader moves an inventory of financial paper or makes transactions on behalf of the bank. The evaluations should note the worth of the holdings being moved, reflect on limits, and ensure that management guidelines on hedging are observed.

Experimentation through computers, algorithms, and heuristics can be of major assistance in this pursuit. All traders and managers should be able to test against existing positions in order to avoid purchasing, event and corresponding party risks.

One AI construct for risk management, developed in Japan for a major financial institution, consists of two parts. It is composed of a statistical analysis component that detects anything unusual from the movement of predefined monitoring indexes and expert system modules that infer reasons for the anomaly and suggest measures that can be used to cope with the situation.

This analytical solution is characterized by its unique hybrid structure: it combines conventional statistical methods with AI, effectively using networked trader workstations, and distributed databases.

A firm's risk management system should be designed to maintain a risk balance on a steady basis. This includes continuously assessing the risk being involved, evaluating assumed risk in a manner integrative with previous transactions, and making post-mortems to verify the accuracy of calculations.

This is doable but requires the use of computers, communications, and mathematical models. Three attributes are essential to success: a global approach, capillary structure for information input, and instantaneous response.

Markets react instinctively when a rumor spreads in Washington, New York, London, Frankfurt, Zurich, or Tokyo. And since the First World's financial markets are networked, any major reaction or developing trend taking place in one of them has a high probability of spreading. If financial institutions are unable or unwilling to continually follow their risks, they will pay a heavy price.

A study done by Staal Bankiers shows that from 1982 to 1987, six Dutch banks, three large and three small, experienced losses because of bad risks. These losses amounted to twice the banks' profits. Consequently, the banks had to provide for retained earnings to cover losses of an estimated $5 billion over the aforementioned time frame.

This brings up the subject of financial staying power. In order to measure capital strength, financial analysts typically employ three criteria total equity-to-assets, common equity-to-assets, and common equity-to-loans. These have been preferred for some time, but now some firms are beginning to incorporate the new risk-adjusted return on capital (RAROC) ratios. Bankers Trust, for example, has built a computer-based system to calculate RAROC.

In any financial institution, a RAROC application will do well to follow the risk categories outlined by Federal Reserve proposals:

1. cash and equivalents
2. money market risk (weight 30 percent)
3. items with mortgage risk (weight 60 percent)
4. standard bank risks (weight 100 percent)

Risk is global and has many aspects, but real-time (and more recently real-space) applications make it possible to detect and control the risks that in large measure are inherent in the financial industry business.

6. Placing Emphasis on Strategic Products

In the 1960s, General Electric had a unit in Santa Barbara, California, that was staffed by former general managers of the company.[6] Their mission was to define what GE would be doing fifteen years down the line and to determine from where the corporation's profits would come. Citibank now has a research laboratory in Santa Monica, California. Its mission is not only to develop new products together with the operating departments of the bank, but also to enrich these products with technology and search for new markets for them. A firm's search for new opportunities is closely tied to refining current plans, developing new products, and capitalizing on market growth. Information systems themselves are a strategic product in the financial industry. Therefore, there should be a close coordination between strategic planning and the direction to be given to technology investments made by *any* institution.

Strategic planning should be given the role of "devil's advocate" on current business plans and financial products. "Even if you are doing well, you risk becoming another big brown industry," says one senior banker. Thus, rather than coasting on the momentum of products and services that are currently doing well, a firm should use this momentum to put in place the next big income earners.

The general manager of Banque Francaise d'Investissements offers the following statistics on the contribution of new financial products to yearly business and to P and L. Month by month, about 35 percent of the income and slightly over 50 percent of the profits came from products that did not exist 18 months earlier. This is a concrete example of how much innovation and renewal can influence the bottom line in investment banking.

Today, the classical banking business is suffering from disintermediation of corporate customers in the capital markets, deregulation of interest rates and banking rules, increased pressure on pricing from new competition, and the steady misuse of technology. There are several ways in which banks cannot only respond to these problems, but also thrive in today's financial climate.

Innovative banking services are essential; banks must think of activities such as securitization and project financing, and caps and collars as products. Also, sophisticated clients demand quality of services. Quality must be planned, supported, and controlled from product design to production and delivery.

Client advising is financial engineering in the investment business. It calls for skills not widely available before; hence, it is wise to use expert system in this area.

Having a market orientation includes not only intensive marketing and calling on customers but also market analysis, product planning, sales planning, and after-sales customer service. At the same time, cost control is important. All costs should be watched; personnel costs must be swamped while at the same time quality of service is increased.

The development of innovative banking services will not take place randomly. There are a number of well-defined steps in designing a banking product or issuing a new one in an established product line such as underwriting.

For example, a bank will originate a suitable issue of bonds or shares; this is the design phase. It will then go through the appropriate regulatory loops to ensure that any relevant information about the company has been made public. Finally, it will do the underwriting, together with a group of other financial institutions.

Each of these institutions promises to buy a slice of the issue in return for a commission. In the meantime, the leading bank guarantees that the money will be available to the issuer on time and distributes the newly created securities to the underwriting group and to investors in the market.

In Tokyo, the Mitsubishi Bank, together with the Mitsubishi Research Institute, developed a very sophisticated solution for Zurich-based Mitsubishi Finance Corporation. The solution, Bond Selection for Underwriting, works in yen, Swiss francs, and Eurodollars, and has been in operation since January 1989. This is a first-class AI construct with thousands of rules consisting of five main subsystems. These include

1. a P and L database of listed companies and associated analyzer,
2. a database with precedence of issued bonds, including all parties in the transactions,
3. a critical evaluation regarding underwriting through questionnaire (the expert system examines financial conditions and cost-evaluates each bond),
4. a proposal evaluation and marketing/scheduling action, and
5. an analysis of precedence and follow-up evaluation.

In a fast-growing and fast-changing domain such as modern banking, product leadership is not a prize that can be won once and then left on the shelf as though it were a trophy. It has to be won again and again—or it will ultimately be lost.

Endnotes

1. Vilfredo Pareto (1848–1923) was a Swiss-Italian economist and mathematician who taught economics and sociology at the University of Lausanne.

2. See also D.N. Chorafas and H. Steinmann, *High Technology at UBS for Excellence in Client Service* (Zurich: Union Bank of Switzerland, 1988).

3. See also D.N. Chorafas, *High Technology in the Securities Business* (Chicago, IL: Probus Publishing Company, 1990).

4. For a discussion of standard costs in banking see D. N. Chorafas, *Bank Profitability* (London and Boston, MA: Butterworths, 1989).

5. See also D. N. Chorafas, *Risk Management in Financial Institutions* (London and Boston: Butterworths, 1990).

6. A GE general manager is typically in charge of a unit that employs 5,000 people or more and operates as an independent profit center.

Index

X

Y

Z